PHILOSOPHY TODAY NO. 1

Philosophy Today No. 1

EDITED BY

Jerry H. Gill

THE MACMILLAN COMPANY, *NEW YORK*

COLLIER-MACMILLAN, LTD., *LONDON*

1) Philosophy, Modern -- 20th Century -- Collections

To

KENNETH MONROE

The Macmillan Company, New York
Collier-Macmillan Canada Ltd., Toronto, Ontario

Printed in the United States of America

CONTENTS

INTRODUCTION

THE present volume is an attempt to provide an introduction to what is going on in the field of philosophy today. As such its compilation has been guided by three main concerns, each of which carries with it an inherent difficulty.

To begin with, the best way to "feel the pulse" of contemporary philosophy is to become acquainted with recent articles in the leading philosophical journals published in English. Thus the following essays have been chosen from eight different journals over a period of the past four years. Although a genuine effort has been made to avoid choosing too many articles from a few journals, the necessity of some thematic unity renders a completely equitable spread impossible.

Secondly, it is important to present a selection of essays that represents the major movements and issues of the day. At the same time, a selection which conforms to a party line must be avoided. The essays that follow were chosen because as a group they represent a large segment of the philosophical spectrum. There are, to be sure, movements and issues it has been necessary to omit.

Finally, care has been taken to select articles which are comprehendable by the nonprofessional student of philosophy. As is the case in any field of thought, professional philosophy journals are often filled with articles only the specialist can understand. Nevertheless, there are often articles of a survey nature, or highly original essays, which are refreshingly free of technical jargon. The essays comprising the present volume were chosen because they exemplify these qualities.

Now a word about the essays themselves. The contemporary scene in philosophy is dominated by two main movements or emphases: linguistic analysis and

existential analysis. The former focuses attention upon
language as both the source and the answer of philosophical puzzles, while the latter focuses on the dimen-
sions of human existence as the real concern of
philosophy. It is only proper that the present volume
contain some essays that express these two main
emphases in a sympathetic and somewhat comprehensive fashion. Thus Parts I and II are devoted to
Linguistic and Existential Analysis respectively.

Part I   The two most influential thinkers of the linguistic bent have been Ludwig Wittgenstein and J. L.
Austin. Thus it is only fitting that each of them have
a chance to speak for himself in Chapter 1, "Wittgenstein's Lecture on Ethics," and Chapter 3, Austin's
"Three Ways of Spilling Ink." Each of these is followed
by an interpretive essay which seeks to come to grips
with the main themes of Wittgenstein's and Austin's
thought. Although Wittgenstein's essay was written in
1929, and thus represents his early, more positivistic
thinking, its creative uniqueness renders mandatory its
inclusion in this volume. Moreover, Dennis O'Brian's
essay on "The Unity of Wittgenstein's Thought" (Chapter 2) serves to trace out the similarities and differences
in Wittgenstein's early and later philosophy. In much
the same fashion, Stanley Cavell's "Austin At Criticism"
(Chapter 4) seeks to evaluate the contribution of
Austin's work.

Part II   One of the fountainheads of existentialistic
thought is Søren Kierkegaard, and Kierkegaard scholarship continues to carry a great deal of interest. In
Chapter 5 Henry E. Allison explores the relationship
between "Christianity and Nonsense" in Kierkegaard's
Concluding Unscientific Postscript. He comes up with
a rather radical but provocative conclusion. Another
fountainhead of existentialist thought is Martin Heidegger. He, too, has undergone something of a radical
change in his thinking so as to make it necessary to
speak of the "turning point" between the early and
later Heidegger. It is this turning point that A.
Borgmann discusses in his "The Transformation of

Heidegger's Thought" in Chapter 6. One other key existentialist thinker is Jean-Paul Sartre, and the relationship between his existentialism and his communistic
tendency has long fascinated philosophical, literary,
and political scholars. In Chapter 7 Arthur Lessing
analyzes this relationship in terms of "Marxist Existentialism." Out of the combination of existentialism
and the thought of Edmund Husserl has come a new
movement known as "phenomenology." Asher Moore
addresses himself to "Existential Phenomenology" in
Chapter 8, and Rollo Handy makes a critical response.
Part III   One of the most interesting areas of contemporary philosophy is that of the relationship between ethical responsibility and rationality. Since this
area is one in which both language philosophy and
existentialism have an interest, it is appropriate to include a group of essays dealing with it. Both Warner
Wick's "Truth's Debt To Freedom" (Chapter 9) and
John R. Searle's "How To Derive 'Ought' From 'Is'"
(Chapter 10) argue against the dichotomy that has
traditionally been placed between matters of fact and
matters of value. Roderick M. Chisholm gives a detailed analysis of the statement "He could have done
otherwise" in his essay by that title (Chapter 11). His
analysis reflects a good deal of work that has been
done in recent years on the logic of ethical responsibility, and in some ways parallels Austin's essay in
Chapter 3. The contemporary distinction between normative ethics and "meta-ethics" has become a philosophical commonplace. William K. Frankena, in his
American Philosophical Association Presidential Address, "On Saying the Ethical Thing" (Chapter 12)
challenges this distinction by suggesting the necessity
of "normative meta-ethics."

Contrary to what many "modern day Jeremiahs"
would have us believe, philosophy today is widely diverse and truly exciting.

PART I
Linguistic Analysis

CHAPTER 1

WITTGENSTEIN'S LECTURE ON ETHICS

LUDWIG WITTGENSTEIN,
FRIEDRICH WAISMANN,
RUSH RHEES*

···—⟡—···

The following lecture, hitherto unpublished, was prepared by Wittgenstein for delivery in Cambridge sometime between September 1929 and December 1930. It was probably read to the society known as "The Heretics," to which Wittgenstein gave an address at that time. The manuscript bears no title. So far as is known, this was the only popular lecture ever composed or delivered by Wittgenstein.

The text that follows the lecture below is a transcript of shorthand notes made by the late Friedrich Waismann during and after conversations with Wittgenstein and Moritz Schlick in 1929 and 1930. They are here reproduced with the kind permission of Waismann's literary executors, Professor Sir Isaiah Berlin, Professor Gilbert Ryle, and Professor Stuart Hampshire. Our thanks are due for assistance by Mr. Brian McGuinness, who is working on the Waismann papers under a grant from the British Academy.

We are indebted to Mr. Rush Rhees for the above in-

* Ludwig Wittgenstein (1889–1951) was born and raised in Austria but studied and taught philosophy at Cambridge University. The notes that follow "Wittgenstein's Lecture on Ethics" were made by the late Friedrich Waismann, an early member of the logical empiricist group known as "The Vienna Circle." The final comments are those of Mr. Rush Rhees, a contemporary British linguistic philosopher. This article originally appeared in *The Philosophical Review*, Vol. 74, No. 1 (January 1965), and is printed here by permission of its editors, along with that of Mr. Rush Rhees and Mr. B. F. McGuinness.

formation and for help in the preparation of the following
materials, and to him and to Wittgenstein's other literary
executors, Miss Elizabeth Anscombe and Professor G. H.
von Wright, for permission to publish the lecture.

THE EDITORS

I: A Lecture on Ethics

BEFORE I begin to speak about my subject proper let
me make a few introductory remarks. I feel I shall
have great difficulties in communicating my thoughts to
you and I think some of them may be diminished by
mentioning them to you beforehand. The first one,
which almost I need not mention, is that English is not
my native tongue and my expression therefore often
lacks that precision and subtlety which would be desirable if one talks about a difficult subject. All I can
do is to ask you to make my task easier by trying to
get at my meaning in spite of the faults which I will
constantly be committing against the English grammar.
The second difficulty I will mention is this, that probably many of you come up to this lecture of mine with
slightly wrong expectations. And to set you right in
this point I will say a few words about the reason for
choosing the subject I have chosen: When your former
secretary honoured me by asking me to read a paper to
your society, my first thought was that I would certainly do it and my second thought was that if I was to
have the opportunity to speak to you I should speak
about something which I am keen on communicating
to you and that I should not misuse this opportunity to
give you a lecture about, say, logic. I call this a misuse,
for to explain a scientific matter to you it would need
a course of lectures and not an hour's paper. Another
alternative would have been to give you what's called
a popular-scientific lecture, that is a lecture intended
to make you believe that you understand a thing which

actually you don't understand, and to gratify what I believe to be one of the lowest desires of modern people, namely the superficial curiosity about the latest discoveries of science. I rejected these alternatives and decided to talk to you about a subject which seems to me to be of general importance, hoping that it may help to clear up your thoughts about this subject (even if you should entirely disagree with what I will say about it). My third and last difficulty is one which, in fact, adheres to most lengthy philosophical lectures and it is this, that the hearer is incapable of seeing both the road he is led and the goal which it leads to. That is to say: he either thinks: "I understand all he says, but what on earth is he driving at" or else he thinks "I see what he's driving at, but how on earth is he going to get there." All I can do is again to ask you to be patient and to hope that in the end you may see both the way and where it leads to.

I will now begin. My subject, as you know, is Ethics and I will adopt the explanation of that term which Professor Moore has given in his book *Principia Ethica.* He says: "Ethics is the general enquiry into what is good." Now I am going to use the term Ethics in a slightly wider sense, in a sense in fact which includes what I believe to be the most essential part of what is generally called Aesthetics. And to make you see as clearly as possible what I take to be the subject matter of Ethics I will put before you a number of more or less synonymous expressions each of which could be substituted for the above definition, and by enumerating them I want to produce the same sort of effect which Galton produced when he took a number of photos of different faces on the same photographic plate in order to get the picture of the typical features they all had in common. And as by showing to you such a collective photo I could make you see what is the typical—say— Chinese face; so if you look through the row of synonyms which I will put before you, you will, I hope, be able to see the characteristic features they all have in common and these are the characteristic features of

Ethics. Now instead of saying "Ethics is the enquiry into what is good" I could have said Ethics is the enquiry into what is valuable, or, into what is really important, or I could have said Ethics is the enquiry into the meaning of life, or into what makes life worth living, or into the right way of living. I believe if you look at all these phrases you will get a rough idea as to what it is that Ethics is concerned with. Now the first thing that strikes one about all these expressions is that each of them is actually used in two very different senses. I will call them the trivial or relative sense on the one hand and the ethical or absolute sense on the other. If for instance I say that this is a *good* chair this means that the chair serves a certain predetermined purpose and the word good here has only meaning so far as this purpose has been previously fixed upon. In fact the word good in the relative sense simply means coming up to a certain predetermined standard. Thus when we say that this man is a good pianist we mean that he can play pieces of a certain degree of difficulty with a certain degree of dexterity. And similarly if I say that it is *important* for me not to catch cold I mean that catching a cold produces certain describable disturbances in my life and if I say that this is the *right* road I mean that it's the right road relative to a certain goal. Used in this way these expressions don't present any difficulty or deep problems. But this is not how Ethics uses them. Supposing that I could play tennis and one of you saw me playing and said "Well, you play pretty badly" and suppose I answered "I know, I'm playing badly but I don't want to play any better," all the other man could say would be "Ah then that's all right." But suppose I had told one of you a preposterous lie and he came up to me and said "You're behaving like a beast" and then I were to say "I know I behave badly, but then I don't want to behave any better," could he then say "Ah, then that's all right"? Certainly not; he would say "Well, you *ought* to want to behave better." Here you have an absolute judgment of value, whereas the first instance was one of a relative judgment. The essence of this difference seems to be obviously this: Every judgment of relative value is a mere statement of facts and can therefore be put in such a form that it loses all the appearance of a judgment of value: Instead of saying "This is the right way to Granchester," I could equally well have said, "This is the right way you have to go if you want to get to Granchester in the shortest time"; "This man is a good runner" simply means that he runs a certain number of miles in a certain number of minutes, etc. Now what I wish to contend is that, although all judgments of relative value can be shown to be mere statements of facts, no statement of fact can ever be, or imply, a judgment of absolute value. Let me explain this: Suppose one of you were an omniscient person and therefore knew all the movements of all the bodies in the world dead or alive and that he also knew all the states of mind of all human beings that ever lived, and suppose this man wrote all he knew in a big book, then this book would contain the whole description of the world; and what I want to say is, that this book would contain nothing that we would call an *ethical* judgment or anything that would logically imply such a judgment. It would of course contain all relative judgments of value and all true scientific propositions and in fact all true propositions that can be made. But all the facts described would, as it were, stand on the same level and in the same way all propositions stand on the same level. There are no propositions which, in any absolute sense, are sublime, important, or trivial. Now perhaps some of you will agree to that and be reminded of Hamlet's words: "Nothing is either good or bad, but thinking makes it so." But this again could lead to a misunderstanding. What Hamlet says seems to imply that good and bad, though not qualities of the world outside us, are attributes to our states of mind. But what I mean is that a state of mind, so far as we mean by that a fact which we can describe, is in no ethical sense good or bad. If for instance in our world-book we read the description of a murder with all its details physical and psychological, the mere description of these facts will contain nothing which we could call an *ethical* proposition. The murder will be on exactly the same level as any other event, for instance the falling of a stone. Certainly the reading of this description might cause us pain or rage or any other emotion, or we might read about the pain or rage caused by this murder in other people when they heard of it, but there will simply be facts, facts, and facts but no Ethics. And now I must say that if I contemplate what Ethics really would have to be if there were such a science, this result seems to me quite obvious. It seems to me obvious that nothing we could ever think or say should be *the* thing. That we cannot write a scientific book, the subject matter of which could be intrinsically sublime and above all other subject matters. I can only describe my feeling by the metaphor, that, if a man could write a book on Ethics which really was a book on Ethics, this book would, with an explosion, destroy all the other books in the world. Our words used as we use them in science, are vessels capable only of containing and conveying meaning and sense, *natural* meaning and sense. Ethics, if it is anything, is supernatural and our words will only express facts; as a teacup will only hold a teacup full of water even if I were to pour out a gallon over it. I said that so far as facts and propositions are concerned there is only relative value and relative good, right, etc. And let me, before I go on, illustrate this by a rather obvious example. The right road is the road which leads to an arbitrarily predetermined end and it is quite clear to us all that there is no sense in talking about the right road apart from such a predetermined goal. Now let us see what we could possibly mean by the expression, "*the* absolutely right road." I think it would be the road which *everybody* on seeing it would, *with logical necessity*, have to go, or be ashamed for not going. And similarly the *absolute good*, if it is a describable state of affairs, would be one which everybody, independent of his tastes and inclinations, would *necessarily* bring about or feel guilty for not bringing about. And I want to say that such a state of affairs is a chimera. No state of affairs has, in itself, what I would like to call the coercive power of an absolute judge. Then what have all of us who, like myself, are still tempted to use such expressions as "absolute good," "absolute value," etc., what have we in mind and what do we try to express? Now whenever I try to make this clear to myself it is natural that I should recall cases in which I would certainly use these expressions and I am then in the situation in which you would be if, for instance, I were to give you a lecture on the psychology of pleasure. What you would do then would be to try and recall some typical situation in which you always felt pleasure. For, bearing this situation in mind, all I should say to you would become concrete and, as it were, controllable. One man would perhaps choose as his stock example the sensation when taking a walk on a fine summer's day. Now in this situation I am, if I want to fix my mind on what I mean by absolute or ethical value. And there, in my case, it always happens that the idea of one particular experience presents itself to me which therefore is, in a sense, my experience *par excellence* and this is the reason why, in talking to you now, I will use this experience as my first and foremost example. (As I have said before, this is an entirely personal matter and others would find other examples more striking.) I will describe this experience in order, if possible, to make you recall the same or similar experiences, so that we may have a common ground for our investigation. I believe the best way of describing it is to say that when I have it *I wonder at the existence of the world.* And I am then inclined to use such phrases as "how extraordinary that anything should exist" or "how extraordinary that the world should exist." I will mention another experience straight away which I also know and which others of you might be acquainted with: it is, what one might call, the experience of feeling *absolutely* safe. I mean the state of mind in which one is inclined to say "I am

safe, nothing can injure me whatever happens." Now
let me consider these experiences, for, I believe, they
exhibit the very characteristics we try to get clear
about. And there the first thing I have to say is, that
the verbal expression which we give to these experiences is nonsense! If I say "I wonder at the existence of
the world" I am misusing language. Let me explain
this: It has a perfectly good and clear sense to say
that I wonder at something being the case, we all
understand what it means to say that I wonder at the
size of a dog which is bigger than anyone I have ever
seen before or at any thing which, in the common sense
of the word, is extraordinary. In every such case I
wonder at something being the case which I *could*
conceive *not* to be the case. I wonder at the size of this
dog because I could conceive of a dog of another,
namely the ordinary size, at which I should not wonder. To say "I wonder at such and such being the
case" has only sense if I can imagine it not to be the
case. In this sense one can wonder at the existence of,
say, a house when one sees it and has not visited it
for a long time and has imagined that it had been
pulled down in the meantime. But it is nonsense to
say that I wonder at the existence of the world, because I cannot imagine it not existing. I could of course
wonder at the world round me being as it is. If for
instance I had this experience while looking into the
blue sky, I could wonder at the sky being blue as opposed to the case when it's clouded. But that's not
what I mean. I am wondering at the sky being *whatever it is*. One might be tempted to say that what I
am wondering at is a tautology, namely at the sky
being blue or not blue. But then it's just nonsense to
say that one is wondering at a tautology. Now the
same applies to the other experience which I have
mentioned, the experience of absolute safety. We all
know what it means in ordinary life to be safe. I am
safe in my room, when I cannot be run over by an
omnibus. I am safe if I have had whooping cough and
cannot therefore get it again. To be safe essentially

means that it is physically impossible that certain things should happen to me and therefore it's nonsense to say that I am safe *whatever* happens. Again this is a misuse of the word "safe" as the other example was of a misuse of the word "existence" or "wondering." Now I want to impress on you that a certain characteristic misuse of our language runs through *all* ethical and religious expressions. All these expressions *seem*, prima facie, to be just *similes*. Thus it seems that when we are using the word *right* in an ethical sense, although, what we mean, is not right in its trivial sense, it's something similar, and when we say "This is a good fellow," although the word good here doesn't mean what it means in the sentence "This is a good football player" there seems to be some similarity. And when we say "This man's life was valuable" we don't mean it in the same sense in which we would speak of some valuable jewelry but there seems to be some sort of analogy. Now all religious terms seem in this sense to be used as similes or allegorically. For when we speak of God and that he sees everything and when we kneel and pray to him all our terms and actions seem to be parts of a great and elaborate allegory which represents him as a human being of great power whose grace we try to win, etc., etc. But this allegory also describes the experience which I have just referred to. For the first of them is, I believe, exactly what people were referring to when they said that God had created the world; and the experience of absolute safety has been described by saying that we feel safe in the hands of God. A third experience of the same kind is that of feeling guilty and again this was described by the phrase that God disapproves of our conduct. Thus in ethical and religious language we seem constantly to be using similes. But a simile must be the simile for *something*. And if I can describe a fact by means of a simile I must also be able to drop the simile and to describe the facts without it. Now in our case as soon as we try to drop the simile and simply to state the facts which stand behind it, we find that there are no such facts. And so, what at first

appeared to be a simile now seems to be mere nonsense. Now the three experiences which I have mentioned to you (and I could have added others) seem to
those who have experienced them, for instance to me,
to have in some sense an intrinsic, absolute value.
But when I say they are experiences, surely, they are
facts; they have taken place then and there, lasted a
certain definite time and consequently are describable.
And so from what I have said some minutes ago I must
admit it is nonsense to say that they have absolute
value. And I will make my point still more acute by
saying "It is the paradox that an experience, a fact,
should seem to have supernatural value." Now there is
a way in which I would be tempted to meet this paradox. Let me first consider, again, our first experience of
wondering at the existence of the world and let me
describe it in a slightly different way; we all know
what in ordinary life would be called a miracle. It
obviously is simply an event the like of which we have
never yet seen. Now suppose such an event happened.
Take the case that one of you suddenly grew a lion's
head and began to roar. Certainly that would be as
extraordinary a thing as I can imagine. Now whenever
we should have recovered from our surprise, what I
would suggest would be to fetch a doctor and have the
case scientifically investigated and if it were not for
hurting him I would have him vivisected. And where
would the miracle have got to? For it is clear that
when we look at it in this way everything miraculous
has disappeared; unless what we mean by this term
is merely that a fact has not yet been explained by
science which again means that we have hitherto failed
to group this fact with others in a scientific system.
This shows that it is absurd to say "Science has proved
that there are no miracles." The truth is that the scientific way of looking at a fact is not the way to look
at it as a miracle. For imagine whatever fact you may,
it is not in itself miraculous in the absolute sense of that
term. For we see now that we have been using the
word "miracle" in a relative and an absolute sense.

And I will now describe the experience of wondering at the existence of the world by saying: it is the experience of seeing the world as a miracle. Now I am tempted to say that the right expression in language for the miracle of the existence of the world, though it is not any proposition *in* language, is the existence of language itself. But what then does it mean to be aware of this miracle at some times and not at other times? For all I have said by shifting the expression of the miraculous from an expression *by means of* language to the expression *by the existence* of language, all I have said is again that we cannot express what we want to express and that all we *say* about the absolute miraculous remains nonsense. Now the answer to all this will seem perfectly clear to many of you. You will say: Well, if certain experiences constantly tempt us to attribute a quality to them which we call absolute or ethical value and importance, this simply shows that by these words we *don't* mean nonsense, that after all what we mean by saying that an experience has absolute value *is just a fact like other facts* and that all it comes to is that we have not yet succeeded in finding the correct logical analysis of what we mean by our ethical and religious expressions. Now when this is urged against me I at once see clearly, as it were in a flash of light, not only that no description that I can think of would do to describe what I mean by absolute value, but that I would reject every significant description that anybody could possibly suggest, *ab initio*, on the ground of its significance. That is to say: I see now that these nonsensical expressions were not nonsensical because I had not yet found the correct expressions, but that their nonsensicality was their very essence. For all I wanted to do with them was just *to go beyond* the world and that is to say beyond significant language. My whole tendency and I believe the tendency of all men who ever tried to write or talk Ethics or Religion was to run against the boundaries of language. This running against the walls of our cage is perfectly, absolutely hopeless.

Ethics so far as it springs from the desire to say something about the ultimate meaning of life, the absolute good, the absolute valuable, can be no science. What it says does not add to our knowledge in any sense. But it is a document of a tendency in the human mind which I personally cannot help respecting deeply and I would not for my life ridicule it.

II: *Notes on Talks with Wittgenstein*[1]

FRIEDRICH WAISMANN

Montag, 30 Dezember, 1929 (bei Schlick).

Der Mensch hat den Trieb, gegen die Grenzen der Sprache anzurennen. Denken Sie z.B. an das Erstaunen, daß etwas existiert. Das Erstaunen kann nicht in Form einer Frage ausgedrückt werden, und es gibt auch gar keine Antwort. Alles, was wir sagen mögen, kann a priori nur Unsinn sein. Trotzdem rennen wir gegen die Grenzen der Sprache an. Dieses Anrennen hat auch Kierkegaard gesehen und es sogar ganz ähnlich (als Anrennen gegen das Paradoxon) bezeichnet. Dieses Anrennen gegen die Grenze der Sprache ist die Ethik. *Ich halte es für sicher wichtig, daß man all dem Geschwätz über Ethik—ob es eine Erkenntnis gebe, ob es Werte gebe, ob sich das Gute definieren lasse etc.—ein Ende macht. In der Ethik macht man immer den Versuch, etwas zu sagen, was das Wesen der Sache nicht betrifft und nie betreffen kann. Es ist a priori gewiß: Was immer man für eine Definition zum Guten geben mag—es ist immer ein Mißverständnis, daß eigentlich, was man in Wirklichkeit meint, entspreche sich im Ausdruck. (Moore). Aber die Tendenz, das Anrennen, deutet auf etwas hin.*

---

[1] Both passages were translated by Max Black.

Monday, 30 December 1929 (at Schlick's).

Man has the urge to thrust against the limits of language. Think for instance about one's astonishment that anything exists. This astonishment cannot be expressed in the form of a question and there is no answer to it. Anything we can say must, a priori, be only nonsense. Nevertheless we thrust against the limits of language. Kierkegaard, too, recognized this thrust and even described it in much the same way (as a thrust against paradox). This thrust against the limits of language is *ethics*. I regard it as very important to put an end to all the chatter about ethics—whether there is knowledge in ethics, whether there are values, whether the Good can be defined, etc. In ethics, one constantly tries to say something that does not concern and can never concern the essence of the matter. It is a priori certain that, whatever definition one may give of the Good, it is always a misunderstanding to suppose that the formulation corresponds to what one really means. (Moore). But the tendency, the thrust, *points to something.*

17 Dezember, 1930.

Über Schlicks Ethik. *Schlick sagt, es gebe in der theologischen Ethik zwei Auffassungen vom Wesen des Guten: nach der flacheren Deutung ist das Gute deshalb gut, weil Gott es will; nach der tieferen Deutung will Gott das Gute deshalb, weil es gut ist.*

Ich meine, daß die erste Auffassung die tiefere ist: Gut ist, was Gott befiehlt. Denn si schneidet den Weg einer jeden Erklärung, 'warum' es gut ist, ab, während gerade die zweite Auffassung die flache, die rationalistische ist, die so tut, als ob das, was gut ist, noch begründet werden könnte.

Die erste Auffassung sagt klar, daß das Wesen des Guten nichts mit den Tatsachen zu tun hat und daher durch kein Satz erklärt werden kann. Wenn es einen Satz gibt, der gerade das ausdrückt, was ich meine, so ist es der Satz: Gut ist, was Gott befiehlt.

Wert. *Wenn ich die Wirklichkeit beschreibe, so beschreibe ich, was ich bei den Menschen vorfinde. Die Soziologie muß ebenso unsere Handlungen und unsere Wertungen beschreiben wie der Neger. Sie kann nur berichten, was geschieht. Aber nie darf in der Beschreibung des Soziologen der Satz vorkommen: 'Das und das bedeutet einen Fortschritt.'*

Was ich beschreiben kann, ist, daß vorgezogen wird. Nehmen Sie an, ich hätte durch Erfahrung gefunden, daß Sie immer von zwei Bildern dasjenige vorziehen, das mehr grün enthält, das eine grünliche Tönung enthält, etc. Dann habe ich nur das beschrieben, aber nicht, daß dieses Bild wertvoller ist.

Was ist das wertvolle an einer Beethoven Sonate? Die Folge der Töne? Nein, sie ist ja nur eine Folge unter vielen. Ja, ich behaupte sogar: Auch die Gefühle Beethovens, die er beim Komponieren der Sonate hatte, waren nicht wertvoller als irgendwelche andere Gefühle. Ebensowenig ist die Tatsache des Vorgezogenwerdens an sich etwas Wertvolles.

Ist der Wert ein bestimmter Geisteszustand? Oder eine Form, die an irgendwelchen Bewußtseinsdaten haftet? Ich würde antworten: Was immer man mir sagen mag, ich würde es ablehnen, und zwar nicht darum, weil die Erklärung falsch ist, sondern weil sie eine Erklärung ist.

Wenn man mir irgendetwas sagt, was eine Theorie ist, so würde ich sagen: Nein, nein! das interessiert mich nicht. Auch wenn die Theorie wahr wäre, würde sie mich nicht interessieren—sie würde nie das sein, was ich suche. Das Ethische kann man nicht lehren. Wenn ich einem Anderen erst durch eine Theorie das Wesen des Ethischen erklären könnte, so hätte das Ethische gar keinen Wert.

Ich habe in meinem Vortrag über Ethik zum Schluß in der ersten Person gesprochen. Ich glaube, daß das etwas ganz Wesentliches ist. Hier läßt sich nichts mehr konstatieren, ich kann nur als Persönlichkeit hervortreten und in der ersten Person sprechen.

Für mich *hat die Theorie keinen Wert. Eine Theorie*

gibt mir nichts. Religion. *Ist das Reden wesentlich für die Religion? Ich kann mir ganz gut eine Religion denken, in der es keine Lehrsätze gibt, in der also nicht gesprochen wird. Das Wesen der Religion kann offenbar nicht damit etwas zu tun haben, daß geredet wird, oder vielmehr: wenn geredet wird, so ist das selbst ein Bestandteil der religiösen Handlung und keine Theorie. Es kommt also auch gar nicht darauf an, ob die Worte wahr oder falsch oder unsinnig sind.*

Die Reden der Religion sind auch kein Gleichnis; denn sonst müßte man es auch in Prosa sagen können. Anrennen gegen die Grenze der Sprache? Die Sprache ist ja kein Käfig.

Ich kann nur sagen: Ich mache mich über diese Tendenz im Menschen nicht lustig; ich ziehe den Hut davor. Und hier ist es wesentlich, daß es keine Beschreibung der Soziologie ist, sondern, daß ich von mir selbst spreche.

Die Tatsachen sind für mich unwichtig. Aber mir liegt das am Herzen, was die Menschen meinen, wenn sie sagen, daß die 'Welt da ist.'

Ich frage Wittgenstein: *Hängt das Dasein der Welt mit dem Ethischen zusammen?*

Wittgenstein: *Daß heir ein Zusammenhang besteht, haben die Menschen gefühlt und das so ausgedrückt: Gottvater hat die Welt erschaffen, Gottsohn (oder das Wort, das von Gott ausgeht) ist das Ethische. Daß man sich die Gottheit gespalten und wieder als Eines denkt, das deutet an, daß hier ein Zusammenhang besteht.*

17 December, 1930.

ON SCHLICK's ETHICS. Schlick says that theological ethics contains two conceptions of the essence of the Good. According to the more superficial interpretation, the Good is good because God wills it; according to the deeper interpretation, God wills the Good because it is good.

I think that the first conception is the deeper one: Good is what God orders. For this cuts off the path to any and every explanation "why" it is good, while the second conception is precisely the superficial, the rationalistic one, which proceeds as if what is good could still be given some foundation.

The first conception says clearly that the essence of the Good has nothing to do with facts and therefore cannot be explained by any proposition. If any proposition expresses just what I mean, it is: Good is what God orders.

VALUE. If I describe reality, I describe what I find among men. Sociology must describe our actions and our valuations just as it does those of the Negroes. It can only report what occurs. But sociological descriptions must never include the assertion: "Such and such constitutes an advance."

What I can describe is that people have preferences. Assume that I had discovered by experience that, of two pictures, you always preferred the one that contained more green, that had a greenish tinge, etc. Then I have described only *that*, but not that this picture is the more valuable.

What has value in a Beethoven sonata? The sequence of notes? No, that is only one sequence among many. And I would even say that Beethoven's feelings while composing the sonata were no more valuable than any other feelings. Similarly, the fact that something is preferred has in itself just as little value.

Is value a particular state of mind? Or a form inhering in certain data of consciousness? My answer is: Whatever one said to me, I would reject it; not indeed because the explanation is false but because it is an *explanation*.

If anybody offers me a *theory*, I would say: No, no, that doesn't interest me. Even if the theory were true that would not interest me—it would not be *what* I seek. The ethical cannot be taught. If I needed a theory in order to explain to another the essence of the ethical, the ethical would have no value at all.

At the end of my lecture on ethics, I spoke in the first person. I believe that is quite essential. Here nothing more can be established, I can only appear as a person speaking for myself.

For me the theory has no value. A theory gives me nothing.

RELIGION. Is speech essential for religion? I can quite well imagine a religion in which there are no doctrines, and hence nothing is said. Obviously the essence of religion can have nothing to do with the fact that speech occurs—or rather: if speech does occur, this itself is a component of religious behavior and not a theory. Therefore nothing turns on whether the words are true, false, or nonsensical.

Neither are religious utterances *figurative*, for else they should be also expressible in prose. Thrusting against the limits of language? Language is not a cage.

I can only say: I don't belittle this human tendency; I take my hat off to it. And here it is essential that this is not a sociological description but that I speak *for myself*.

For me the facts are unimportant. But what men mean when they say that *"The world is there"* lies close to my heart.

I ask Wittgenstein: Is the existence of the world connected with the ethical?

Wittgenstein: Men have felt a connection here and have expressed it in this way: God the Father created the world, while God the Son (or the Word proceeding from God) is the ethical. That men have first divided the Godhead and then united it, points to there being a connection here.

III: Some Developments in Wittgenstein's View of Ethics

RUSH RHEES

In the *Tractatus* (6.42) Wittgenstein says "there can be no ethical propositions," but he still thinks that

speaking of good and evil means something. He has
just said that "in the world everything is as it is, and
things happen as they do; *in* the world there is no
value—and if there were any, it would have no value."
(Instead of "a value that has value" he might have said
"that has value in itself" or "absolute value.") What
there is, the kinds of things there are, and the ways in
which things happen might have been otherwise:
there is nothing special about their being as they are.
He might have said that an expression like "a value
which has value" is nonsense born of a confusion of
grammar, which a logical analysis would replace by
something else. Instead he says that "if there is a
value which has any value, it must lie outside the
whole sphere of what happens." And it is because of
what judgments of good and evil do mean that it is
pointless to look for their meaning in any events or
facts that might be found by science. "There are no
distinctions of absolute value" does not mean "the
phrase 'distinctions of absolute value' means nothing."

"There are no ethical propositions" was a commentary to 6.4: "All propositions are of equal value."
This means first that all *logical* propositions are of
equal value. No one logical principle and no special
set of logical principles is the fundamental one and
source of all the rest. None occupies an "exceptional
position." But when he turns 6.4 toward "ethical propositions" he does not refer to the equal value of all
logical propositions but to that of all statements of
fact. Perhaps no one would take an ethical judgment
for the assertion of a logical principle, but one might
think it some kind of description of what has happened. Here again Wittgenstein is guided by what
we do mean in these judgments.

Compare "absolute value lies outside the world of
facts" and "logical necessity lies outside the world
of facts." Neither can be expressed, but logical necessity can be shown as absolute value cannot. We may
show the necessity of logical principles by writing
tautologies and contradictions in the T-F notation. The

T-F notation is a logical symbol, not an explanation, and it is one in which we may write any other form of proposition as well. It is a notation in which they are shown to *be* propositions. It shows both how logical principles are distinguished from other propositions and how they are related to the form of proposition—to what it is to be a proposition at all. But the T-F notation is no help in ethical judgments; for where there is a judgment of absolute value, the question "Is it true or false?" means nothing.

If I could express an ethical judgment, you might deny it, and of course it would mean nothing to say we were both right. But in the *Tractatus*, and in much of the "Lecture on Ethics," Wittgenstein thinks of "true or false" in the sense in which a prediction in science may be shown to be true or false. It would make no sense to ask if a judgment of absolute value had been corroborated by something that happened or something that had been discovered. We cannot ask this of logical principles either; but the T-F notation takes account of this, and it serves for logical principles because these are (as he later called them) rules of grammar of propositions which do allow of corroboration or falsification.

The explanation (of the difference between logical necessity and absolute value) by reference to the T-F notation is probably too simple. There are ethical statements, but they are expressed no differently from statements of fact; the ethical character is not shown in the symbolism. If we consider (6.422) an ethical law of the form "You ought . . ." the first thought is, "And what if I don't?"—as though it were a statement of *relative* value. With a judgment of absolute value the question makes no sense. But we might almost ask: "By what logic?"

If I say, "then the angles *must* be equal," there is no alternative; that is, "the alternative" means nothing. If I say, "You *ought* to want to behave better," there is no alternative either. The other may think, "What if I don't?" if only because in fact he does not and there is nothing to make him. Or he may be denying what I said: it may be a way of saying, "There is no 'ought' about it." But if he means it as a question, he has mistaken what I said: he can ask it only because he thinks I meant something else.

"You ought to make sure that the strip is firmly clamped before you start drilling." "What if I don't?" When I tell you what will happen if you don't, you see what I mean.

But: "You ought to want to behave better." "What if I don't?" What more could I tell you?

Yet "There *is* no alternative" does not mean what it does in logic. "If the legs of the triangle are equal, the base angles *must* be equal." Suppose my first thought were: "What if I make one with the legs perfectly equal and the base angles are not equal?" You say, "Don't talk nonsense"; or you get me to look more closely at what I was trying to ask, and I say, "Oh, yes." When the man asked, "What if I don't?" the question made no sense in that connection, although it would in others. But when I tried to ask about the logical conclusion, it was not a question at all. (I do not think "indirect proofs" make any difference here.)

We express (or try to express) judgments of value, not just any time, but in circumstances in which it makes sense to do so. Then there are certain replies one can make and certain questions one can ask, and others which would mean nothing. This is implied, at least, in the *Tractatus*. It is not worked out, and it hardly could be, with the views he then held about language and about sense.

He had changed them by the time of the "Lecture on Ethics." He did not think one could give a general account of propositions in terms of truth functions. Every proposition belongs to some system of propositions, and there are a number of these systems. The formal rules or internal relations of one system are not those of another. He spoke of them as "systems of measurement" and as "independent coordinates of description." Several will come into the description of

one and the same state of affairs: the description is
determined by several co-ordinates. He could not speak
in this sense of a system of ethical propositions or
judgments of value, as though we might determine the
object's value along with its weight and temperature.
And he still thought of language primarily as description. But the "Lecture on Ethics" starts from examples
more than the *Tractatus* does.

For instance, when someone says, "I know I'm playing tennis badly, but I don't want to play any better,"
all the other man could say would be, "Ah, then, that's
all right." He is making a judgment of value—not
telling anyone what he has seen. And the "could"
expresses a rule of grammar. Then, when someone
says, "I know I behave badly, but then I don't want
to behave any better," Wittgenstein asks whether you
could make the same reply here, and answers "certainly not," meaning that such a reply would make no
sense. This has nothing to do with what would be
intelligible in a description of facts. It is a question of
what is intelligible in this game of ethical judgments.
Toward the end of the lecture he does show how in
our expressions of value judgments we may take a
familiar word like "safe" and join it with "absolutely"
—which is a distortion or a destruction of its meaning.
But the example by which he first showed what he
meant by a judgment of absolute value—"Well, you
ought to want to behave better"—is a natural remark
to make in the circumstances; the only remark you
could make, in fact. It is not a distortion or misuse of
language.

He says in the later examples that he would reject
any analysis which showed that they were not nonsense—that they describe such and such experiences—
because in those expressions he wishes to "go beyond
the world . . . that is to say, beyond significant language." I think this goes with a view of judgments
of value as expressions of will.

The *Tractatus* distinguishes the will that is good or
evil from the will of which I have experience (this is

a grammatical distinction). He had written in the *Notebooks* (p. 87) that "the will is a position the subject adopts towards the world" (or he might have said, "towards life"). I know only that "I *have* to go that way." I cannot do certain things without feeling ashamed. This is part of how I look on life, what I recognize that I must meet. In the same way, I may find problems where another would find none—or it may be the other way about. I praise the character a man has just shown, or I tell him "You ought to want to behave better." This refers to what he did or said here just now. But I am claiming that the significance of what he did "goes beyond" these circumstances. A little earlier in the *Notebooks* (p. 83) he said that "a good life is the world seen *sub specie aeternitatis*. . . . The ordinary way of looking at things sees objects so to speak from within their midst, the view *sub specie aeternitatis* from outside. So that they have the whole world as their background." I suppose he disliked this phrasing, and the *Tractatus* phrasing is different. It may still do something to show why he separates judgments of value from statements of fact, and what he means when he says they cannot be expressed.

He criticized remarks of this sort later. If you have said what it is that cannot be expressed, we begin to wonder how expressing it would differ from saying what it is. Of course I may say, "There is no one sentence which could convey all I meant when I thanked him." To understand any judgment of value we have to know something of the culture, perhaps the religion, within which it is made, as well as the particular circumstances that called it forth; what the man had done, what the question was when I spoke to him, and so on. But suppose I have explained all this, we might still ask whether I have said something which has, for me and for some who heard me, a significance which "goes beyond" all circumstances. What would it mean if I said it did have a significance of that kind? One answer is: that it goes deep with me when I say it; that it is anything but a *trivial* remark. This will

appear especially in the way I behave after I have
spoken: my behavior toward the man I addressed and
toward the one he wronged, for instance. (Here
again: it has to be an occasion on which a remark
could have that significance. To behave in this way
otherwise would be ridiculous and annoying.)

If you said that the moral rebuke, if it is justified,
has a significance beyond any circumstances, many
would understand you. And if we describe the difference it makes when the remark is of this kind, we
shall know what is meant by describing it as "going
beyond."

The *Tractatus* is unclear in this because it does not
mention the occasions or the problems in connection
with which a man might make such a judgment. We
are not *always* viewing actions as we do in a judgment of value. The *Tractatus* speaks of "problems of
life." But it does not ask—as Wittgenstein later did—
when, or in what circumstances, anyone would speak
about problems of life.

Once (in 1942) when I had asked something about
the study of ethics, Wittgenstein said it was strange
that you could find books on ethics in which there
was no mention of a genuine ethical or moral problem.
He wanted to speak of a problem only where you
could imagine or recognize a solution, I think. When
I suggested the question whether Brutus' stabbing
Caesar was a noble action (as Plutarch thought) or a
particularly evil one (as Dante thought), Wittgenstein said this was not even something you could
discuss. "You would not know for your life what went
on in his mind before he decided to kill Caesar. What
would be have had to feel in order that you should
say that killing his friend was noble?"[2] Wittgenstein
mentioned the question of one of Kierkegaard's essays:
"Has a man a right to let himself be put to death for
the truth?" and he said, "For me this is not even a

[2] I am quoting from what I wrote down a few hours
after the conversation. The quotation marks mean no more
than that.

problem. I don't know what it would be *like* to let
oneself be put to death for the truth. I don't know
how such a man would have to feel, what state of
mind he would be in, and so forth. This may reach a
point at which the whole problem wavers and ceases
to be a problem at all. Like asking which of two
sticks is the longer when they are seen through the
'shimmer' of air rising from a hot pavement. You say,
'But surely one of them *must* be longer.' How are we
to understand this?" I suggested the problem facing a
man who has come to the conclusion that he must
either leave his wife or abandon his work of cancer
research. "Thanks," said Wittgenstein, "Let's discuss
this.

"Such a man's attitude will vary at different times.
Suppose I am his friend, and I say to him, 'Look,
you've taken this girl out of her home, and now, by
God, you've got to stick to her.' This would be called
taking up an ethical attitude. He may reply, 'But what
of suffering humanity? how can I abandon my research?' In saying this he may be making it easy for
himself: he wants to carry on that work anyway. (I
may have reminded him that there are others who
can carry it on if he gives up.) And he may be inclined to view the effect on his wife relatively easily:
'It probably won't be fatal for her. She'll get over it,
probably marry again,' and so on. On the other hand
it may not be this way. It may be that he has a deep
love for her. And yet he may think that if he were to
give up his work he would be no husband for her.
That is his life, and if he gives that up he will drag her
down. Here we may say that we have all the materials
of a tragedy; and we could only say: 'Well, God help
you.'

"Whatever he finally does, the way things then turn
out may affect his attitude. He may say, 'Well, thank
God I left her: it was better all around.' Or maybe,
'Thank God I stuck to her.' Or he may not be able to
say 'thank God' at all, but just the opposite.

"I want to say that this is the solution of an ethical problem.

"Or rather: it is so with regard to the man who does not have an ethics. If he has, say, the Christian ethics, then he may say it is absolutely clear: he has got to stick to her come what may. And then his problem is different. It is: how to make the best of this situation, what he should do in order to be a decent husband in these greatly altered circumstances, and so forth. The question 'Should I leave her or not?' is not a problem here.

"Someone might ask whether the treatment of such a question in Christian ethics is *right* or not. I want to say this question does not make sense. The man who asks it might say: 'Suppose I view his problem with a different ethics—perhaps Nietzsche's—and I say: "No, it is not clear that he must stick to her; on the contrary, . . . and so forth." Surely one of the two answers must be the right one. It must be possible to decide which of them is right and which is wrong.'

"But we do not know what this decision would be like—how it would be determined, what sort of criteria would be used, and so on. Compare saying that it must be possible to decide which of two standards of accuracy is the right one. We do not even know what a person who asks this question is after."

He came back to this question of "the right ethics" later. He did so once (in 1945) when he was discussing the relations of ethics and psychology and sociology. "People have had the notion of an ethical theory—the idea of finding the true nature of goodness or of duty. Plato wanted to do this—to set ethical inquiry in the direction of finding the true nature of goodness —so as to achieve objectivity and avoid relativity. He thought relativity must be avoided at all costs, since it would destroy the *imperative* in morality.

"Suppose you simply described the *Sitten und Gebräuche* (ways and customs) of various tribes: this would not be ethics. Studying ways and customs would not be the same as studying rules or laws. A rule is neither a command—because there is no one who gives the command—nor is it an empirical statement of how the majority of people behave. Both those interpretations ignore the different grammars, the different ways in which rules are used. They are not used as commands are and they are not used as sociological descriptions are. If I buy a game in Woolworth's, I may find on the inside cover a set of rules beginning: 'First set out the pieces in such and such a way.' Is this an order? Is it a description—an assertion that anybody ever has acted or ever will act in that way?

"Someone may say, 'There is still the difference between truth and falsity. Any ethical judgment in whatever system may be true or false.' Remember that '*p* is true' means simply '*p*.' If I say: 'Although I believe that so and so is good, I may be wrong': this says no more than that what I assert may be denied.

"Or suppose someone says, 'One of the ethical systems must be the right one—or nearer to the right one.' Well, suppose I say Christian ethics is the right one. Then I am making a judgment of value. It amounts to *adopting* Christian ethics. It is not like saying that one of these physical theories must be the right one. The way in which some reality corresponds—or conflicts—with a physical theory has no counterpart here.

"If you say there are various systems of ethics you are not saying they are all equally right. That means nothing. Just as it would have no meaning to say that each was right from his own standpoint. That could only mean that each judges as he does."

These samples (perhaps not well chosen) from his later discussions show parallels with his later discussions of language and of logic and mathematics. There is no one system in which you can study in its purity and its essence what ethics is. We use the term "ethics" for a variety of systems, and for philosophy this variety is important. Obviously different ethical systems have points in common. There must be grounds for saying that people who follow a particular system are making ethical judgments: that they regard this or that as good, and so forth. But it does not follow that what those people say must be an expression of something more ultimate. He used to say that what we might call "the anthropological method" had proved particularly fruitful in philosophy: that is, imagining "a tribe among whom it is carried on in this way: . . . ." And once when I mentioned Goering's *"Recht ist das, was uns gefällt,"* Wittgenstein said that "even that is a kind of ethics. It is helpful in silencing objections to a certain attitude. And it should be considered along with other ethical judgments and discussions, in the anthropological study of ethical discussions which we may have to conduct."

In the period leading up to the *Investigations* he would try to set down the way he had thought about logic in the *Tractatus*. For example: "In logic we have a *theory*, and this must be simple and neat, for I want to know that whereby language is language. That all this which we call language has imperfections and slag on it, I agree, but I want to come to know *that* which *has* been adulterated. That whereby I am able to *say something.*" What the *Tractatus* says of "the real sign" (*das eigentliche Zeichen*) or "the real proposition" would illustrate this. And there is a similar tendency in what it says of ethics. "The Ethical," which cannot be expressed, is that whereby I am able to think of good and evil at all, even in the impure and nonsensical expressions I have to use.

In the *Tractatus* he would consider different ways of saying something, in order to find what is essential to its expression. As we can see what the various ways of expressing it have in common, we can see what is arbitrary in each of them and distinguish it from what is necessary. Near the beginning of the "Lecture on Ethics" (pp. 4–5 above) he says: "if you look through the row of synonyms which I will put before you, you will, I hope, be able to see the characteristic features which they all have in common and these are the characteristic features of Ethics."

When he wrote the *Brown Book* he would constantly describe "different ways of doing it," but he did not call them different ways of saying the same thing. Nor did he think we could reach the heart of the matter by seeing what they all have in common. He did not see them as so many fumbling attempts to say what none of them ever does say perfectly. The variety is important—not in order to fix your gaze on the unadulterated form, but to keep you from looking for it.

When he says there that any given language game or system of human communication is "complete," he means that you fall into confusion if you try to provide a more ample and more perfect system for what may be said in it. Whatever may be said in your new system, it will not be what was said in the original language game. (Think of the advertisements for formalized languages.) When we study ethical systems other than our own, there is a special temptation to interpret them. We are inclined to think that expressions as they are used in those ethical discussions have some significance which they suggest to *us*— instead of looking at what is done with them there. Wittgenstein mentioned *L'homme est bon* and *La femme est bonne.* "Consider the temptation to think that this must really mean that the man has a masculine goodness and that the woman has a feminine goodness. There may be a very strong temptation to think this. And yet this is not what the French say. What they really mean is what they really say: *l'homme est bon'* and *'la femme est bonne.'* In considering a different system of ethics there may be a strong temptation to think that what seems to *us* to express the justification of an action must be what really justifies it there, whereas the real reasons are the reasons that are given. These *are* the reasons for or against the action. 'Reason' doesn't always mean the same thing; and in ethics we have to keep from assuming that reasons must really be of a different sort from what they are seen to be."

CHAPTER 2

THE UNITY OF WITTGENSTEIN'S THOUGHT

DENNIS O'BRIEN*

J. O. URMSON's historical account of the development of philosophical analysis in Britain between the two World Wars casts Wittgenstein as the founder of two opposed views of the notion of philosophical analysis —a "metaphysical" reductive analysis akin to Russell's "logical atomism," and an "ordinary language," descriptive analysis akin to the analyses of Austin or Ryle.[1] The *Tractatus Logico-Philosophicus*[2] is the cornerstone of atomism; the *Philosophical Investigations*[3] is a rejection of the *Tractatus* in favor of a new mode of philosophy. Urmson notes, however, that new interpretations of the *Tractatus* in the light of the later *Investigations* appearing at the time his book was written tended to question the radical disparity between early and late Wittgenstein, but he justifies his

* Dennis O'Brien is Professor of Philosophy and Dean of the College at Middlebury College, Vermont. This article originally appeared in *The International Philosophical Quarterly*, Vol. 6, No. 1 (March 1966), and is printed here by permission of the editor and author.

[1] J. O. Urmson, *Philosophical Analysis: Its Development between the Two World Wars* (Oxford: Clarendon Press, 1956).

[2] Ludwig Wittgenstein, *Tractatus Logico-Philosophicus*, newly translated by D. F. Pears and B. F. McGuiness (New York: Humanities Press, 1961). All references to the *Tractatus* will be to this edition.

[3] Ludwig Wittgenstein, *Philosophical Investigations*, trans. G. E. M. Anscombe (New York: Macmillan, 1953). Afterward cited as *PI*.

own account on the ground that his reading of the development of analysis was the one held by the philosophers of the period. There is no doubt that Urmson reports correctly on the general opinion current until very recently that Wittgenstein rejected and even disparaged his early work.[4] Interpreters of the *Tractatus* have had to work in the face of Wittgenstein's own seeming rejection. Still, Wittgenstein did want the *Tractatus* published as a background to the *Investigations*[5] and Stenius expresses the "newer" view when he says, "I share the often-expressed feeling that Wittgenstein overshoots the mark when in his later work he criticizes his earlier thought."[6]

On some of the most crucial points of seeming change the record is unclear. Is it the espousal of ordinary language that marks the new philosophy? *Tractatus* 5.5563 reads: "In fact, all propositions of our everyday language, just as they stand, are in perfect logical order."[7] Clearly the *Investigations* rejects the notion of sense-data, but according to Anscombe so does the author of the *Tractatus*.[8] In this article, I

[4] David Pole, *The Later Philosophy of Wittgenstein* (London: University of London, 1958) is an account of the philosophy of the *Investigations* which regards it as a wholly independent endeavor totally divorced from the rejected *Tractatus*.

[5] "It suddenly seemed to me that I should publish those old thoughts [*Tractatus*] and the new ones [*Investigations*] together: that the latter could be seen in the right light only in contrast with and against the background of my old way of thinking." *PI*, x.

[6] Erik Stenius, *Wittgenstein's Tractatus* (Ithaca, N.Y.: Cornell U. Press, 1960), p. 16.

[7] Frank Ramsey objected to Russell's claim that the *Tractatus* was concerned with "ideal languages" on the basis of this statement. See the reprint of Ramsey's review of the *Tractatus* in F. Ramsey, *Foundations of Mathematics* (New York: Harcourt, 1931).

[8] G. E. M. Anscombe, *An Introduction to Wittgenstein's Tractatus* (London: Hutchinson Univ. Library, 1959), Ch. 1. Anscombe criticizes Popper's sense-data interpretation of "atomic facts" which she cites as "the most common view of the *Tractatus*" (p. 25).

should like in a very brief and sketchy way to indicate a fundamental unity that runs through all of Wittgenstein. It will be seen that the unity is most clear in what is uniformly *rejected* by both the *Tractatus* and the *Investigations*. On the more "positive" side, a fundamental unity or at least continuity can be discerned in Wittgenstein's notion of the task and method of philosophy. Bringing out this unity is not simply a hollow meta-philosophical victory, since in a philosophy which offers no theses the notion of how to philosophize is central.

I. How to Reject Nonsense

An historian of philosophy writing as a Wittgensteinian faces great difficulties describing the relation between the *Tractatus* and the later works. He says of the propositions in the *Tractatus*: "6.54 My propositions serve as elucidations in the following way: anyone who understands me eventually recognizes them as nonsensical, when he has used them—as steps—to climb up beyond them." He contrasts philosophical propositions with propositions of the natural sciences (6.53) on the ground that the propositions of the sciences say something, while philosophical propositions do not and are without meaning. If Wittgenstein is serious here, and I believe he is, as I will show below, then it does not seem that he could *refute* the *Tractatus* by showing that the propositions in it were false. Scientific theories say something, they make a claim about how the world is, and these theories can be verified or refuted. It is the misfortune of philosophical statements that they are neither verifiable or refutable. Wittgenstein does say, that "the *truth* of the thoughts that are here [in the *Tractatus*] set forth seems to me unassailable and definitive" (p. 5). Just how that claim is to be interpreted is very puzzling since it hardly seems possible that propositions which he characterizes as "nonsense" can be "true." The simplest way of accounting for this discrepancy is to hold that what he says in a general way about the *Tractatus* in the Preface does not conform to the strict conventions of the text itself. Strictly, philosophical propositions are elucidations and Wittgenstein's are *true* elucidations, i.e., the right and proper elucidations, but we should not think than an elucidation is itself a statement of *fact* which conforms to the canons of verification. It is no inconsistency, no matter how paradoxical it sounds, to say that the *Tractatus* gives the true elucidation of philosophical problems while offering no truths. As we shall see, this notion of elucidation is critical.

If no truths are offered by the *Tractatus* then there is no possibility of showing their falsity at a later date. Of course one could abandon this purely elucidatory notion of philosophy and conclude that philosophy really *does* offer truths. From such a standpoint one could say that it was a philosophical *truth* that purely elucidatory conceptions of philosophy are misconceived in some fashion. Wittgenstein, of course, does not criticize the *Tractatus* in this fashion, and he says in the *Investigations,* § 128: "If one tried to advance *theses* in philosophy, it would never be possible to question them, because everyone would agree to them." This statement implies that philosophy does not, in fact, advance theses—statements that could be taken as truth claims—and *if* it did, they would be very odd claims, since they would seem so unassailable that everyone would agree right off and wonder why any claim needed to be made at all. This general agreement to philosophical "theses" is comparable to the "truth" of the propositions of the *Tractatus* which is definitive and unassailable—and for that reason not properly comparable to even the most well verified scientific statements. We will have to choose from the category of rejection some notion other than "false" or "refuted" to describe Wittgenstein's attitude toward the *Tractatus* or else we will undercut his own notion that philosophy does not offer theses. The statement, "I have refuted a philosophical thesis," is anomalous for Wittgenstein throughout.

Just how to characterize the undoubted rejection of the *Tractatus* is very puzzling. If we were to state it in ways suggested by the *Investigations* it would seem that the earlier work was too *narrow*. Whatever "truth" it contained was restricted to only one very limited problem, the meaning of declarative sentences in the context of the strict sciences. In the later work we are asked to consider the whole variety of language games from giving orders to guessing riddles, making jokes, thanking, cursing, greeting, praying, of which scientific claims are only a small group (*PI*, 23). As Wittgenstein comments after listing these various language games: "It is interesting to compare the multiplicity of the tools in language and the ways they are used, the multiplicity of kinds of word and sentence, with what logicians have said about the structure of language. (Including the author of the *Tractatus Logico-Philosophicus*.)" What is "false" about the *Tractatus* may be mistaking part for whole. Even in ordinary cases, decisions about parts and wholes are not straightforward empirical matters. It is clearly a mistake to say that an arm is the whole of what we know as the body, but it is not like the mistake of describing an arm as if it worked by steel springs. Perhaps the *Tractatus* should be looked on as a wrong *decision*, which, like a wrong decision about parts and wholes in a scientific case, proved unfruitful—though not in the scientific sense of unfruitful.

II. "The Meaning of P Is —"

The simplest key to the whole of Wittgenstein's philosophy lies in the evaluation of sentences of this type. It is a perfectly ordinary type of sentence which is used everyday and, like St. Augustine's problems with the notion of time, it never bothers us unless we are asked to explain it. (Wittgenstein, of course, uses Augustine's famous query about time as an illustration of a *philosophical* problem: *PI*, 89.) Philosophers have taken the explanation of this sentence as their particular task and have produced various theories of meaning, behavioristic, mentalistic and so on. To understand Wittgenstein properly we must realize that he consistently holds that *all* these attempts are beside the point. The notion of a *theory* of meaning is empty or an instance of language on a holiday. "Theory" is a perfectly comprehensible word and so is "meaning" despite our temptation to think of it as queer (*PI*, 93); but the two gears don't mesh. When the two notions are brought together neither one does its proper work and so the machine idles.

To state in summary fashion what will be developed below, the sentence, "The meaning of *p* is —," has been wrongly interpreted by philosophers as a statement admitting truth values. It looks like a declarative sentence, like "The color of the rug is blue," and so philosophers have tried to indicate what sorts of facts could be used to substantiate a claim that the meaning of something was such-and-such. In the *Tractatus*, Wittgenstein holds that such sentences *about* meaning are themselves meaningless since they do not, as meaningful sentences do, picture any facts. Sentences about meaning and theories of meaning in general are not *theoretical* because they do not have any factual basis; they are part of "the mystical." There is a *prima facie* case that there is an analogous position in the *Investigations* where we are told to completely abjure looking for the meaning of words and sentences and to concentrate on how they are used. The heart of the misinterpretations of the *Tractatus* and the *Investigations* lies in assuming in various ways that some theory of meaning is being presented. For the *Tractatus* it has been sense-data which are the *facts* which substantiate the claim that the meaning of *p* is ⸺, while in the *Investigations* it is a behavioral criterion. Both notions are fundamentally misconceived.

III. *Psychological and Logical Theories of Meaning*

In order to understand the *Tractatus* it is necessary to remind ourselves of Russell's views on the nature of meaning from which Wittgenstein was attempting to escape. It is a well known fact, which Russell himself gratefully acknowledged, that Wittgenstein's criticism caused him to change his mind on certain issues. Yet in his introductory remarks to the *Tractatus* Russell managed to suggest a way of reading that book which was much closer to his own views than Wittgenstein's. Russell's views we can fairly characterize as a psychological theory of meaning, while Wittgenstein's we can call a logical theory for lack of a better term, though we must realize that in the last analysis it is not a theory. That Russell's theory of meaning was psychological *even after* the impact of Wittgenstein's ideas is testified to by this remark from the lectures on logical atomism in which he publicly acknowledged his debt to Wittgenstein: "The notion of meaning is always more or less psychological, and . . . it is not possible to get a pure logical theory of meaning."[9] It is a psychological theory of meaning via sense processes that Russell suggested as a proper reading of the *Tractatus*. As Anscombe tries to show in her commentary—and I agree with her in this—no such reading can be supported by the text.

We will fail to appreciate the radical nature of Witt-

[9] Bertrand Russell, "The Philosophy of Logical Atomism," reprinted in B. Russell, *Logic and Knowledge*, ed. R. C. Marsh (London: Allen & Unwin, 1956), p. 186.

genstein's proposals in the *Tractatus* unless we are caught by the plausibility of Russell's views about meaning. A word is only a noise, a fact like any other, but as a word it has the capacity to *stand for something*, to be a sign. How does this marvelous capacity arise? Russell's account is straightforward and seemingly correct. The noise attaches itself to the object which it stands for through some process in the brain. As red objects cause red sensations, so the word "red" can cause, bring to mind, red sensations and thus make us turn to consider the world. It is obvious why such a view is labelled "psychological"; it is also clear that it is a straightforward *theory* since like all theories it describes a factual or causal connection. There is nothing mysterious about the claim that "red" has a meaning; it amounts to the factual claim that this sound "red" causes a psychological event which in turn is or has been causally related to certain facts in the world. To say that "red" has a meaning is to make a factual claim about the relation of a certain sound to the brain and through the brain to the world. This gives a picture of how words have meaning that seems inescapable; yet if we pursue it we run into grave problems.

As a theory of meaning this psychological view offers a convenient way of handling meaninglessness. A word is meaningless if the causal connection fails to obtain. If words have meaning when they refer to objects in the world, then a noise which cannot be traced to the world via sensations will be empty noise, meaningless. Words like "god" must be analyzed into sense qualities in order that they can be given meaning; if they cannot be so analyzed they are vacuous. If a word has meaning ultimately via a connection to objects through sensations our ordinary names of objects like "dog" will need analysis into sense qualities, and finally even the normal sense words like "red" prove insufficient. The sound "red" may cause some sensation in my brain—no doubt "god" causes some vague images to swim into view— but I can only be sure that a sound has a meaning if the quality of the sensation is the kind caused by the world. If not, then my language hooks on to nothing. The only way of finally verifying that a sensation is caused by the world is in present experience. There is no *real* way of doubting that this present impression is from the world, so the word which signifies via this sensation has a meaning.[10] Thus Russell felt it imperative to replace the ordinary names of our language like "dog" or "Socrates" with logically proper names like "this" whose function is clearly directed toward what is immediate in experience. Sentences compounded out of logically proper names which indubitably had a meaning guaranteed by present experience were the end point of analysis. It was in this way that those strange sounds that we call words could hook onto a world and have meaning. If meaning consists in the factual connection of sound, sensation, and object, then, like all factual assertions, it must ultimately be grounded in the immediate observation of just such a connection.

If basic or atomic propositions are compounded of logically proper names construed in the fashion suggested, then it follows that not only must they be meaningful, since they stand at the point of causal linkage between the brain and the world, but they must also be *true*. Any proposition formed out of such logically proper names directs us at once to the present reality which gives them meaning by hooking them on to the world *and* presents us with the data which will confirm the proposition. We are to imagine a proposition like "This is thus" in which the words definitely have a meaning because they hook onto the world in our immediate awareness. But, if this is the case, while I am gathering in the meaning of the names I will also inspect the very data which will confirm the judgment. Indeed, I will always discover that such judgments are true. If I look about and see that this is *such*, not thus, I am in no position to say that the original propo-

[10] I pass by as irrelevant the problem of the existence of the external world as the cause of these direct sensations.

sition is false. I can reply, "But what do you mean? I see a *this* that is *such*, is that what you mean by 'thus'? If so then your proposition is surely true, if not then I don't know what I am to look for." Russell did maintain just such a view of basic propositions even as late as the *Inquiry into Meaning and Truth*.

A basic proposition must have two properties: (1) it must be caused by some sensible occurrence; (2) it must be of such a form that no other basic proposition can contradict it.

As to (1): I do not wish to insist upon the word "caused," but the belief must arise on the occasion of some sensible occurrence, and must be such that, if questioned, it will be defended by the argument, "why, I see it" or something similar.

As to (2): . . . No previous or subsequent occurrence, and no experience of others, can prove the falsehood of a basic proposition. . . . When we have analyzed a judgment of perception in this way we are left with something that cannot be *proved* to be false.[11]

There are many anomalies about this theory, including the fact that such basic propositions cannot be uttered because by the time the words are formulated the experience has flitted by. But the most striking for our purposes is that a basic proposition is a factual statement that cannot be *proved* to be false. Indeed, it would turn out on Russell's view that if we had an ideal language, not only would all propositions have clear empirical meanings, but there would be no false propositions. Any molecular proposition either can be analyzed into a compound of basic propositions all of which *must* be true so that the equivalent complex must be true, or it simply cannot be analyzed at all and is meaningless. Ironically, it is precisely on the matter of atomic propositions that Russell and Wittgenstein differ so radically and yet where they were interpreted as basically identical. Russell's basic propositions are defined by certain *factual* considerations, psychological

[11] B. Russell, *Inquiry into Meaning and Truth*, (London: Allen & Unwin, 1940) pp. 138–39.

immediacy, and causal relation to the world; Wittgenstein's are defined by the *logical* property of having one and only one way of being falsified. This point is made in very different ways by Anscombe[12] and by Stenius in his account of how an atomic proposition determines a "yes-no space."[13]

We shall discuss Wittgenstein's notion of atomic propositions below. Yet we should emphasize the striking contrast between two theories which rest on atomic propositions, but for one of which these propositions must be true, where for the other they must always be univocally falsifiable. The misunderstanding is vividly pointed up in the correspondence between Russell and Wittgenstein about the *Tractatus*. Russell asks, "But a *Gedanke* (thought) is a *Tatsache* (fact): what are its constituents and components, and what is their relation to those of the pictured *Tatsache*?" Wittgenstein replied;

I don't know what the constituents of a thought are but I know *that* it must have constituents which correspond to the words of our language. Again the kind of relation of the constituents of the thought and of the pictured fact is irrelevant. It would be a matter of psychology to find out.[14]

And as Wittgenstein says in the *Tractatus*: "4.1121 Psychology is no more closely related to philosophy than any other natural science." If you have a psychological and causal theory of meaning, as we claim Russell has, then it is absolutely vital to find out the constituents of the thought-fact. How else will you make the causal connection which defines meaning? For Wittgenstein, however, the relation of the factual constituents of a thought and a pictured fact are "irrelevant." A psychologist might discover what they were but it would not assist the philosopher in his task of elucidating meanings. As he says in the *Investigations*,

[12] Anscombe, *op. cit.*, pp. 34–36.
[13] Stenius, *op. cit.*, ch. IV.
[14] Quoted in Anscombe, *op. cit.*, p. 28.

"Try not to think of understanding as a 'mental process' at all" (*PI*, 154).

There is no doubt that at first blush one could imagine that Wittgenstein and Russell had the same notion of meaning. For Russell, language hooks onto the world via logically proper names which must have meaning, which are guaranteed to stand for things in the world. And Wittgenstein says:

2.1514 The pictorial relationship consists of the correlations of the picture's elements with things [*Sachen*].

2.1515 These correlations are, as it were, the feelers of the picture's elements, with which the picture touches reality.

The elements of the picture are the names out of which it is concatenated, these names are correlated to things, and by this means language hooks onto the world. But the contrast can be brought clearly into focus by looking at the difference in the two men's "doctrine" of *objects*. For Russell, if I know that "red" has a meaning then I know as a *fact* that red objects exist or have existed. In the final analysis if a word has a meaning it is because a causal connection can be traced to the world which entitles us to make some sort of true existence statement. Meaning is a *factual* relation between a sound fact and some occurrence of a sense object. These objects which stand as the meaning of the sounds are quite concrete, positive existents—if they weren't they could hardly enter into the factual claim involved in saying that some sound had a meaning. The essence of basic objects is that they are directly observable qualia. In Wittgenstein, on the other hand, objects are not positive concrete entities at all. What exist are facts. "1.1 The world is the totality of facts, not things." When I know an object I am not directly acquainted with a sense quale; rather

2.0123 If I know an object I also know all its possible occurrences in states of affairs.

(Everyone of these possibilities must be part of the nature of the object.)

2.0124 If all objects are given, then at the same time all *possible* states of affairs are also given.

At least for the purposes of meaning analysis, objects are defined as the *possibilities* of states of affairs. Wittgenstein doesn't deny that they may have positive qualities, perhaps like Russell's basic sense qualia, but "2.01231 If I am to know an object, though I need not know its external properties, I must know all its internal properties." Knowing the internal properties of an object is knowing its possible occurrences in states of affairs. If, then, propositions do touch reality via the names which are correlated with objects, it is not to actual reality, to existents, but to possible states of affairs.[15]

Because Russell's objects, which are the meanings of words, are positive existents, it follows that anytime we know the meaning of the word we also know some truth about the world, or conversely, for any word or

[15] The fact that for purposes of analysis "objects" are defined by their internal properties as possible states of affairs rather than any positive, external characteristics, calls into question a common interpretation of the famous opening section of the *Investigations*. There Wittgenstein criticizes Augustine's notion that we learn the meaning of words by an association between the concrete objects pointed at by parents and teachers and the sounds which they utter—a virtual paradigm of the psychological theory we have been discussing. It has been widely taken as an attack against the *Tractatus*, where meaning was supposedly the correlation of name and object. But Augustine, like Russell, is talking about concrete, existent objects and a factual association between a sound and a thing, while the positive characteristics of objects are quite beside the point in the *Tractatus*, where their whole function seems to be as something that enters into possible states of affairs. There is an enormous difference between a theory in which a sound has meaning in virtue of a straightforward factual relation to some concrete object, and one in which a word has meaning because it is seen as relating to a possible state of affairs. Clearly the *Investigations* is attacking sense data and psychological theories of meaning, but so, it seems to me, is the *Tractatus*.

proposition to have meaning some other proposition must be true, viz., the one which asserts the factual connection which is the meaning of the words. Since Wittgenstein's objects are not concrete existents, when we know the meaning of a word via its relation to objects we do not know any facts, since the relation of the picture-fact to a *possibility* can hardly be a fact. Thus Wittgenstein can make precisely the opposite claim about what we can "know," given the relation between names and objects.

2.021 Objects make up the substance of the world. That is why they cannot be composite.

2.0211 If the world had no substance, then whether a proposition has sense would depend on whether another proposition was true.

2.0212 In that case we could not sketch out any picture of the world (true or false).

One of the paradoxes of *any* position which maintains that the sentence, "The meaning of *p* is —," is a truth claim of some sort (about sensations, behavior and so on) is that *simply* from admitting that some sign has a meaning we can derive a true factual statement about the world. Indeed, we seem to be able to derive an infinite set of true statements from the admission that a sign *S* has a meaning. If *S* has a meaning then the proposition " '*S*' is related to *s* (the object which is its meaning)" must be true. And if this proposition is true it must have a meaning—how could a meaningless proposition be true?—and some further true propositions stating this meaning must be derivable and so on. We are involved in an infinite regress in which to know that a proposition is meaningful we must know the truth of another meaningful proposition which involves the truth of another meaningful proposition and so on. Either we accept the infinite regress or stop the process by means of some propositions in which truth and meaning are identical, as Russell does in his basic proposition. To Wittgenstein it seemed preferable to simply deny that ascertaining meaning involved the truth of any proposition, in particular, the proposition "the meaning of *p* is —." But if "the meaning of *p* is —" cannot be true or false it does not share the "logic" of sentences which have sense. 4.5 says, "The general form of a proposition is: This is how things stand." Our claims about the meaning of *p* do not express how things stand, they are neither verifiable or falsifiable, and thus are strictly without sense. If we cannot make truth claims about the meaning of this or that word or sentence then we must also lack any factual basis for a theory of meaning which would describe in a general way the factual process by means of which sounds get associated with the world. Wittgenstein believed that past philosophies had in various ways attempted such theories and hence were not simply false but nonsense.[16]

We have so far used the blanket term "meaning" to cover the notion of what it is that a word as distinguished from a mere sound accomplishes. Before proceeding to a further discussion of Wittgenstein we must take note of the distinction between sense (*Sinn*) and reference (*Bedeutung*) which Wittgenstein borrowed from Frege. Words are distinguished from mere noises in that they are *means* by which we take account of something. A proper name like "Socrates" is used to refer to someone but normally we do not think it has any sense, i.e., that it describes some quality. I can call my cat "Socrates," and that may be odd, ironic, and funny but it isn't false. On the other hand, "wise" has sense, so that referring to my cat as wise would be false. As Anscombe points out, Russell uses only one notion of meaning and "holds that the meaning of words must always be objects that one is directly acquainted with."[17] All meaning is finally referential; that is why the ultimate constituents of meaning must

---

[16] This belief seems to me substantially false. Stenius has already pointed out the resemblance between Wittgenstein and Kant: see Stenius, *op. cit.*, ch. XI. Philosophers have been remarkably ingenious in distinguishing their metaphysical or critical endeavors from scientific theory.

[17] Anscombe, *op. cit.*, p. 17.

be logically proper names, i.e., just those words which fail to function if they have no reference. The attempt to ground meaning in factual relations requires just this reduction of all meaning to referential meaning because a sound has a meaning only when it directs us toward an object in the world. Just as "Socrates" is simply a noise if it isn't used to refer to some object, so, Russell thinks, all words fail to have "meaning" if they cannot be grounded in an object referred to. Wittgenstein's position is at first sight closer to common sense since he holds that names have reference but no sense, while propositions have sense but no reference. The "meaning" of a proper name is to pick out the bearer, but the meaning of a proposition does not pick out any object; it conveys a sense which we can see is either confirmed or not confirmed by reality.

This distinction between sense and reference seems obviously correct *at first sight*, but we must credit Russell with showing that on deeper reflection it is puzzling. Russell, after all, consciously rejected the distinction which he knew from Frege. Why? Well, we are back at our initial problem: How do these noises hook onto the world? If the names out of which a proposition is compounded do not serve to pick out objects in the world, how can propositions ever have meaning or be verified? If names which direct us to present experience in the fashion that "Socrates" directs us to its bearer are not the ultimate meaningful units out of which everything else is compounded, then how does language direct us to the world at all? Referential meaning is *the* sense of meaning because it involves this necessary linkage between a noise and something for which that noise is a sign. Nevertheless, if we are bewitched by Russell's solution we will have to accept all of its paradoxes. Let us turn, then, directly to Wittgenstein's treatment of these questions.

A proposition has sense but no reference. "3.3 Only propositions have sense (*Sinn*)." Or, as Russell put it after accepting Wittgenstein's criticism, propositions are not names of facts.

It is quite obvious as soon as it is pointed out to you, but as a matter of fact I never realized it until it was pointed out to me by a former pupil of mine, Wittgenstein. It is perfectly evident as soon as you think of it, that a proposition is not a name of a fact, from the mere circumstance that there are *two* propositions corresponding to each fact. Suppose it is a fact that Socrates is dead. You have two propositions: "Socrates is dead" and "Socrates is not dead." And these two propositions corresponding to the same fact, there is one fact in the world that makes one true and one false.[18]

The point can be made clear by reversing Russell's example. Let us ask ourselves what makes the name "Socrates" work (have a meaning) and the proposition "Socrates is white" work. "Socrates" works when there is a Socrates to which it refers, but, curiously enough, "Socrates is white" works when there is a white Socrates *or* when there is a black, yellow, or red Socrates. Using the blanket notion of meaning, we say that "Socrates" has no meaning if it doesn't actually function to pick out somebody, but "Socrates is white" becomes false, not meaningless when it serves to pick out the red Socrates. If we were to say that our *proposition* had *referential* meaning, then we would have to say that the "objects" to which it referred were a white Socrates or a red Socrates or a yellow Socrates, etc. This would have to be the case, since it is the existence of any of these states that makes the proposition meaningful, although frequently false. When we know that a proposition has sense we know nothing about the world one way or the other. If *p* is meaningful then either P or not-P; if "Socrates is white" is meaningful, then either Socrates is white or Socrates is not white. And of course this doesn't tell me anything:

[18] Russell, "The Philosophy of Logical Atomism," *op. cit.*, p. 187. Either the point didn't sink in deeply enough or Russell forgot these good words when he came to treating "basic propositions," which certainly appear to function as names of atomic facts.

"4.461 I know nothing about the weather when I know that it is either raining or not raining."

If p is meaningful when a P or a non-P state of affairs obtains in the world, we could still wonder why there isn't a sort of factual check on whether a proposition has meaning. Imagine a universe U consisting of two objects, a and b, and two predicates, blue and red. Now consider the propositions "a is green" or "c is blue" or "c is green": are they meaningful in U? It would seem so. For U it is certainly the case that these propositions are false. All these propositions are meaningful in U because they are all false in U; and if a proposition can be false, it must be meaningful. Whatever the state of the facts in U, whether a is red or blue, b is red or blue, we can see that "a is green" is false, so that in a backhanded fashion a knowledge of the facts in U tells us that these propositions which seem to have nothing at all to do with U are meaningful. This is a paradoxical result. Wittgenstein's answer is the notion of atomic propositions. If we wish to see whether any proposition is meaningful we must analyze it into atomic propositions. Complex propositions have an indefinite sense. "3.24 When a propositional element signifies a complex, this can be seen from an indeterminateness in the propositions in which it occurs. In such cases we *know* that the proposition leaves something undetermined." As Anscombe suggests, "One kind of indefiniteness in a proposition might be that there was more than one way of its being false."[19] In U we know *the* meaning of "a is red" when it is false, viz., that a is blue. The two opposed colors form an analogy of a Yes-No space of possibilities such that the recognition that "a is red" is false can mean only one thing, that it is blue. In contrast, "c is blue" is false in U not because c is red, but because c just isn't. When I am told that "c is blue" is false, I would normally think that this was because c

---

[19] Anscombe, *op. cit.*, p. 34. My discussion at this point is particularly indebted to Anscombe's analysis of the *Tractatus*.

was red or some other color, but it appears that there
are two ways in which it could be falsified, namely,
when c is some other color or when there isn't any c
at all. This shows that when I know that the proposition is false I do not yet know what is being asserted
—I don't know whether I am to conclude that c is
another color or that c is non-existent. An atomic proposition is one in which no such ambiguity exists.

Adopting Anscombe's terminology, we say that "c is
blue" is not meaningful in respect to U because it is
radically false.[20] If it were meaningful it could be
analyzed into atomic propositions which, if they were
false, would be false in the ordinary way, i.e., "a is red"
is false because a is blue.[21] If we assumed that the
assertion of the color predicates of a or b exhausted the
atomic propositions in U, then "c is blue" must be
analyzed in terms of these—in which case its falsehood
will be ordinary falsehood—or else it cannot be so
analyzed and it will be meaningless in U. Thus when
we say that a proposition p is meaningful, we tacitly

[20] *Ibid.*, p. 49.
[21] My example is only an analogue of an atomic proposition intended to suggest the sense of "ordinary" as opposed
to "radical falsehood." 6.3751 rules out statements like "a
is red" as atomic propositions. In U "a is red" and "a is
blue" are possible propositions and I am imagining that
they are atomic. In fact they can't be because their logical
product is contradictory and "the logical product of two
elementary propositions can be neither a tautology nor a
contradiction." One of the real anomalies about Wittgenstein's atomic propositions is that from the falsity of such a
proposition we can make no *positive* inferences. If "a is
red" is false we would normally imagine it was blue or
some other color, but for Wittgenstein it would simply be
"not-red" if it were atomic. My example in which there
are only two possible color predicates comes closer to
Wittgenstein's thought than our ordinary world in which
the falsity of "a is red" leaves a great deal undetermined.
Wittgenstein believed when writing the *Tractatus* that determinate meaning required this yes-no space as opposed
to a multi-valued logical space. This is clearly one of the
things on which he changed his mind. *PI*, 88: "If I tell
someone 'Stand roughly there'—may not this explanation
work perfectly? And cannot every other one fail too?"

affirm that either a P or a non-P state of affairs obtains in the world, which, we say, tells us nothing, just as the fact that it is raining or not raining tells us nothing about the weather—except of course that raining is a *possible* state of the weather. The insistence on analysis to atomic propositions is meant to rule out having to hold that p is meaningful because it is radically falsified as an impossible state of affairs. The "non-P" state of affairs that falsified an atomic proposition is simply the non-holding of the state of affairs pictured. "4.25 If an elementary proposition is true, the state of affairs exists: if an elementary proposition is false, the state of affairs does not exist (*so besteht der Sachverhalt nicht*)."

To recapitulate: for Russell, if p has a meaning then some other proposition q (which states the factual relation constituting the meaning of p) must be true. For Wittgenstein, if p is meaningful then I must admit the truth of either p or not-p. From the fact that a proposition has meaning I can conclude nothing about the world, *except* either p or not-p which is a tautology supposedly true of every situation. But Wittgenstein says in 6.124:

The propositions of logic describe the scaffolding of the world, or rather they represent it (*darstellen*). They have no "subject matter." They presuppose that names have meaning and elementary propositions sense; and that is their connexion with the world. It is clear that something about the world must be indicated by the fact that certain combinations of symbols—whose essence involves the possession of a determinate character—are tautologies. This contains the decisive point.

The "fact" that when I say p has a meaning I am admitting that either p or not-p is true does indicate something about the world: it indicates the "scaffolding" of the world, the framework of possibilities. In U, "c is blue or c is not blue" not only does not convey any information about U; it is totally useless, not part of any symbolism for U. The tautology which follows from the admission that an atomic proposition is mean-

ingful excludes the case in which p is false because
p-conditions are impossible. Propositions hook onto the
world when we see that either p or not-p is true. Meaning determines no facts in the world but it determines
"the limits of the world." As we pointed out above,
Russell and Wittgenstein both have the proposition
touch reality via names of objects, but where Russell's
objects function as existent termini of a causal relation,
for Wittgenstein, "Objects contain the possibility of all
situations." (2.014) Propositions relate to reality via
the scaffold of possibilities which is given by the
objects. "2.0124 If all objects are given, then at the
same time all *possible* states of affairs are also given."[22]

IV. *"Don't Ask for the Meaning,*
Ask for the Use"

The whole discussion of the *Tractatus* can be
summed up by reminding ourselves that under no conditions can a sentence of the form "The meaning of
p is —" be meaningful. In order to be meaningful it
would have to determine some truth conditions, but
statements about meaning are "true" only if the fact
pictured exists *or* doesn't exist, i.e., that p is meaningful
determines no truth conditions, only a tautology. "4.461
Propositions show what they say: tautologies and contradictions show that they say nothing. A tautology
has no truth conditions, since it is unconditionally
true." From this very simple consideration the mysti-
cism of the *Tractatus* and its conclusions about a proper

[22] The fact that "logic" and a "knowledge of objects"
present us with the scaffolding of the world suggests that
even in the *Tractatus* "logic" does not mean simply a
formal study of inference but is being conceived of more
broadly, or more concretely, in the direction of the later
sense of "logic" in which certain *subject matters* determine
a "logic." In Kantian language it is more like transcendental
logic than formal logic.

philosophical method follow. If the philosopher's job is one of analysis, getting meanings clear, not settling factual problems like a scientist, then the function of his sentences cannot be to *describe* anything. The philosopher elucidates; he tries to make clear how a sentence is meaningful, what possibilities it sketches out. Wittgenstein thinks of this as an activity rather than a *theory* because theory suggests that we are offering truths, factual statements, in philosophy.

Russell was rightly disturbed by the mystical turn of the *Tractatus* since it implicitly categorized Russell's philosophy as nonsense, and he suggested that a hierarchy of language might allow us to formulate sentences of the type "The meaning of *p* is——" in a proper manner. This suggestion was taken up by Carnap:

According to [Wittgenstein], the investigations of the logic of science contain no sentences, but merely more or less vague explanations which the reader must recognize as pseudo-sentences . . . when in what follows [i.e., in Carnap's own work] it is shown that the logic can be formulated not in senseless, if practically indispensable pseudo-sentences, but in perfectly correct sentences.[23]

He then goes on to add that if we follow Wittgenstein we will be unable to distinguish between the useful logic of science and the sentences of the speculative metaphysician. A Wittgensteinian rejoinder to Carnap's suggestion offers a convenient bridge between the *Tractatus* and the *Investigations*.

Wittgenstein thought that the only "correct sentences" were like the propositions of the natural sciences, i.e., propositions which pictured a fact and stated a truth claim (6.53). If statements about meaning are to be formulated in "perfectly correct sentences," then they will have to picture a fact and make truth claims, and we will be right back in all

[23] Carnap, *Logical Syntax of Language* (London: Routledge and Kegan Paul, 1937), p. 283.

the paradoxes of Russell's psychological theory of meaning with its infinite regress and/or basic propositions in which the distinction between meaning and truth collapses. And as far as the distinction between metaphysical statements and Wittgenstein's elucidations are concerned, it is not Wittgenstein who confuses the point but Russell. The *Tractatus* is anti-metaphysical because it opposes factual statements that are *necessarily* true.

We could distinguish three kinds of sentences in connection with the *Tractatus*: (1) *Factual sentences*: the propositions of the natural sciences that picture a fact and make a truth claim. Sentences like "The cow is brown." (2) *Elucidatory sentences*: sentences which *show* something by the fact that we accept them. "If *p* is meaningful then either P is the case or P is not the case: If 'Socrates is white' is meaningful then either Socrates is white or he isn't." These sentences clearly picture no fact; they do not make any truth claims and hence "say nothing." But "It is clear that something about the world must be indicated by the fact that certain combinations of symbols—whose essence involves the possession of a determinate character—are tautologies" (6.124). (3) *Metaphysical sentences*: factual propositions which are true because their falsehood would be impossible or inconceivable. Russell's basic propositions are an excellent example. Russell said that "a judgment of perception . . . cannot be *proved* to be false." Now of course any verified factual claim cannot be *proved* to be false because it is, in fact, true, but Russell's basic propositions cannot be proved false because their falsity is inconceivable. If we understand the meaning of "This is thus," it must be true, or, conversely, we could not understand the proposition and say that it was false. A Russellian basic proposition we can say is "radically true" because its negation is "radically false"—but it is just such sentences that Wittgenstein declares are meaningless. Metaphysics is a pseudo-science because it offers synthetic *a priori* judgments, factual propositions which are necessarily true. Metaphysical sentences fail because they *appear* to make factual claims, but when we examine their truth conditions we discover that their truth rests on a question of meaning, not fact. Wittgenstein's elucidatory sentences, he is very careful to note, are *not* factual claims at all.

In the light of this rejoinder to Carnap's charge of metaphysics consider the following passage from *The Blue Book*:

We have been told by popular scientists that the floor on which we stand is not solid, as it appears to common sense, as it has been discovered that the wood consists of particles filling space so thinly that it can almost be called empty. This is liable to perplex us, for in a way we know of course that the floor is solid, or that if it isn't solid, this may be due to the wood being rotten but not to its being composed of electrons. To say on the latter ground that the floor is not solid, is to misuse language. . . .

As in this example the word "solidity" was used wrongly and it seemed that we had been shown that nothing really was solid, just in this way in stating our puzzles about the *general vagueness* of sense experience, and about the flux of phenomena, we are using the words "flux" and "vagueness" wrongly, in a typically metaphysical way, namely without an antithesis; whereas in their correct and everyday use vagueness is opposed to clearness, flux to stability, inaccuracy to accuracy, and *problem* to solution. The very word "problem," one might say, is misapplied when used with our philosophical troubles. These difficulties as long as they are seen as problems, are tantalizing, and appear insoluble.[24]

It is obvious that the criticism of "metaphysics" made in these preliminary studies for the *Investigations* has a close *family resemblance* to the criticism of metaphysics we have extracted from the *Tractatus*. Why is the statement "All floors are unsolid" metaphysical and

[24] L. Wittgenstein, Preliminary Studies for the "Philosophical Investigations," known as *The Blue and Brown Books* (Oxford: Blackwell, 1958), pp. 45–46.

meaningless? Not because the words in it lack sense content—Carnap and Russell's criterion for "metaphysical." Not only is the sentence perfectly sensible but it could conceivably be true. What makes the sentence metaphysical is that in trying to *prove* its truth, the scientist construes the word "unsolid" in such a way that the solidity of a floor would be inconceivable.

For even if the particles were as big as grains of sand, and as close together as those in a sandheap, the floor would not be solid if it were composed of them in the sense in which a sandheap is composed of grains. Our perplexity was based on a misunderstanding; the picture of the thinly filled space was wrongly *applied*.[25]

In *Tractatus* 6.1232 Wittgenstein distinguishes between the "essential general validity" of logical propositions and the "accidental general validity" of such propositions as "All men are mortal." The statement "All floors are unsolid" looks like a statement of accidental general validity. There is no reason why careful investigation might not establish this fact, but the truth of the statement offered has "essential general validity." It is "metaphysical" because it appears to make a factual claim whereas the truth conditions suggested leave no way for the claim to be falsified—it is a paradigm case of a factual statement whose meaning guarantees its truth, of a synthetic *a priori* judgment, of a necessary fact, in short, of metaphysics.

Wittgenstein labels the fault "metaphysical" and adopts his later terminology when he calls it a misuse of language. We should note how close the notion of "misuse" is to "metaphysical meaninglessness" as construed in the *Tractatus*. Words fail to have a use or are meaningless when they are used "without antithesis." The great shift that has come since the *Tractatus* is that Wittgenstein is willing to consider a range of possible antitheses, states which could be positively characterized and would exclude the truth of the judgment offered, where before we were asked

25 *Ibid.*

to believe that atomic propositions, the ultimates on which all determinate meaning rested, involved only one negation which was not equivalent to any state of affairs that could be described positively. No matter how necessary atomic propositions may have seemed to Wittgenstein he was not able to suggest any examples and we have no cases of analysis actually being carried out to the level of atomic propositions. If the requirement is loosened so that meaning does not depend on a Yes-No space but on a multi-valued space —a series of possible alternatives—then actual examples of analysis can be offered.[26] Once a *range* of antitheses is opened up, we will no longer be able to give *the* analysis of the meaning of a proposition, but we can construct various language games specifying various possible antitheses and request the auditor to show us which game he is playing.

Now it looks as if when someone says "Bring me a slab" he could only mean that expression as *one* long word corresponding to the single word "slab"—then can we mean it sometimes as four? And how does one usually mean it?—I should think that we would be inclined to say when it is used in contrast with other sentences such as "Hand me the slab," etc.; that is in contrast with other sentences containing the separate words of our command in other combinations (*PI*, § 20).

"Bring me a slab" will have a range of meanings depending on how you lay out the contrasts. Metaphysical utterances can be rejected because there is *no* game being played with them, no contrasts are suggested. We dissolve metaphysical "problems" by treating them *as if* they made factual claims, i.e., as if the words had antitheses, and if the metaphysician says he is playing the suggested language game we can show that his judgment is false or harmlessly true.

[26] Not only is a range of possible states of affairs which would falsify a declarative sentence allowed, but all sorts of other linguistic entities like commands, thanking, cursing, praying can be seen to function contrastively.

V. "And Don't Ask for the Use Either!"

The fact that most of Wittgenstein's interpreters have
been brought up in the British philosophical tradition
has produced a characteristic misinterpretation of both
the *Tractatus* and the *Investigations*. Hume's simple
impressions up-dated as sense data were seen as the
key to the earlier book, and the later studies seemed
to be part of the "common sense" tradition most recently exemplified by Moore. When we are told (*PI*,
124), "Philosophy may in no way interfere with the
actual use of language," it may appear that this common sense interpretation is proper. Nevertheless there
is a fundamental difference between Moore and Wittgenstein.[27] Moore was interested in defending the
truth of common sense against metaphysical *doubts*.
Can any metaphysician really make me doubt the truth
of the judgment that this is my hand in front of me?
And if not, in what way can I have any doubts about
the existence of the external world? Moore's technique
was to take some common sense judgment supposedly
rendered dubious by a metaphysician and just ask us
to examine it in the light of present experience to see
if we could really sense this doubt. As Paul correctly
points out, Wittgenstein's technique was quite different.
Where Moore invited his auditor to concentrate his
attention on some present fact which could scarcely
be doubted, Wittgenstein used his language games to
assemble cases.

Instead of concentrating into a gaze, I am to make a
wide survey; and it is not that cases just come before
me in their arrangement, for there are cases to be invented by me and arrangements of them to be made

[27] This difference is pointed out in an excellent chapter by
G. A. Paul on Wittgenstein in A. J. Ayer *et al.*, *Revolution
in Philosophy* (London: Macmillan, 1956).

by me. Here is why Wittgenstein produces no method in philosophy, there is no method for inventing cases, no method for arranging them.[28]

And a passage in *The Blue Book* is almost a direct attack on Moore and the techniques of common sense philosophy:

There is no common sense answer to a philosophical problem. One can defend common sense against the attacks of philosophers only by solving their puzzles, i.e., by curing them of the temptation to attack common sense; not by restating the view of common sense.[29]

Wittgenstein continues to hold as he did in the *Tractatus* that the philosopher has no direct interest in the *truth* of common sense, or science or whatever. Common sense cannot be defended against metaphysical attack by attempting a *verification* of the truths of common sense in present experience or by a more subtle view of the facts, but by showing the metaphysician that he has failed to make any claim, true or false, and hence his utterance is meaningless. "What *we* do is to bring words back from their metaphysical to their everyday use" (*PI*, 116).

I think we should take this last statement quite literally: Wittgenstein is interested in the everyday *use* of language, not in the truth which may or may not be conveyed in everyday judgments. If, using his own criterion, "*ordinary* language" is to have a meaning, we must search for the contrast that is being pointed to. It is obvious that the contrast is "metaphysical language." The ordinary use of language is to point up something *rather than* something else: "Go left!" also says "Don't go right!" But metaphysical language is language on a holiday because it *seems* to be saying something, rather than another, but we can try to show that in fact it is not functioning at all. The virtue of "everyday" is that language *functions* there, not that it always states truths. And if the espousal of "ordinary

[28] *Ibid.*, p. 96.
[29] *The Blue Book*, p. 58.

language" is not an espousal of common sense truths, it is also not clearly a rejection of technical language. Technical languages like mathematics or psychology have an ordinary use. Thus he says: "An investigation is possible in connection with mathematics which is clearly analogous to our investigation of psychology. It is just as little a *mathematical* investigation as the other is a psychological one" (*PI*, pt. II, xiv). Technical studies like mathematics and psychology may be subject to a philosophical analysis if their language functions metaphysically and not in the ordinary way.[30] "Ordinary language," then, points neither to everyday truths or prosaic vocabularies, but to the ordinary way in which language has meaning as against the extraordinary and metaphysical ways that philosophers misuse language.

The task of the philosopher remains, as it was in the *Tractatus*, one of elucidating meaning—and how do we do that? In a broader and looser fashion we are right back to the same "meaningless" statements about meanings that we saw in the *Tractatus*. Under what states of affairs is the command "Go left!" meaningful? When the person who hears the command goes left—or when he goes right, just stands there or lies down or something, i.e., that the command if meaningful is compatible with seemingly any state of affairs. I always find myself saying that he understood my command if

---

[30] Much of the *Foundations of Mathematics* (Oxford: Blackwell, 1956) is concerned with "metaphysical claims" that mathematicians make about what they are doing. A metaphysical claim always involves the notion of a *necessary* truth. Wittgenstein held in the *Tractatus* and later that "necessary" was a matter of our chosen meanings for terms and we should never think that because we have chosen to make certain patterns meaningful that we have therefore established a truth. *FM* I, 5: "'But doesn't it follow with logical necessity that you get two when you add one to one?' . . . The proposition: 'It is true that this follows from that' means simply: this follows from that." Mathematicians like to think that "One plus one is two" is a necessary truth—but if it is necessary, it is not a truth and if it is a truth it is not necessary.

he did it or if he didn't do it—he disobeyed, forgot, and so on. But if "Go left!" is meaningful when he goes left or he doesn't go left, then the "fact" that it is meaningful determines no state of affairs at all. Rather, we say that the command is meaningful if the person knows how to play the game of obeying directions. The noise "Go left" does not have meaning like a conditioned reflex—a causal connection between a sound fact and a behavioral fact—but because it is seen as a move in a game. We say that the command has meaning, not because it determines any behavior or state of affairs, but because the person who understands it fits into a game where there is obeying orders *and* disobeying orders, forgetting them, mishearing them, and so on. That an order is meaningful determines the limits of my world, my language game—it determines a range of possible behavior that would be regarded as obeying and disobeying and so on.

The notion that the *Investigations* substitutes a behavioristic psychological theory of meaning for the *Tractatus'* sensationalist psychology is clearly incorrect. Wittgenstein is perfectly clear in the *Investigations* that philosophy offers no theses, and clearly behaviorism offers a *theory* of meaning based on factual data. One can reconstruct the paradoxes of a psychological theory of meaning for behaviorism. For example, if noises become commands by causal association to behavior, then commands must always be infallibly obeyed, as in any causal process: if you topple the first domino they all come down necessarily. The behavior we call "disobeying" is really obeying some other (possibly internal) command. The only thing that can interfere with a causal process being carried through is another causal process. One is tempted to construct the notion of "atomic commands" in which disobedience is simply not doing what you are told, rather than obeying some other command. It becomes metaphysical in a behavioristic theory to say that the subject "obeys" the command since "disobeying a command" has no function. The subject can *only* obey commands and if the commands are incompatible he must of course do one and not the other, but there is no disobedience involved. Commands subject only to "radical obedience" are not linguistic entities having a meaning any more than atomic propositions which cannot be proved false.

If admitting that some sound has a meaning is a matter of seeing it as a piece in a game, then we should see that the motto "Don't ask for the meaning, ask for the use!" should be amended, "And don't ask for the use either!" Behavioristic misinterpretation of the *Investigations* assumes that the intent of this new slogan is to direct us away from something going on inside the subject's head, the unobservable psychic process, to the observable behavior associated with the word. Behaviorism, however, assumes that "The meaning of *p* is —" is a statement setting forth truth conditions, when all a statement about meaning does is show forth a language game. For behaviorism the meaning of "Go left!" is that the subject goes left (no other causes interfering): for Wittgenstein the meaning of "Go left" is that the subject goes left or he doesn't go left *but* he sees his behavior as a move in a language game. Meaning is not a factual connection between sound and behavior; it is seeing a fact *as* a piece in a game. The second part of the *Investigations* discusses the notion of "seeing *x* as" at length in order to point out that seeing something *as* is not a matter of discovering a new fact about it. " 'Seeing as . . .' is not part of perception" (*PI,* 197). For a psychological theory of meaning, grasping the meaning of a sound is ultimately *seeing* the sound in connection with another fact (sense object or action), so that meaning becomes a perceptible fact.

The slogan "Ask for . . . the use!" can mislead us, then, if we think that this asking will be settled by a declarative reply, "The use is. . . ." The reason that there is no reply is not only that we cannot say what *the* use is since there are many games that could be played with this counter—a point sufficiently emphasized by interpreters of Wittgenstein—but that we could not *say* what a use is since noting that a word has a use is seeing it as a piece in a game and *that* a mark is a piece in a game is not a describable fact about the mark. We can, however, try to *show* what the meaning or use of a word is by assembling a variety of language games that could be played with the word. Failure to understand the meaning of a word is failing to see how it directs us one way and not another—we don't understand what contrasts are being pointed to by the scientist who claims the floor is unsolid because it is made of electrons. In order to appreciate the range of contrasts in a particular game we may surround it with other games which vary slightly in certain ways. Our interest will not be in games actually played but in imaginary and even bizarre cases, since they point up more sharply the contrasts in the game under investigation.

A main source of our failure to understand is that we do not *command a clear view* of the use of our words.—Our grammar is lacking in this sort of perspicuity. Hence the importance of finding and inventing *intermediate cases* (*PI*, § 122).

We see what we *do* mean by showing what we could mean if we played different games with different contrasts being pointed to. We come to understand the game we are playing by appreciating what games we aren't playing; this gives us the perspicuous aspect that allows a clear view of our use of words.

Wittgenstein's advocacy of ordinary language differs markedly, in my judgment, from that of many contemporary philosophers who would claim his blessing. He is not interested in the truths of everyday discourse. He would find no *philosophical* assistance in the surveys of the descriptive linguist or the compilations of the *O. E. D.* of what is or has been uttered. He clearly thinks the philosopher's job lies in, *inventing* intermediate—even absurd—cases not toting up actual uses. And how can we be sure that the utter-

ances of the linguist's informant or the quotations from
F. H. Bradley in the *O. E. D.* are not metaphysical
"uses" of language? The philosopher's task of elucidating meaning remains logical, i.e., non-factual. He
neither establishes facts, nor can he depend on facts
from physiology, psychology, or the history of language
to reveal meanings.

In this steadfast contrast between the philosopher's
concern with meaning and the scientist's concern with
facts lies a key to the unity of Wittgenstein's philosophy. Philosophy is not a theory offering truths about
meanings, because meanings are not truths about the
world. Philosophy must be an *activity*, because its
"subject matter," meaning, is not factual. The notion
that meaning is *use*, not fact, seems to me implicit in
the *Tractatus*. If coming to understand a meaning is a
matter of engaging in an activity, rather than coming
to know a truth, then the language games of the *Investigations* fit into the over-all conception of philosophy outlined in the *Tractatus*.

THREE WAYS OF
SPILLING INK

J. L. AUSTIN*

Parts I, II, and III of the following paper are taken, almost verbatim, from J. L. Austin's longhand draft, found among his papers after his death, of a lecture he gave to the American Society of Political and Legal Philosophy, which met in Chicago in 1958. Authenticity of expression can be claimed for these sections, though no doubt Austin would have changed much had he himself completed his revisions for publication in the yearbook of the Society: *Responsibility (Nomos* III), edited by Carl Friedrich (New York, 1960). An outline of this lecture, which was "distributed at the meeting and available to the participants," was published as an appendix to this volume.

The introductory section was not fully written out in Austin's manuscript, but has been pieced together from notes made on several separate sheets, and with the help also of Austin's notes for seminars he conducted at Oxford, over a period of many years, under the general title "Excuses." In these seminars he discussed not only material incorporated in the present paper, but also much on which "A Plea for Excuses" was based.

The manuscript bears the title "Responsibility," since this was the general topic of the meeting of the Society at which the lecture was given. The published appendix, however, is entitled "Three Ways of Spilling Ink," and this is

---

* J. L. Austin (1911–1960) was Professor of Philosophy at Oxford University and has become, next to Wittgenstein, the most influential of all linguistic philosophers. This article first appeared in *The Philosophical Review*, Vol. 75, No. 4 (October 1966), and is printed here by permission of the editors, together with Mrs. J. L. Austin and Mr. G. J. Warnock.

most probably the title Austin himself would have chosen had he published the paper.

The editor is grateful to Mrs. Austin for permission to submit the paper for publication and to Mr. G. J. Warnock, who has read both the manuscript and the present paper and has made many valuable suggestions for its improvement.

L. W. FORGUSON

MOST of what I have to say about responsibility in general I have said in another place.[1] But of course the point of what I had to say there was that there isn't much point in discussing it in general terms. I shall repeat it here only in summary. It is a view which I have not so much merely held, but used in practice for some twenty years, and have found it consistently to pay off. Briefly, it is the idea which Aristotle had in a primitive way, without having to fight free of the toils of sophistication that now encumber us: namely, that questions of whether a person was responsible for this or that are prior to questions of freedom. Whatever Aristotle's idea may have been it *worked* this way: to discover whether someone acted freely or not, we must discover whether this, that, or the other plea will pass —for example, duress, or mistake, or accident, and so forth.

We may hope to profit then, in this area of inquiry, from the careful study of what we may call, for the sake of a word, *excuses*—of the different ways, and different words, in which on occasion we may try to get out of things, to show that we didn't act "freely" or were not "responsible." But if we are going to consider this subject and these expressions, we ought to attend as well to what might be called words of *aggravation*—words, that is, that not only don't get us out of things, but may actually make things worse for us, or at any rate may often bring in the very things that excuses, if we had any, would be designed to rule out. I shall concentrate here on a pretty narrow topic, since

---

[1] "A Plea for Excuses" (1956), in *Philosophical Papers*, ed. by J. O. Urmson and G. J. Warnock (Oxford, 1961).

I don't know enough (or even *think* I know enough) about the whole subject: what follows is a sample only of some contributions that might be of use.

In considering responsibility, few things are considered more important than to establish whether a man *intended* to do *A*, or whether he did *A* intentionally. But there are at least two other familiar words important in this respect. Let us distinguish between acting *intentionally* and acting *deliberately* or *on purpose*, as far as this can be done by attending to what language can teach us.

A schoolteacher may ask a child who has spilled the ink in class: "Did you do that intentionally?" or "Did you do that deliberately?" or "Did you do that on purpose (or purposely)?" It appears at first sight to matter little which question is asked. They appear to mean the same or at least to come down to the same in this case. But do they really? There are in fact techniques available for distinguishing between these expressions. I cannot exploit these by any means fully here, but only indicate the resources available. We may consider, for instance, for a start: (i) imagined or actual cases, and (ii) the "grammar," "etymology," and so forth of the words.

I

First let us consider some cases. Actual cases would of course be excellent: we might observe what words have actually been used by commentators on real incidents, or by narrators of fictitious incidents. However, we do not have the time or space to do that here. We must instead imagine some cases (imagine them carefully and in detail and comprehensively) and try to reach agreement upon what we should in fact say concerning them. If we can reach this agreement, we shall have some *data* ("experimental" data, in fact) which we can then go on to *explain*. Here, the explanation will be an account of the meanings of these expressions, which we shall hope to reach by using such methods as those of "Agreement" and "Difference": what is in fact present in the cases where we do use, say, "deliberately," and what is absent when we don't. Of course, we shall then have arrived at nothing more than an account of certain ordinary "concepts" employed by English speakers: but also at no less a thing. And it is not so little. These concepts will have evolved over a long time: that is, they will have faced the test of practical use, of continual hard cases better than their vanished rivals.

Here, then, are some cases.

(1) Suppose I tie a string across a stairhead. A fragile relative, from whom I have expectations, trips over it, falls, and perishes. Should we ask whether I tied the string there intentionally? Well, but it's hard to see how I could have done such a thing unintentionally, or even (what is not the same) not done it intentionally. You don't do that sort of thing—by accident? By mistake? Inadvertently? On the other hand, would I be bound to admit I did it "on purpose" or "purposely"? That has an ugly sound. What could the purpose have been if not to trip at least someone? Maybe I had better claim I was simply passing the time, playing cat's cradle, practicing tying knots.

(2) I needed money to play the ponies, so I dipped into the till. Of course, I *intended* (all the time) to put it back as soon as I had collected my winnings. That was my intention: I took it with the intention of putting it back. But was that my *purpose* in taking it? Did I take it for the purpose of, or on purpose to, put it back? Plainly not.

(3) As I drive up, I see that there is broken glass on the roadway outside my home; so I throw it onto the sidewalk, and a pedestrian later stumbles over it and is injured. Very likely I did throw the glass onto the sidewalk all right, etc. But did I do it on purpose, purposely? Did I do it deliberately? Conceivably, but

in the way we should naturally imagine the incident, certainly not either.

(4) The notice says, "Do not feed the penguins." I, however, feed them peanuts. Now peanuts happen to be, and these prove, fatal to these birds. Did I feed them peanuts intentionally? Beyond a doubt: I am no casual peanut shedder. But deliberately? Well, that seems perhaps to raise the question, "Had I read the notice?" Why does it? Or "on purpose?" That seems to insinuate that I knew what fatal results would ensue. Again, why?

We may also consider cases that are stereotypes, the ones evoked by clichés. Here are some.

We say that A wounded B with the intention of killing him, or of causing him grave bodily injury; or, more formally, with intent to kill him, and so forth. We do not say, "A wounded B for the purpose of killing him." Why not? Because the killing and the wounding are "not sufficiently separate"—are "too intimately connected"; because there are not "*two things*" that are done? But what does this really mean?

Again, we ask this young man who is paying attentions to our daughter to declare his intentions. What are his intentions? Are his intentions honorable? Here, would it make any difference if we asked him what was the purpose of these attentions, whether he has some purpose in view, whether he is doing these things on purpose or for a purpose? This makes his conduct seem more calculated, frames him as an adventurer or seducer. Instead of asking him to clarify the position, perhaps to himself as well as to us, are we not now asking him to divulge a guilty secret?

Another cliché: we find ourselves fairly often speaking of a "deliberate intention"; "with the deliberate intention of forcing the lock," for example. Just as we may speak of a deliberate choice or a deliberate decision. *But* we do not speak of an intentional deliberation; nor (except in special cases which cannot here be discussed) of an intentional decision or an intentional choice.

Perhaps it would help to think of kinds of cases in which a thing is done intentionally but not deliberately, and so forth: cases, that is, where these adverbial expressions are expressly dissociated. The way this happens will commonly reveal some "opposite" of one of the three expressions which is *not* an "opposite" of the other two.

For example, suppose I do a thing impulsively, and possibly even on impulse. Then I shall not be doing it deliberately—and indeed to *say* that I did it impulsively (and perhaps even on impulse) would surely be to rule out the suggestion that I did it deliberately. For example, at a certain juncture in the course of our quarrel, moved perhaps by some turn of emotion or memory, I impulsively stretch out my hand to make things up, and exert all my tact to the same end. Now this is intentional enough: I intend to put out my hand, to bury the hatchet. Actually, I did even stretch out my hand on purpose, purposely. Yet it was not done deliberately: within twenty minutes I may be regretting it. The impulse is strong: I didn't stop to think (but about what?). I act precipitately, so probably not deliberately, but of course I knew what I was doing and meant to do it, even perhaps used my wits in doing it adroitly. (I may have stopped to think about *that*: the impulse may have been merely to make friends, holding out my hand something I thought up to do the trick.) If I acted not even on impulse, but quite *spontaneously* (rather tricky, this), and so even more evidently not deliberately, it is at least plausible to say that I still acted intentionally (cf. Sir Walter Raleigh). Again, a man put into agony of mind and fearful indecision[2] by some crisis may adopt some course such as running back into the blaze. No doubt he runs back into the blaze intentionally enough; he even (*perhaps*) decides to run back—though of course this is not necessary for him to do so "inten-

---

[2] Perhaps owing to someone else's fault: but for reasons given below we will *exclude* this possibility, and suppose it an "accidental" crisis, such as fire.

tionally." But I think it might well be agreed he did not do so deliberately. These examples will suffice to show that what is done intentionally and purposely need not be done deliberately. Moreover, they appear to show some common characteristics: there is something "precipitate" about the act in every case.

On the other hand, it is fully possible to act both deliberately and intentionally yet "not on purpose," or at least (*if* this is the same thing—there are distinctions here which we shall have to neglect) for no purpose, without any purpose, purposelessly. So to act may be, typically, to act wantonly. A gang of boys decapitates, seriatim, every one of the line of young trees newly planted along our street: this is deliberate, wanton damage. But they have, we may say, no interest in killing the trees; very likely they haven't given the matter a thought. Do children pull the wings off flies "on purpose?" Yet see them at it, and it is patent that they do it intentionally, and also deliberately.

So far we have shown that a thing done intentionally need not be done deliberately or on purpose, but what about conversely? Can something be done deliberately or purposely but not intentionally? Can we think of a case in which something is done *deliberately* but not intentionally? Certainly this seems more difficult. However, there are cases.

I am summoned to quell a riot in India. Speed is imperative. My mind runs on the action to be taken five miles down the road at the Residency. As I set off down the drive, my cookboy's child's new gocart, the apple of her eye, is right across the road. I realize I could stop, get out, and move it, but to hell with that: I must push on. It's too bad, that's all: I drive right over it and am on my way. In this case, a snap decision is taken on what is essentially an *incidental* matter. I did drive over the gocart deliberately, but not intentionally—nor, of course, unintentionally either. It was never part of my intention to drive over the gocart. At no time did I intend to drive over it. It was incidental to anything I intended to do, which was simply to get to the scene of the riot in order to quell it. However "odd" it may sound, I feel little doubt that we should say here that we did run over the gocart deliberately *and* that we should not care to say we ran over it intentionally. We never intended to run over it.

A similar account should probably be given, too, of some things that will, it can be foreseen, follow as consequences or results of our doing certain actions—namely, that these things are "done" by us deliberately but not intentionally. For example, I realize that by insisting on payment of due debts I am going to "ruin" my debtor—that is, he will be ruined as a consequence of being compelled to pay. I have absolutely no wish to ruin him, even wish not to: but maybe if I don't get payment both I and others are going to suffer severely; and very likely I think he has been faintly improvident. So I demand payment. He is ruined and, if you like, I ruined him. If this is said—I might resist and resent the imputation a bit—I think it must be admitted that I did ruin him deliberately; not, however, that I ruined him intentionally. At no time did I intend to ruin him; it was never any part of my intention. (This, if it be admitted, is an especially interesting case: for plainly I am *not* here responsible for his ruin.)

Finally, can a thing be done on purpose, but yet not intentionally? This seems even more difficult, and may actually be impossible. However, the expression "accidentally on purpose" hints, at least ironically, that something of the sort may be possible; for, if done accidentally, it is not done intentionally. But how ironical is this expression? (Perhaps a case comparable to the debt-collection case could be constructed here.)

II

We now turn to our second general source of information: grammar and philology. Here we find that "purpose," "intend," and "deliberate" exhibit numerous and striking differences.

(1) *Deliberate* and *deliberation,* the verb and the noun, differ from both *intend/intention* and *purpose/purpose* in some ways in which the latter pair resemble each other. Thus, "I am deliberating" could only be used to describe a process that is going on: but "I am intending" and (if it exists) "I am purposing" could not be used to describe a process. In line with this is the fact that deliberations may be protracted, but intentions and purposes cannot be so.

(1*a*) The use of "I intend" (and, so far as it exists, of "I purpose") is quite different from "I deliberate," which if *it* exists could only be a habitual present, describing what I ordinarily do, as in "I deliberate before I act." "I intend to X" is, as it were, a sort of "future tense" of the verb "to X." It has a vector, committal effect like "I promise to X," and, again, like "I promise to X," it is one of the possible formulae for making explicit, on occasion, the force of "I shall X": (namely, that it was a declaration of intention and not, for example, a forecast or an undertaking). We might feel inclined to say: it is almost an "auxiliary verb." But the fact of the matter is that terms like "future tense" and "auxiliary verb" were not invented with the need to do justice to such a word as "intend" in mind. A complete reclassification of these archaic terms is needed. That reclassification is needed is shown, for example, by the fact that there is some oddity about the combination "I shall intend."

(2) If we next consider the adjectival terminations found in "deliber*ate*," "intention*al*," and "purpose*ful*" or "purpos*ive*," (which are also of course incorporated in the corresponding adverbs), it would seem significant that they are different. "Deliber*ate*" is of course formed on the Latin past participle: words of this kind commonly mean that something has happened or been done. We should suspect that the process of deliberation, whatever that may be, has been gone through.

So consider*ate* behavior is behavior which shows that there has been consideration (of the feelings of others, as affected by my proposed activities).

The termination -ful, on the other hand, is commonly used in cases where something may be present or may not be present: an accretion or extra. "Thoughtful," "careful," "purposeful" alike refer to things we may (but equally may not) be doing *when* doing X: we may be taking thought for the interests and feelings of others, taking care to guard against possible accidents, or pursuing a purpose.

The termination -al, as in "intentional," qualifies, or classifies, as we may say, the act so described much more "directly" and intimately than -ful or -ate. (Incidental note: -ive, as in "purposive," would perform a similar function. But of course it is a term of psychological art, and to my mind requires some justification: because all our ordinary terminology, not merely the adjectival termination, certainly suggests that intention is related to our action in a more intimate way than its purpose, and in quite a different way.)

(2a) The same lesson is pointed by the negative forms of the adjectives (and adverbs). There is no accepted negative form of "deliberate." "Purpose" takes -less; I may "have no purpose (whatsoever)" in doing something, just as I may take no care. But I don't "have no intention (whatsoever)" in doing something.

Here something of a general justification may be required. Why should we suppose it is significant of anything whatsoever that, for example, these adjectives and their negatives take different forms? Why shouldn't it just be that "thought," for example, is not a Latin word and so can't readily take the Latin -ate termination, whereas "consider" can? Why shouldn't it all be "euphony," or chance, or meaningless luxuriation?

Now we can admit, and indeed positively welcome, all these suggestions, and yet adhere to our superstition that the forms of words and expressions are highly significant for their meaning. Briefly, let us assume, for

the sake of argument and because we actually have no
right to assume anything else, that "in origin" speech
consisted in any person making any noise in any situation to signify anything. Let us also assume, what in a
sense is a tautology, that *in the very long run*, the
forms of speech which survive will be the *fittest* (most
efficient) forms of speech. Now one general criterion
of efficiency[3] is simply this, stated loosely: that any
unit of speech *U* should sound *tanto quanto* like every
other unit of speech that "means" anything like what *U*
means, and unlike *tanto quanto* every other unit of
speech that means anything unlike what *U* means: or
that small variations in meaning should be signified by
small concomitant variations in sound. This principle
will account, on my view, not merely for the phenomenon of the survival of words in groups where similar-
sounding words mean similar things (for example,
"fumble," "tumble," "stumble," and the like) but for
much of what ought to be included in etymology, and
for the whole general evolution of morphology, syntax,
and grammar.

In this account of the origin of speech forms on evo-
lutionary lines, it will be seen that *allowance* may be
—indeed, to some extent is already fully—made for
chance, for luxuriance, for sound preferences (euphony), and for borrowings. *But still*, in the long run,
the expressions which survive will be such that their
grammatical and morphological characteristics are of
the highest significance for their meaning.

(3) The prepositions used with "intention," "purpose," and "deliberation" to form adverbial or other
expressions likewise point to distinctions between the
three words, and associate them with quite distinct
families of words. We say *on* purpose (to), *for* the
purpose of, but *with* the intention of: (possibly also
with the purpose of). It seems clear that "on" and

---

[3] There are others of great importance: brevity, learn-
ability, etc. But of these, some are closely connected with
the above in a variety of ways.

"for" (compare "on the principle," "on orders," "for the sake of") *dissociate* or *sever* my purpose from my current action in a way that "with" does not do. There are many expressions containing "purpose" ("for the *usual* purposes," "to good purpose," "to some purpose," and so forth) which seem to make purpose as it were *im*personal in a way that is never done with intention.

With "deliberation," perhaps the only, and unexciting, preposition used is "after." "With deliberation" is indeed found, but then the words are used to describe a certain slow style of performance, which makes an impression on the observer. "Deliberately" is used in the same way, as when someone eats his soup deliberately. (Compare the case where he deliberately eats my soup. Here, if he is well advised, he will make haste over it.) Now this sort of secondary sense is fairly common with adverbs of this kind; and "purposefully" is in fact also used in this way. We know the kind of performance it describes: a purposeful air is one of getting the preliminaries, the first stages, each stage *over with*, in order to proceed to the next and get the whole business achieved: it is an air of pressing on. Strikingly enough, however, there is no expression connected with "intentional" which can be used in this manner. The explanation, whatever it is, would seem to lie in the same direction as that of the adjectival terminations referred to above: intention is too intimately associated with ordinary action in general for there to be any *special* style of performance associated with it.

(4) Finally, we might consider the trailing etymologies of the three words: for no word ever achieves entire forgetfulness of its origins. The metaphor in "deliberate" is one from "weighing" or "weighing up," that in "intend" (one which keeps breaking through in many cognate words) is from bending or straining toward (compare "intent of mischief" and "bent on mischief"). In "purpose," the idea is that of setting something up before oneself.

III

Now let us try to understand the three notions of purpose, intention, and deliberation in the light of our investigations so far. We shan't get so far as defining them though, I fear.

The most subtle of our notions is that of intention. As I go through life, doing, as we suppose, one thing after another, I in general always have an idea—some idea, my idea, or picture, or notion, or conception—of what I'm up to, what I'm engaged in, what I'm about, or in general "what I'm doing." I don't "know what I'm doing" as a result of looking to see or otherwise conducting observations:[4] only in rare and perturbing cases do I *discover* what I've done or *come to realize* what I am or have been doing in this way. It is not in such fashion that *I* know what I'm doing when I strike the match in the vicinity of the haystack. (This is the sense in which in general and obviously I know what I'm doing: *contrast* the sense in which you *suppose*, dubiously, that I know what I'm doing when I strike the match so close to the gasoline.) I must be supposed to have *as it were* a plan, an operation—order or something of the kind on which I'm acting, which I am seeking to put into effect, carry out in action: only of course nothing necessarily or, usually, even faintly, so full blooded as a plan proper. When we draw attention to this aspect of action, we use the words connected with intention.[5]

[4] I profited when I once heard this remarked by Miss G. E. M. Anscombe.
[5] At this point, the manuscript contains the unfinished sentence, "When we use the great majority of 'active' verbs, e.g., 'kick' . . ." What Austin probably had in mind was the fact that most "active" verbs include, as part of their sense, some notion of a design or plan to be carried out. Thus, it is generally a mistake to consider them as purely

Now although I say that the "intention" words are connected with this notion of my idea of what I'm doing, it should not be supposed that it will always make sense to stick in "intentionally" after every verb of action in every ordinary sentence with an active personal verb. Only when there is some suggestion that it might have been unintentional does it make non-misleading sense to say, for example, "I ate my dinner intentionally." To this extent, it is true that "intentionally" serves to rule out "unintentionally." What would be wholly untrue is to suggest that "unintentionally" is the word that "wears the trousers"—that is, that until we have grasped certain specific ways of doing things unintentionally, and except as a way of ruling these out, "intentionally" has no positive meaning. There are words of this description: "real," for example, is one. But in the present case, to mention nothing more, there is the verb "intend" to take into account, and it must obviously have a highly "positive" sense; it cannot just be used to rule out "don't (or didn't) intend."

Although we have this notion of my idea of what I'm doing—and indeed we have as a general rule such an idea, as it were a miner's lamp on our forehead which illuminates always just so far ahead as we go along—it is not to be supposed that there are any precise rules about the extent and degree of illumination it sheds. The only general rule is that the illumination is always *limited,* and that in several ways. It will never extend indefinitely far ahead. Of course, all that is to follow, or to be done thereafter, is not what I am intending to do, but perhaps consequences or results or effects thereof. Moreover, it does not illuminate *all* of my surroundings. Whatever I am doing is being done and to be done amidst a back-

---

"behavioristic." That I kick someone does not mean merely that my foot moves sharply into contact with his shin. Perhaps this is why, in normal contexts, adding the adverb "intentionally" is somewhat redundant. This point was suggested to me by G. J. Warnock. (L. W. F.)

ground of *circumstances* (including of course activities
by other agents). This is what necessitates *care,* to
ward off impingements, upsets, accidents. Furthermore,
the doing of it will involve *incidentally* all kinds of
minutiae of, at the least, bodily movements, and often
many other things besides. These will be below the
level of any intention, *however* detailed (and it need
not of course be detailed at all), that I may have
formed.

There is a good deal of freedom in "structuring"
the history of someone's activities by means of words
like "intention," just as when we consider a whole war
we can divide it into campaigns, operations, actions,
and the like; but this is fairly arbitrary except in so
far as it is based upon the plans of the contestants.
So with human activities; we can assess them in terms
of intentions, purposes, ultimate objectives, and the
like, but there is much that is arbitrary about this
unless we take the way the agent himself did actually
structure it in his mind before the event. Now the
word "intention" has from this point of view a most
important *bracketing effect:* when the till-dipper claims
that he *intended all along* to put the money back, what
ho is claiming is that his action—the action that he
was engaged upon—is to be judged *as a whole,* not just
a part of it carved out of the whole. Nearly always, of
course, such a contention as this will carry with it a
contention that his action (as a whole) is not to be
described by the term chosen to describe (only a part
of) it: for example, here, it was not "robbing" the till,
because the action taken as a whole would not result
in the absence of any money from the till. *Reculer
pour mieux sauter* is not to retreat.

Quite distinct is the use of the word "purpose." Certainly, *when* I am doing something for a purpose, this
will be known to me, like my intentions, and will
guide my conduct. Indeed, like an objective, a purpose will influence the forming of intentions. But my
purpose is something to be achieved or effected as a
result of what I'm doing, like the death of my aunt,

or the sickness of the penguins if I did indeed feed them peanuts on purpose. (Very commonly my purpose is to put myself into a position to be able to go on with the next action, the next operation in the campaign.) I need not, however, have any purpose in acting (even intentionally);[6] just as I need not take care or thought. I act for or on (a) purpose, I achieve it; I act with the intention, I carry it out, realize it.

I act *deliberately* when I have deliberated—which means when I have stopped to ask myself, "Shall I or shan't I?" and then decided to do X, which I did. That is to say, I weighed up, in however rudimentary (sometimes almost notional or fictional) a fashion, the pros and cons. And it is understood that there must be some cons, even when what I do deliberately is something unexceptionable, such as paying my taxes. The pros and cons are not confined to *moral* pros and cons, nor need I decide in favor of what I think best or what has the most reasons in favor of it. (Nor, of course, when I have decided to do it, *must* I necessarily carry it out.) Deliberation is not just *any* kind of thinking prior to action: to act with forethought or with premeditation, or to think about ways and means—all these show that we *took thought,* perhaps over a period of time, but none of these shows that we were acting deliberately, and indeed are quite distinct matters from deliberation. Ways and means are a matter for the planning staff; decision is a matter for the commander. That there should be slowness in moving into action or conducting it (so much relied on by lawyers) is the merest symptom.

I will close by adding a general word of warning: there are overriding considerations, which may be operative in any situation in which I act, which may put all three words out of joint, in spite of the other standard conditions for their use being satisfied. For instance, I may be acting under a threat: however much I weight up the pros and cons, if I act under

[6] E.g., feeding starving children: I need have no purpose here.

the influence of a threat I do not do that act deliberately. This sort of overriding consideration must always be allowed for in any case.[7]

[7] The manuscript contains a few further remarks, but not enough to reconstruct a conclusion that could claim to reflect at all adequately Austin's own intentions for a conclusion. It can be said from these remarks, however, that *one* thing Austin most likely had in mind was this: we should not only compare and contrast these three expressions—"intentionally," "deliberately," "on purpose"— with each other, but each should be compared and contrasted with other expressions as well (e.g., "motive" with both "intention" and "purpose," "premeditation" with "deliberation," and "to mean" with "to intend"). These are Austin's own examples, reproduced also, though inaccurately, in the *Nomos* Appendix. Austin often used in his manuscript notes the marks ") ("—e.g., "x) (y"—as a way of saying "contrast x with y," or "x as opposed to y." In the appendix, these are printed—without explanation and looking most peculiar—simply as reversed parentheses. (L. W. F.)

CHAPTER 4

AUSTIN AT CRITICISM

STANLEY CAVELL*

EXCEPT FOR the notable translation of Frege's *Foundations of Arithmetic* and whatever reviews there are, *Philosophical Papers* collects all the work Austin published during his lifetime.[1] In addition, this modest volume includes two papers which will have been heard about, but not heard, outside Oxford and Cambridge. The first is one of the two pieces written before the war ("Meaning," 1940) and shows more clearly than the one published a year earlier ("Are There A Priori Concepts?" 1939) that the characteristic philosophical turns for which Austin became famous were deep in preparation.[2] The second previously unpublished paper ("Unfair to Facts," 1954) is Austin's rejoinder to P. F. Strawson's part in their symposium on truth, a debate which, I believe, Austin is widely thought to have lost initially, and to lose finally with this rejoinder. Austin clearly did not concur in this opinion, repeating the brunt of his countercharge at the end of the course of lectures he gave at Berkeley

* Stanley Cavell is Professor of Philosophy at Harvard University. This article originally appeared in *The Philosophical Review*, Vol. 74, No. 2 (April 1965), and is printed here by permission of the editors and the author.
[1] J. L. Austin, *Philosophical Papers*, ed. by J. O. Urmson and G. J. Warnock (Oxford, 1961).
[2] Curiously, the 1940 paper is the most Wittgensteinian of Austin's writings, in presenting an explicit theory of what causes philosophical disability and in the particular theory it offers (sc., "We are using a working-model which fails to fit the facts that we really wish to talk about").

in 1958–1959.[3] The remaining five papers have all
become part of the canon of the philosophy produced
in English during the past generation, yielding the
purest version of what is called "Oxford philosophy"
or "ordinary language philosophy." I will assume that
anyone sharing anything like his direction from the
English tradition of philosophy, and forced into his
impatience with philosophy as it stands (or patience
with the subject as it could become), will have found
Austin's accomplishment and example inescapable.

As with any inheritance, it is often ambiguous and
obscure in its effects. Two of these provide the subjects
of my remarks here: the first concerns Austin's methods
or purposes in philosophy; the second, related effect
concerns the attitudes toward traditional philosophy
which he inspires and sanctions.

I

I wish not so much to try to characterize Austin's
procedures as to warn against too hasty or simple a
description of them: their characterization is itself, or
ought to be, as outstanding a philosophical problem as
any to be ventured from within those procedures.

[3] These lectures, which he gave for many years at Oxford, were published posthumously under their Oxford title,
Sense and Sensibilia, edited by G. J. Warnock. Austin's
original paper on "Truth" (1950) is, of course, reprinted
in the book under review. The remaining previously published papers are: "Other Minds" (1946), "A Plea for
Excuses" (1956), "Ifs and Cans" (1956), "How to Talk—
Some Simple Ways" (1953), and "Pretending" (1958).
All page references to these papers are cited according to
their occurrence in *Philosophical Papers*. The concluding
paper—"Performative Utterances"—is the transcript of a
talk Austin gave for the B.B.C. in 1956; it is now super-
seded by the publication of the full set of lectures he used
to give on this topic, and gave as the William James Lectures at Harvard in 1955, under the title *How to Do
Things with Words*, edited by J. O. Urmson.

To go on saying that Austin attends to ordinary or everyday language is to go on saying, roughly, nothing —most simply because this fails to distinguish Austin's work from anything with which it could be confused. It does not, in the first place, distinguish his work from ordinary empirical investigations of language, a matter which has come to seem of growing importance since Austin's visits to the United States in 1955 and 1958. I do not say there is *no* relation between Austin's address to natural language and that of the descriptive linguist; he himself seems to have thought there was, or could be, a firmer intimacy than I find between them. The differences which, intuitively, seem to me critical, however, are these. In proceeding from ordinary language, so far as that is philosophically pertinent, one is in a frame of mind in which it seems (1) that one can as appropriately or truly be said to be looking at the world as looking at language; (2) that one is seeking necessary truths "about" the world (or "about" language) and therefore cannot be satisfied with anything I, at least, would recognize as a description of how people in fact talk—one might say one is seeking one kind of explanation of *why* people speak as they do; and even (3) that one is not finally interested *at all* in how "other" people talk, but in determining where and why one wishes, or hesitates, to use a particular expression oneself. What investigations pursued in such frames of mind are supposed to show, I cannot say—perhaps whatever philosophy is supposed to show. My assumption is that there is something special that philosophy is about, and that Austin's procedures, far from avoiding this oldest question of philosophy, plunge us newly into it. I emphasize therefore that Austin himself was, so far as I know, never anxious to underscore philosophy's uniqueness, in particular not its difference from science; he seemed, indeed, so far as I could tell, to like denying any such difference (except that there is as yet no *established* science—of linguistics or grammar perhaps—to which philosophy may aspire to be assimilated).

The qualification "ordinary language," secondly, does not distinguish this mode of philosophizing from any other of its modes—or, I should like to say, does not distinguish it philosophically. It does tell us enough to distinguish hawks from handsaws—Austin from Carnap, say—but not enough to start a hint about *how* ordinary language is appealed to, how one produces and uses its critical and characteristic forms of example, and why; nor about how and just where and how far this interest conflicts with that of any other temper of philosophy. The phrase "ordinary language" is, of course, of no special interest; the problem is that its use has so often quickly suggested that the answers to the fundamental questions it raises, or ought to raise, are known, whereas they are barely imagined. Austin's only positive suggestion for a title to his methods was, I believe, "linguistic phenomenology" ("Excuses," p. 130), and although he apologizes that "that is rather a mouthful" (what he was shy about, I cannot help feeling, was that it sounds rather pretentious, or anyway philosophical) he does not retract it. This title has never caught on, partly, surely, because Austin himself invests no effort in formulating the significance of the phenomenological impulses and data in his work—data, perhaps, of the sort suggested above in distinguishing his work from the work of linguistic science.

Another characterization of Austin's procedures has impressive authority behind it. Professor Stuart Hampshire, in the memorial written for the *Proceedings of the Aristotelian Society* (1959–1960) on the occasion of Austin's death, provides various kinds of consideration—personal, social, historical, philosophical—for assessing Austin's achievement in philosophy. The device he adopts in his own assessment is to "distinguish two slightly different theses that can plausibly be attributed to him: a strong and weak thesis" (p. iii). The strong thesis is this: "For every distinction of word and idiom that we find in common speech, there is a reason to be found, if we look far enough, to explain why this distinction exists. The investigation will always show that the greatest possible number of distinctions have been obtained by the most economical linguistic means" (*ibid.*). "The weaker, or negative, thesis is that we must first have the facts, and all the facts, accurately stated before we erect a theory upon the basis of them" (p. vi). The weaker thesis is "negative," presumably, because it counsels study of ordinary language as a preliminary to philosophical advance, whereas the stronger claims "that the multiplicity of fine distinctions, which such a study would disclose, would by itself answer philosophical questions about free-will, perception, naming and describing, conditional statements" (p. ix).

Hampshire's characterizations were quickly repudiated by Austin's literary executors (J. O. Urmson and G. J. Warnock, *Mind* [1961], 256–257), the weaker thesis on the ground that it is an "unambitious statement which cannot properly, or even plausibly, be magnified into a guiding *doctrine* . . . or recipe," the stronger on various grounds according to its various parts or formulations, but primarily on two: that Austin did sanction at least *some* new distinctions, and that he certainly did not claim that *all* philosophical questions could be answered by attention to fine distinctions. Urmson and Warnock are concerned, it emerges, to repudiate the idea that any such "large assertions" are contained or implied in Austin's writings (or conversations). They conclude by saying: "Austin sometimes gave . . . his own explanations. Why should they not be taken as meaning just what they say?"

I want in Section II to take up that challenge explicitly, if briefly. Immediately, it seems clear to me that Urmson and Warnock have trivialized Hampshire's formulations, whatever their several shortcomings. His weak thesis is hardly affected by being called an "unambitious statement" rather than a doctrine or a recipe, partly because it is not unambitious in Austin's practice, and partly because of Austin's conviction, and suggestion, that most philosophers have not merely

proceeded in the absence of "all the facts," but in the
presence of practically *no facts at all,* or facts so poorly
formulated and randomly collected as to defy comprehension. The issue raised is nothing less, I suggest,
than the question: what is a philosophical fact? What
are the data from which philosophy may, and must,
proceed? It would be presumptuous to praise Austin
for having pressed such questions to attention, but it
is just the plain truth that nothing he says in "his own
explanations" begins to answer them.[4]

The strong thesis, in turn, is unaffected by switch-
ing its quantification from "all" to "some," for the issue
raised is whether attention to fine distinctions can "by
itself" answer *any* philosophical question. At the place
where Urmson and Warnock confidently assert that
some questions can be answered in this way—a matter
they take as "scarcely controversial"—they omit the
qualification "philosophical," and offer no suggestion
as to the particular way in which such answers are
effected.[5] Finally, were we to let Urmson and Warnock's deflations distract us from philosophical curiosity

[4] If such questions strike a philosopher as fundamental
to his subject, or even as relevant, then I do not see how
it can be denied that their answer is going to entail "large
assertions" for which, moreover, so far as they concern
Austin's practice, all the facts are directly at hand, sc., in
Austin's practice. To accept Austin's explanations as full and
accurate guides to his practice would be not only to confuse
advice (which is about all he gave in this line) with
philosophical analysis and literary-critical description
(which is what is needed), but to confer upon Austin
an unrivaled power of self-discernment. It is a mystery to
me that what a philosopher says about his methods is so
commonly taken at face value. Austin ought to be the last
philosopher whose reflexive remarks are treated with this
complacency, partly because there are so many of them,
and partly because they suffer not merely the usual hazards
of self-description but the further deflections of polemical
animus. I return to this in the following section.

[5] Part of Hampshire's suggestion is that accepted philo-
sophical theses and comparisons are drained, set against
Austin's distinctions, of philosophical interest (cf. p. iv).
This is a familiar enough fact of contemporary philosophiz-

about Austin's procedures, that could only inflame our psychological curiosity past composure; for the gap between Austin's unruffled advice to philosophical modesty and his obsession, to say the least, with the fineness of ordinary language and his claims to its revelation would then widen to dream-like proportions. His repeated disclaimer that ordinary language is certainly not the last word, "only it *is* the *first* word" (alluded to by Urmson and Warnock), is reassuring only during polemical enthusiasm. For the issue is why the first, or *any*, word can have the kind of power Austin attributes to it. I share his sense that it has, but I cannot see that he has anywhere tried to describe the sources or domain of that power.

My excuse for butting into this controversy is that both sides seem to me to sanction a description of Austin's concerns which is just made to misdirect a further understanding of it and which is the more harmful because of its obvious plausibility, or rather its partial truth. I have in mind simply the suggestion that Austin's fundamental philosophical interest lay in drawing distinctions. Given this description of the method, and asked to justify it, what *can* one answer except: these are all the distinctions there are, or all that are real or important or necessary, and so forth, against which, it cannot be denied, Austin's own words can be leveled. Too obviously, Austin *is* continuously concerned to draw distinctions, and the finer the merrier, just as he often explains and justifies what he is doing by praising the virtues of natural distinctions over homemade ones. What I mean by saying that this interest is not philosophically fundamental is that his drawing of distinctions is always in the service of further purposes, and in particular two. (1) *Part* of the

ing, and it suggests to me that one requirement of new philosophical answers is that they elicit a new source of philosophical interest, or elicit this old interest in a new way. Which is, perhaps, only a way of affirming that a change of *style* in philosophy is a profound change, and itself a subject of philosophical investigation.

effort of any philosopher will consist in showing up differences, and one of Austin's most furious perceptions is of the slovenliness, the grotesque crudity and fatuousness, of the usual distinctions philosophers have traditionally thrown up. Consequently, one form his investigations take is that of repudiating the distinctions lying around philosophy—dispossessing them, as it were, by drawing better ones. And better not merely because finer, but because more solid, having, so to speak, a greater natural weight; appearing normal, even inevitable, when the others are luridly arbitrary; useful where the others seem twisted; real where the others are academic; fruitful where the others stop cold. This if, if you like, a negative purpose. (2) The positive purpose in Austin's distinctions resembles the art critic's purpose in comparing and distinguishing works of art, namely, that in this crosslight the capacities and salience of an individual object in question are brought to attention and focus. Why comparison and distinction serve such purposes is, doubtless, not easy to say.[6] But it is, I take it, amply clear that their

---

[6] That it is as much a matter of *comparing* as of distinguishing is clear—and takes its importance—from the way in which examples and, most characteristically, stories set the stage for Austin's distinctions. This is plainly different from their entrance in, say, philosophers like Russell or Broad or even Moore, whose distinctions do not serve to compare and (as it were) to elicit differences but rather, one could say, to provide labels for differences previously, somehow, unnoticed. One sometimes has the feeling that Austin's differences penetrate the phenomena they record—a feeling from within which the traditional philosopher will be the one who seems to be talking about mere words. The differing role of examples in these philosophical procedures is a topic of inexaggeratable importance, and no amount of words about "ordinary language" or "make all the distinctions" will convey to anyone who does not have the hang of it how to produce or test such examples. Anyone who has tried to teach from such materials and methods will appreciate this lack, which makes it the more surprising that no one, to my knowledge, has tried to compose a useful set of directions or, rather, to investigate exactly the ways one wishes to describe the

unique value is not accidentally joined to a particular task of criticism. They will not do everything, but nothing else evidently so surely defines areas of importance, suggests terms of description, or locates foci of purpose and stresses of composition: other works tell what the given work is about. In Austin's hands, I am suggesting, other words, compared and distinguished, tell what a given word is about. To know why they do, to trace how these procedures function, would be to see something of what it is he wishes words to teach, and hints at an explanation for our feeling, expressed earlier, that what we learn will not be new empirical facts about the world, and yet illuminating facts about the world. It is true that he asks for the difference between doing something by mistake and doing it by accident, but what transpires is a characterization of *what a mistake is* and (as contrasted, or so far as contrasted with this) what an accident is. He asks for the difference between being sure and being certain, but what is uncovered is an initial survey of the complex and mutual alignments between mind and world that are necessary to successful knowledge. He asks for the difference between expressing belief and expressing knowledge (or between saying "I believe" and saying "I know") and what comes up is a new sense and assessment of the human limitations, or human responsibilities, of human knowledge; and so on.

As important as any of these topics or results within his investigations is the opportunity his purity of example affords for the investigation of philosophical method generally. Here we have, or could have—ap-

---

procedure and notice their varying effectiveness for others, or faithfulness to one's sense of one's own procedures. Perhaps what is wanted really is a matter of conveying "the hang" of something, and that is a very particular dimension of a subject to teach—familiar, for example, in conservatories of music, but also, I should guess, in learning a new game or entering any new territory or technique or apprenticing in a trade.

pearing before our eyes in terms and steps of deliberate, circumstantial obviousness—conclusions arrived at whose generality and convincingness depend, at least intuitively, upon a play of the mind characteristically philosophical, furnished with the usual armchairs and examples and distinctions and wonder. But how can such results have appeared? How can we learn something (about how we—how I—use words) which we cannot have failed to know? How can asking when we would *say* "by mistake" (or what we call "doing something by mistake") tell us what in the world a mistake *is*? How, given such obvious data, have philosophers (apparently) so long ignored it, forgetting that successful knowledge is a human affair, of human complexity, meeting human need and exacting human responsibility, bypassing it in theories of certainty which compare knowledge (unfavorably) with an inhuman ideal; or elaborated moral philosophies so abstracted from life as to leave, for example, no room for so homely, but altogether a central, moral activity as the entering of an excuse? What is philosophy that it can appear periodically so profound and so trivial, sometimes so close and sometimes so laughably remote, so wise and so stone stupid? What is philosophy that it causes those characteristic hatreds, yet mysterious intimacies, among its rivals? What kind of phenomenon is it whose past cannot be absorbed or escaped (as in the case of science) or parts of it freely admired and envied while other parts are despised and banished (as in art), but remains in standing competition, behind every closed argument waiting to haunt its living heirs?

II

One pass to these questions is opened by picking at the particular charges Austin brings against his competitors, past and present. His terms of criticism are

often radical and pervasive, but this should not blunt
an awareness that they are quite particular, characteristic, and finite. And each of them, as is true of
any charge, implies a specific view taken of a situation. This is, indeed, one of Austin's best discoveries,
and nothing is of more value in the example of his
original investigations than his perfect faithfulness to
that perception: it is what his "phenomenology" turns
on. That it fails him in criticizing other philosophers
will have had various causes, but the productive possibility for us is that he has shown us the value of the
procedure and that we are free to apply it for our better
judgment.

I must limit myself to just one example of what I
have in mind. Take Austin's accusing philosophers of
"mistakes." It is worth noticing that the man who
could inspire revelation by telling us a pair of donkey
stories which lead us to take in the difference between
doing something "by mistake" and doing it "by accident" ("Excuses," p. 133, n. 1) uses the term "mistake" in describing what happens when, for example,
Moore is discussing the question whether someone
could have done something other than what in fact
he did ("Ifs and Cans"). Now in the case of shooting
your donkey when I meant to shoot mine, the correctness of the term "mistake" is bound to the fact that
questions like the following have definite answers.
What mistake was made? (I shot your donkey.) What
was mistaken for what? (Your donkey was mistaken
for mine.) How can the mistake have occurred? (The
donkeys look alike.) (How) could it have been pre-
vented? (By walking closer and making sure, which a
responsible man might or might not have been expected to do.) But there are no such answers to these
questions asked about Moore's discussion—or perhaps
we should say that the answers we would have to
give would seem forced and more or less empty, a
fact that ought to impress a philosopher like Austin.

What has Moore mistaken for what? Should we,
for example, say that he mistakes the expression

"could have" for "could have if I had chosen"? Then
how and why and when can such a mistake have
occurred? Was it because Moore has been hasty,
thoughtless, sloppy, prejudiced . . . ? But though these
are the sorts of answers we are now forced to give
(explanations which certainly account for mistakes,
and which Austin is free with in accounting for the
disasters of other philosophers), they are fantastic in
this context; because there is no plausibility to the
suggestion, taken seriously, that, whatever Moore has
done, he has made a mistake: these charges are thus,
so far, left completely in the air. Such charges can
equally account for someone's having been involved in
an accident or an inadvertence or the like. But, as
Austin is fond of saying, each of these requires its own
story; and does either of them fit the conduct of
Moore's argument any better than the term "mistake"?
Then perhaps the mistake lies in Moore's thinking that
"could have" *means* "could have if I had chosen."
But now this suggests not that Moore *took one thing
for another* but that he took a tack he should not or
need not have taken. This might be better expressed,
as Austin does sometimes express it, by saying that
Moore *was mistaken* in this, or perhaps by saying that
it was a mistake for him to. But to say someone is
mistaken requires again its own kind of story, different
from the case of doing something by mistake or from
making a mistake. In particular it suggests a context
in which it is obvious, not that one thing looks like
another, but why one would be led to do the mistaken, unhappy thing in question. The clearest case I
think of is one of poor strategy: "It is a mistake to
castle at this stage." This charge depends upon there
being definite answers to questions like the following.
Why does it seem to be a good thing to do? Why is it
nevertheless not a good thing to do? What would
be a better (safer, less costly, more subtle, stronger)
thing to do instead? Such questions do fit certain procedures of certain intellectual enterprises, for example,

the wisdom of taking a certain term as undefined, the dangers of appealing to the natural rights or the cult emotions of a certain section of the voting population, the difficulties of employing a rhyme scheme of a particular sort. What is Moore trying to do to which such a consideration of plusses and minuses would be relevant?

One may feel: "Of course it is not a matter of better or worse. If Moore (or any philosopher) is wrong he is just wrong. What is absurd about the suggestion that he may have reasons for doing things his way is the idea that he may wish to tally up the advantages of being right over those of being wrong, where being right (that is, arriving at the truth) is the whole point. Cannot to say he has made a mistake—or, rather, to say he is mistaken—just mean that he is just wrong?" But it seems, rather, that "mistaken" requires the idea of a wrong alternative (either taking one thing for another, or taking one tack rather than another). Is such an alternative, perhaps, provided by Austin's account of "could have" (as sometimes indicative rather than subjunctive), and is Moore to be considered mistaken because he did not adopt or see Austin's line? But of course the problem of alternatives is a problem of what alternatives are open to a particular person at a particular moment: and what is "open to" a particular person at a particular moment is a matter of some delicacy to determine—nothing less than determining whether someone could have done or seen something. However this may be, we still need, if we are to say "mistaken," an account of why he took the "alternative" he did. There seem to be just two main sorts of answers to such a question: either you admit that it is an attractive or plausible or seemingly inevitable one, *and account for such facts,* or you will find nothing of attraction or plausibility or seeming inevitability in it and assign its choice to ignorance, stupidity, incompetence, prejudice, and so forth. When Austin is discussing Moore, his respect pushes him to suggest the former sort of explanation, but he is clearly impatient with the effort to arrive at one and drops it as soon as possible (see, for example, pp. 154, 157).

Calling philosophers prejudiced or thoughtless or childish is a common enough salute among classical philosophers: one thinks of Bacon's or Descartes's or Hume's attitudes to other, especially to past, philosophers. It is time, perhaps, to start wondering why such charges should be characteristic of the way a philosophy responds to a past from which it has grown different or to a position with which it is incommensurable.

Other terms of criticism are implied in Austin's occasional recommendations of his own procedures. For example, one reason for following out the branches of Excuses thoroughly and separately is that "Here at last we should be able to unfreeze, to loosen up and get going on agreeing about discoveries, however small, and on agreeing about how to reach agreement." It is hard to convey to anyone who has not experienced it the rightness and relief words like these can have for students who have gone over the same distinctions, rehearsed the same fallacies, trotted out the same topics seminar after term paper, teaching assistant after lecturer, book after article. And the rightness and relief were completed in his confession that the subject of Excuses "has long afforded me what philosophy is so often thought, and made, barren of— the fun of discovery, the pleasure of cooperation, and the satisfaction of reaching agreements." These are real satisfactions, and I can testify that they were present throughout the hours of his seminar on this topic. It would hardly have occurred to anyone, in the initial grip of such satisfactions, to question whether they are appropriate to philosophy (as they obviously are to logic or physics or historical scholarship) any more than they are, in those ways or proportions, to politics or religion or art; to wonder whether their striking presence in our work now did not suggest that we had changed our subject.

The implied terms of criticism in this recommendation are, of course, that we are frozen, tied up, stopped. Granted a shared sense that this describes our position, one wants to know how we arrived at it. Sometimes Austin attributes this to our distended respect for the great figures of the past (see, for example, "Excuses," p. 131), sometimes to general and apparently congenital weaknesses of philosophy itself: "oversimplification, schematization, and constant obsessive repetition of the same small range of jejune 'examples' are . . . far too common to be dismissed as an occasional weakness of philosophers." And this characteristic weakness—something he refers to as "scholastic," following the call of the major line of British Empiricists —he attributes "first, to an obsession with a few particular words, the uses of which are over-simplified, not really understood or carefully studied or correctly described; and second, to an obsession with a few (and nearly always the same) half-studied 'facts'" (*Sense and Sensibilia*, p. 3). So far the criticisms proceed on familiar Baconian or Cartesian ground; the philosopher of good will and the man of common sense will work together to see through philosophy and prejudice to the world as it is.

At some point Austin strikes into criticisms which go beyond the impatience and doubt which begin modern philosophy, new ones necessary perhaps just because philosophy seems to have survived that impatience and doubt (or emasculated them, in turn, into academic subjects). I find three main lines here. (1) Most notably in *Sense and Sensibilia,* he enters charges against philosophers which make it seem not merely that their weakness is somehow natural to the enterprise, imposed on men of ordinary decency by an ill-governed subject, but that their work is still more deeply corrupt: we hear of philosophers having "glibly trotted out" new uses of phrases (p. 19); of subtle "insinuation" which is "well calculated" to get us "where the sense-datum theorist wants to have us" (p. 25); of bogus dichotomies, grotesque exaggeration,

gratuitous ideas (p. 54)—phrases which, at this point,
carry the suggestion that they are deliberate or willful
exaggerations and the like, and pursued with an absence of obvious motivation matched only by an Iago.
(2) On more than one occasion he suggests that
philosophical delinquency arises from a tendency to
Dionysian abandon: we are warned of the blindness
created in the *"ivresse des grandes profondeurs"* (p.
127) and instructed in the size of problems philosophers should aim at—'*In vino*,' possibly, '*veritas*,'
but in a sober symposium '*verum*'" ("Truth," p. 85).
(3) Finally, and quite generally, he conveys the impression that the philosophers he is attacking are not
really serious, that, one may say, they have written
inauthentically (cf. *Sense and Sensibilia*, p. 29).

I cannot attempt here to complete the list of Austin's
terms of criticism, any more than I can now attempt
to trace the particular target each of them has; and I
have left open all assessment of their relative seriousness and all delineation of the particular points of
view from which they are launched. I hope, however,
that the bare suggestion that Austin's work raises, and
helps to settle, such topics will have served my purposes here, which, in summary, are these: (1) To
argue that, without such tracing and assessment and
delineation, we cannot know the extent to which these
criticisms are valid and the extent to which they
project Austin's own temper. (2) To point out that
Austin often gives no reasons whatever for thinking
one or other of them true, never making out the application to a philosopher of a term like "mistaken"
or "imprecise" or "bogus" or the like according to anything like the standards he imposes in his own con-
structions. This discrepancy is not, I believe, peculiar
to Austin, however clearer in him than in other philosophers; my feeling is that if it could be understood
here, one would understand something about the real
limitations, or liabilities, of the exercise of philosophy.
(3) To register the fact that his characteristic terms
of criticism are new terms, new for our time at least,

though not in all cases his alone; and that these new modes of criticism are deeply characteristic of modern philosophy. (4) To suggest that if such terms do not seem formidable directions of criticism, and perhaps not philosophical at all (as compared, say, with terms such as "meaningless," "contradiction," "circular," and so forth), that may be because philosophy is only just learning, for all its history of self-criticism and self-consciousness, to become conscious of itself in a new way, at further ranges of its activity. One could say that attention is being shifted from the character of a philosopher's argument to the character of the philosopher arguing. Such a shift can, and perhaps in the Anglo-American tradition of philosophy it generally does, serve the purest political or personal motive: such criticism would therefore rightly seem philosophically irrelevant, if sometimes academically charming or wicked. The shift could also, one feels, open a new literary-philosophical criticism, in a tradition which knows how to claim, for example, the best of Kierkegaard and Nietzsche. Whatever the outcome, however, what I am confident of is that the relevance of the shift should itself become a philosophical problem. (5) To urge, therefore, a certain caution or discrimination in following Austin's procedures, using his attempts to define in new and freer and more accurate terms the various failings—and hence the various powers—of philosophy, without imitating his complacency, and even prejudice, in attaching them where he sees (but has not proven) fit. It suggests itself that a sound procedure would be this: to enter all criticisms which seem right, but to treat them phenomenologically, as temptations or feelings; in a word, as data, not as answers.

These purposes are meant to leave us, or put us, quite in the dark about the sources of philosophical failure, and about the relation between the tradition of philosophy and the new critics of that tradition, and indeed about the relation between any conflicting philosophies. For quite in the dark is where we ought

to know we are. If, for example, that failure of
Moore's which we discussed earlier is not to be understood as a mistake, then what is it? No doubt it would
be pleasanter were we able not to ask such a question—except that philosophy seems unable to proceed
far without criticizing its past, any more than art can
proceed without imitating it, or science without sum-
marizing it. And anything would be pleasanter than
the continuing rehearsals—performable on cue by any
graduate student in good standing—of how Descartes
was mistaken about dreams, or Locke about truth, or
Berkeley about God, or Kant about things-in-them-
selves or about moral worth, or Hegel about "logic,"
or Mill about "desirable," and so forth; or about
how Berkeley mistook Locke, or Kant Hume, or Mill
Kant, or everybody Mill, and so forth. Such "explanations" are no doubt essential, and they may account
for everything we need to know, except why any man
of intelligence and vision has ever been attracted to
the subject of philosophy. Austin's criticisms, where
they stand, are perhaps as external and snap as any
others, but he has done more than any philosopher
(excepting Wittgenstein) in the Anglo-American tradition to make clear that there is a coherent tradition to
be dealt with. If he has held it at arm's length, and
falsely assessed it, that is just a fault which must bear
its own assessment; it remains true that he has given
us hands for assessing it in subtler ways than we had
known. The first step would be to grant to philosophers
the ordinary rights of language and vision Austin grants
all other men: to ask of them, in his spirit, why they
should say what they say where and when they say it,
and to give the *full story* before claiming satisfaction.
That Austin pretends to know the story, to have heard
it all before, is no better than his usual antagonist's
assumption that there is no story necessary to tell, that
everything is fine and unproblematic in the tradition,
that philosophers may use words as they please, pos-
sessing the right or power—denied to other mortals—

of knowing, without investigating, the full source and significance of their words and deeds.

It is characteristic of work like Austin's—and this perhaps carries a certain justice—that criticism of it will often take the form of repudiating it as philosophy altogether. Let me conclude by attempting to make one such line of criticism less attractive than it has seemed to some philosophers to be.

A serviceable instance is provided by a sensational book published a few years ago by Mr. Ernest Gellner (*Words and Things*, London, 1959) in which this author congratulates himself for daring to unmask the sterility and mystique of contemporary English philosophy by exposing it to sociology. First of all, unmasking is a well-turned modern art, perhaps *the* modern intellectual art, and its practitioners must learn not to be misled themselves by masks, and to see their own. I mean both that unmasking is itself a phenomenon whose sociology needs drawing, and also that the philosophy Gellner "criticizes" is itself devoted to unmasking. If, as one supposes, this modern art develops with the weakening or growing irrelevance of given conventions and institutions, then the position of the unmasker is by its nature socially unhinged, and his responsibility for his position becomes progressively rooted in his single existence. This is the occasion for finding a mask or pose of one's own (sage, prophet, saint, and so forth). Austin was an Englishman, an English professor. If I say he *used* this as a mask, I mean to register my feeling that he must, somewhere, have known his criticisms to be as unjustified as they were radical, but felt them to be necessary in order that his work get free, and heard. It would have served him perfectly, because its Englishness made it unnoticeable as a pose, because what he wanted from his audience required patience and cooperation, not depth and upheaval, and because it served as a counterpoise to Wittgenstein's strategies of the sage and the ascetic (which Nietzsche isolated as the traditional mask of the Knower; that is, as the only form in which it could carry authority).

Far from a condemnation, this is said from a sense that in a modern age to speak the truth may require the protection of a pose, and even that the necessity to posture may be an authentic mark of the possession of truth. It may not, too; that goes without saying. And it always is dangerous, and perhaps self-destructive. But to the extent it is necessary, it is not the adoption of pose which is to be condemned, but the age which makes it necessary. (Kierkegaard and Nietzsche, with terrible consciousness, condemned both themselves and the age for their necessities; and both maintained, at great cost, the doubt that their poses were really necessary—which is what it must feel like to know your pose.)

The relation of unmasking to evaluation is always delicate to trace. Gellner vulgarly imagines that his sociological reduction in itself proves the intellectual inconsequence and social irrelevance or political conservatism of English philosophy. (His feeling is common enough; why such psychological or sociological analyses appear to their performers—and to some of their audience—as reductive in this way is itself a promising subject of psychological and sociological investigation.) Grant for the argument that his analysis of this philosophy as a function of the Oxford and Cambridge tutorial system, the conventions of Oxford conversation, the distrust of ideology, the training in classics and its companion ignorance of science, and so forth, is accurate and relevant enough. Such an analysis would at most show the conditions or outline the limitations—one could say it makes explicit the conventions—within which this work was produced or initiated. To touch the question of its value, the value of those conventions themselves, as they enter the texture of the work, would have to be established. This is something that Marx and Nietzsche and Freud, our teachers of unmasking, knew better than their progeny.

Still, it can seem surprising that radical and permanent philosophy can be cast in a mode which merges comfortably in the proprieties of the common room—in the way it can seem surprising that an old man, sick and out of fortune, constructing sayings (in consort with others) polite enough for the game in a lady's drawing room, and entertaining enough to get him invited back, should have been saying the maxims of La Rochefoucauld.

Seven published papers are not many, and those who care about Austin's work will have felt an unfairness in his early death, a sense that he should have had more time. But I think it would be wrong to say that his work remains incomplete. He once said to me, and doubtless to others: "I had to decide early on whether I was going to write books or to teach people how to do philosophy usefully." Why he found this choice necessary may not be clear. But it is as clear as a clear Berkeley day that he was above all a teacher, as is shown not merely in any such choice, but in everything he wrote and (in my hearing) spoke, with its didactic directions for profitable study, its lists of exercises, its liking for sound preparation and its disapproval of sloppy work and lazy efforts. In example and precept, his work is complete, in a measure hard to imagine matched. I do not see that it is anywhere being followed with the completeness it describes and exemplifies. There must be, if this is so, various reasons for it. And it would be something of an irony if it turned out that Wittgenstein's manner were easier to imitate than Austin's; in its way, something of a triumph for the implacable professor.

PART II

Existential Analysis

CHAPTER 5

CHRISTIANITY AND NONSENSE

HENRY E. ALLISON*

> My propositions serve as elucidations in the following
> way: anyone who understands me eventually recognizes
> them as nonsensical, when he has used them—as steps—to
> climb up beyond them. (He must, so to speak, throw away
> the ladder after he has climbed up it.)
>
> LUDWIG WITTGENSTEIN

THE *Concluding Unscientific Postscript* is generally regarded as the most philosophically significant of Kierkegaard's works. In terms of a subjectivistic orientation
it seems to present both an elaborate critique of the
pretensions of the Hegelian philosophy and an existential analysis which points to the Christian faith as
the only solution to the "human predicament." Furthermore, on the basis of such a straightforward reading
of the text, Kierkegaard has been both vilified as an
irrationalist and praised as a profound existential
thinker who has uncovered the only legitimate starting
point for a philosophical analysis of the religious life
and a Christian apologetic.

The aim of this paper is to suggest that any such
reading involves a radical misunderstanding of Kierkegaard's intent. Given the supposition that the *Post-*

* Henry E. Allison, formerly of Pennsylvania State University, is now a member of the Philosophy Department
at the University of Florida. This article was initially published in *The Review of Metaphysics*, Vol. 20, No. 3
(March 1967), and is printed here by permission of both
the editor and the author.

script is to be regarded as a contribution to religious
or existential philosophy, the charge of irrationalism is
irrefutable. Viewed as an anti-idealistic philosophical
thesis, the "doctrine" that "truth is subjectivity" not
only leads to a consistent misologism, but also implies
the ultimate identification of Christianity and nonsense. However, when this result is understood in light
of Johannes Climacus' (the pseudonymous author)
self-proclaimed role as a humorist, and of the discussion of indirect communication and "double reflection"
which is prefaced to the "argument," the doctrinal
content of the work must be regarded as an ironical
jest, which essentially takes the form of a carefully
constructed parody of the *Phenomenology of Mind*.
Moreover, the real purpose of this jest is not to convince the reader of a philosophical or religious truth,
but to prevent him from theorizing, even in an "existential" sense about Christianity, and instead to help
him to come to grips, in the isolation of his own
subjectivity, with the question of what it means to
become a Christian. Thus, far from being a contribution, good, bad or indifferent, to a philosophy of
existence, the *Postscript* emerges as Kierkegaard's attempt at a *reductio ad absurdum* of any such enterprise.

I

The *Postscript* is essentially concerned with the
problem of becoming a Christian. This is called the
"subjective problem," and is sharply distinguished from
the objective problem of the truth of the Christian
religion. The latter question, which is the central concern of historical criticism and speculative philosophy,
is rather cursorily dismissed with the reflection that an
objective investigation of the historical claims of

Christianity can never yield more than approximation (a certain degree of probability), and that any mere approximation is incommensurable with the "infinite personal interest in an eternal happiness" which characterizes a believing Christian. Furthermore, any such objective approach to Christianity is not only futile but perverse, for the disinterestedness demanded of an objective observer is diametrically opposed to the decisiveness and total commitment which constitutes the very essence of Christian faith.

This analysis of the two approaches to Christianity gives rise to the distinction between subjective and objective reflection, and it is within the framework of this distinction that the "argument" of the work unfolds. The tendency towards objective thought finds its culmination in Hegel. In the Hegelian philosophy we are shown the necessity of transcending our finite particularity and viewing things from the standpoint of the Idea. There one will come to see the unity of thought and being and the identity of subject and object. The goal of the *Phenomenology of Mind* is precisely to lead the individual along the "highway of despair," to see the inadequacy of all finite forms of consciousness, and eventually to the promised land of Absolute Spirit, where all finite oppositions are reconciled. From this standpoint it is encumbent upon the individual to "forget himself,"[1] in the sense of his finite particularity, to become disinterested in his personal existence and absorbed in the Idea.

It is precisely this viewpoint which is the main target of Climacus' attack. His basic objection, and here it must be remembered that this objection is directed as much against the Danish Hegelians, e.g., Heiberg and Martenson, as Hegel himself, is that this ultimate conformity of thought and being can never be realized by an existing human being, for it is precisely existence which keeps the moments of thought and being, of

[1] Hegel, *The Phenomenology of Mind*, trans. by J. B. Baillie (London and New York, 1931), p. 130.

ideality and reality apart. Thus, the attempt to realize
their union and to achieve the standpoint of pure
thought necessarily involves the comical attempt to
forget that one happens to be an existing human being.
Climacus epitomizes this contention with the reflection
that: "If the Hegelian philosophy has emancipated itself
from every presupposition, it has won this freedom by
means of one lunatic postulate: the initial transition to
pure thought" (p. 279).

However, while the objective thinker tends to lose
himself in his speculations, the subjectively oriented
thinker "is essentially interested in his own thinking,
existing as he does in his thought" (p. 67). This means
that the subjective thinker is not concerned with the
results yielded by disinterested reflection, but with the
realization of the truth in his own existence. Objective
reflection is concerned with "the matter at issue," i.e.,
whether a particular theory is true or false, but for the
subjective thinker, his very subjectivity becomes "the
matter at issue." Hence Climacus proclaims:

This must constantly be borne in mind, namely that
the subjective problem is not something about an
objective issue, but is the subjectivity itself. For since
the problem in question poses a decision, and since all
decisiveness, as shown above, inheres in subjectivity, it
is essential that every trace of an objective issue should
be eliminated. If any such trace remains, it is at once
a sign that the subject seeks to shirk something of the
pain and crisis of the decision: that is, he seeks to make
the problem to some degree objective. (p. 115)

With this the wedge is firmly placed between the
two modes of reflection. They are not only heterogene-
ous, but incommensurable. Instead of the Hegelian
both/and whereby the individual finds himself in the
infinite after forgetting himself in the finite, Climacus
offers the existential either/or wherein the forgetfulness
of self, characteristic of speculative thought, is viewed
as a fantastic flight from one's existential situation, and
the authentic task of the subjective thinker is to "im-

merse himself in existence," i.e., to become increasingly
conscious of his existential situation.

Climacus offers several illustrations of what he means
by subjective reflection or becoming subjective, and
perhaps the most illuminating of them is his analysis
of the question: "What does it mean to die," wherein he
clearly anticipates the well known discussion of
Heidegger. Objectively, Climacus suggests, we know
all sorts of things about death. We know, for instance,
that we shall die if we swallow a dose of sulphuric acid
or if we drown ourselves. We also know from history
books that Napoleon always went about with poison
ready at hand, and that in certain circumstances the
Stoics regarded suicide as a courageous act. Furthermore, we are all aware of the fact that we will eventually die, and even that it might happen at any
moment. Yet to possess all these items of information,
to objectively recognize the inevitability and the uncertainty of death, is not to have understood it. Such
understanding is radically different from understanding
any item of information. It requires the ability to so
exist that one regards death as an ever present possibility. This does not mean, however, that one simply
acknowledges in passing that one must think about it
at every moment, but that one really does so think
about it. This intensity of subjective reflection is
necessary according to Climacus, for

. . . if I am a mortal creature, then it is impossible to
understand this uncertainty in terms of a mere generality unless indeed I, too, happen to be merely a
human being in general. . . . And if initially my human nature is merely an abstract something, it is at
any rate the task which life sets me to become subjective; and in the same degree that I become subjective,
the uncertainty of death comes more and more to
interpenetrate my subjectivity dialectically. It thus becomes more and more important for me to think it in
connection with every factor and phase of my life; for
since this uncertainty is there in every moment, it can
only be overcome by overcoming it in every moment
(p. 149).

II

This analysis of the two kinds of reflection leads Climacus to a consideration of the kind of truth appropriate to each. From the point of view of objective reflection, truth is viewed in the traditional manner as the conformity of thought and being. The precise meaning of this formula, however, is dependent upon an understanding of "being." Here Climacus recognizes two possibilities: either "being" is understood as real or empirical being or as ideal being. Because of the uncertainty of all empirical generalizations (an uncertainty which is grounded for Climacus, as for Plato, in the changing character of the world of sense), if "being" is understood in the former sense (as empirical being) truth becomes a *desideratum*, something to be approximated but never finally achieved by any existing individual. (Hence "an existential system is impossible.") If, however, it is understood in the latter sense (as ideal being) its conformity with thought becomes an empty tautology, "an abstract self-identity." In either case, however, the Hegelian attempt to mediate between thought and being must be rejected. Such mediation may be valid *sub specie aeterni*, but this is irrelevant to the poor existing individual, who is "confined to the straightjacket of existence" and cannot attain that exalted standpoint.

What is needed, therefore, is an explanation of how the eternal, i.e., ethico-religious, truth is to be understood by an existing individual, and this is provided by the contention that truth lies in subjectivity. Since objective reflection necessarily leads away from the subject and culminates in a disinterested contemplation, a truth which is true for the subject, i.e., existentially relevant, can only be acquired through inwardness or subjective reflection:

The subjective reflection turns its attention inwardly to the subject, and desires in this intensification of inwardness to realize the truth. And it proceeds in such fashion that, just as in the preceding objective reflection, when the objectivity had come into being, the subjectivity had vanished, so here the subjectivity of the subject becomes the final stage and objectivity a vanishing factor (pp. 175–176).

Now inwardness culminates in passion, and it is only in the moment of passion that an individual is able to existentially realize the union of the finite and the infinite which is the goal of the Hegelian dialectic. "In passion," Climacus contends, "the existing individual is rendered infinite in the eternity of the imaginative representation, and yet is at the same time most definitely himself" (p. 176). This unique quality of passion is grounded in its dual nature as both the culmination of inwardness and the means to self-transcendence. Because of this dual nature Climacus can regard the individual during the moment of passion as at the same time fully at one with himself and in a genuine relationship with God. This conception follows from Climacus' definition of inwardness as "the relationship of an individual to himself before God" (p. 391) and points to Kierkegaard's oft expressed conviction that man, as a "synthesis of the finite and the infinite" is only really at one with himself when he exists in full consciousness of his God-relationship. Finally, since he often describes an individual's "God-relationship" as a "possibility relationship" and God as "infinite possibility," and since he regards imagination as the organ of possibility in man, it follows that for Climacus the union of God and man, the finite and the infinite, can only take place in the imagination.[2]

From this it can be readily seen that subjective reflection provides the only possible approach to ethico-

[2] My interpretation of this passage, and especially the phrase "in the eternity of imaginative representation" (*i Phantasiens Evighed*) is indebted to Professor Louis Mackey of Rice University.

religious knowledge, which is the only knowledge that has "an essential relationship to the existence of the knower." However, whereas from the objective point of view reflection is directed towards the result of one's investigation, conceived of as a body of truth maintaining its validity apart from the individual's relationship to it, subjective reflection is directed towards the relationship itself, with the paradoxical result that "if only the mode of the relationship is in the truth, the individual is in the truth, even if he should happen to be related to what is not true" (p. 178). In other words, one can say that while objective reflection is directed towards the "what" or content of a doctrine, subjective reflection is concerned with the "how," the way in which it is existentially appropriated by the individual. Thus, it is the "passion of the infinite," or the genuineness of the commitment which is decisive, and not the specific nature of that to which one is committed. As an illustration of this Climacus utters the well-known, yet highly misleading dictum:

If one who lives in the midst of Christendom goes up to the house of God, the house of the true God, with the true conception of God in his knowledge, and prays, but prays in a false spirit; and one who lives in an idolatrous community prays with the entire passion of the infinite, although his eyes rest upon the image of an idol: where is there more truth? The one prays in truth to God though he worships an idol; the other prays falsely to the true God, and hence worships in fact an idol (pp. 179–180).

This statement is misleading because it appears to endorse the unqualified rejection of the "what" of belief in favor of the "how," with the obvious implication that it is better to be a "true," passionately committed Nazi than to be a lukewarm Christian. This, however, is not Climacus' intent, and he goes to great lengths to obviate any such misunderstanding. First, he endeavors to distinguish between true inwardness and madness. Climacus points to Don Quixote as the prototype of "subjective madness," and argues that the basic

characteristic of such madness is the concentration of
one's passion upon a particular finite object, an *idée
fixe*. Thus, madness becomes characterized as an "aber-
rant inwardness," wherein one becomes infinitely concerned over something which is of no decisive significance. In contrast with this, true inwardness is
always directed towards the infinite, i.e., towards one's
God-relationship, and, Climacus concludes: "At its
maximum this inward 'how' is the passion of the
infinite, and the passion of the infinite is the truth.
But the passion of the infinite is precisely subjectivity,
and thus subjectivity becomes the truth" (p. 181).

Second, and most important, this passionate "how"
is so qualified that Christianity, as the ultimate "what,"
becomes its only satisfactory correlate, and thus, what
began as an attack upon objective reflection, ends up
as a rather peculiar "demonstration" of the subjective
truth of Christianity. This is not accomplished, however, by an immediate reconciliation of the "how" and
the "what," the commitment and its object, but by
further accentuating their opposition, thereby suggesting an eventual *coincidentia oppositorum*. The basic
premise of this "argument" is Climacus' contention:
"An objective uncertainty held fast in an appropriation process of the most passionate inwardness is the
truth, the highest truth attainable for an existing individual" (p. 182).

This definition of truth which, Climacus tells us, is
an equivalent expression for faith determines the opposition between subjective and objective reflection, "the
fork in the road where the way swings off." Just as the
scientific quest for objective truth requires the rejection
of all subjective or private interests, so "when subjectivity is the truth, *the conceptual determination of
the truth must include an expression for the antithesis
to objectivity*" (p. 182). Thus, there is a direct correlation between objective uncertainty and subjective
truth, the objective uncertainty serving to increase "the
tension of that infinite passion which is inwardness."
When systematically applied such a conception leads

to a radical misologism, and as we shall see, this is precisely the direction in which the discussion proceeds.

Climacus had begun his analysis of subjectivity by arguing quite cogently that the decisiveness of religious or ethical commitment is incompatible with the disinterested reflection of objective thought. Thus, one can neither speculate one's way into Christianity, nor treat the content of Christian faith in a speculative manner, à la Hegel, without completely perverting its very essence. However, where St. Thomas Aquinas was content to point out that one cannot know and believe the same thing at the same time, and where Kant sought to deny knowledge in order to make room for faith, Climacus argues for a direct relationship between theoretical implausability and religious faith. Thus Climacus can assert: "Faith is precisely the contradiction between the infinite passion of the individual's inwardness and the objective uncertainty." Moreover, since such objective uncertainty is the inevitable lot of all existing beings, the attempt to deny it can only be regarded as absentmindedness, and thus the true believer "must constantly be intent upon holding fast the objective uncertainty, so as to remain out upon the deep, over seventy thousand fathoms of water . . . still preserving his faith" (pp. 182–83).

Armed with this conception of truth, Climacus returns to the problem of his earlier work, the *Philosophical Fragments*: the question of the relationship between the Socratic and the specifically Christian religiosity. Both here and in the *Fragments* Socrates is viewed by Climacus as the very prototype of the subjective or existential thinker outside of Christianity. His great merit over against both Plato and the modern speculative thinkers is that he never forgets that he is an existing individual, but rather "concentrates essentially upon existence."

The heart of Socratic thought is to be found in the notion that the truth lies within. As Climacus tells us in the *Fragments*: "In the Socratic view each individual is his own center, and the entire world centers in his views, his self-knowledge is a knowledge of God" (p. 14). Thus, the task confronting a Socratic thinker is to become subjective, in the sense of continually realizing in existence his God-relationship. This, according to Climacus, is the profound significance of Socrates' doctrine that knowledge is recollection, and which clearly differentiates it from the speculative use made of that doctrine by Plato. Existentially understood it means that the knower is potentially in possession of the eternal truth, i.e., his God-relationship, and is confronted with no difficulty other than the fact that he exists. This minor difficulty, however, turns out to be decisive, and provides the clue to understanding Socrates' frequent professions of ignorance. This ignorance is viewed by Climacus as a consequence of the previously established contention that for one engaged in the business of existing, the eternal truth remains objectively uncertain. Moreover, since a total commitment is demanded to what is objectively uncertain, Climacus contends that from the point of view of the existing individual the truth becomes a paradox. This paradox was thoroughly grasped by Socrates, who totally committed himself to the truth despite his recognition of its objective uncertainty (the manner in which he faced death in the *Phaedo* being Climacus' favorite illustration), and for this reason: "Socrates was in the truth by virtue of his ignorance, in the highest sense in which this was possible within paganism" (p. 183).

But paganism is not Christianity, and although Climacus points to the analogies between Socratic inwardness and Christian faith, his main goal seems to be to show the superiority of the latter. The basic limitation of the Socratic position lies in the theory of recollection. This theory has a two-fold existential significance. First, as was shown in the *Fragments*, it clearly implies that neither an historical event nor another person can have any decisive significance for an existing individual. Since the truth lies within, one person can do no more than provide the occasion whereby another comes to recollect it (the slave boy incident in the *Meno* being the paradigm case), and thus the maieutic relationship is the highest possible between men. Second, because the truth lies within, temporal existence lacks any ultimate seriousness, for the possibility of "taking oneself back into eternity through recollection is always there" (p. 184). To be sure, Socrates with his passionate inwardness did not make use of this possibility, but according to Climacus its very presence serves to mitigate the seriousness of his inwardness.

This limitation raises the question of the possibility of a higher level of inwardness. Since the limitation of the Socratic position stems from the contention that the individual is initially in possession of the truth, any deeper expression of inwardness or subjectivity must involve a denial of this possession. However, the denial that the individual is in possession of the truth is *eo ipso* a denial of the contention that truth is subjectivity, and thus we are led by the inexorable "logic" of Climacus to the paradoxical conclusion that the deepest possible expression of the notion that subjectivity is truth, is precisely the proposition that subjectivity is untruth. This, however, is not to be understood as implying a regression to the speculative standpoint, wherein subjectivity is also untruth, for the decisive characteristic of this level of ultimate inwardness is that here "subjectivity is beginning upon the task of becoming the truth through a subjectifying process, is in the difficulty that it is already untruth" (pp. 185–186). The result is not the abandonment, but the further accentuation of existence, and hence of inwardness. The subject cannot be regarded as eternally being in untruth, as this would apparently imply that he was created thusly by God, nor does it make sense to regard the loss of the "eternal essential truth" as the result of an unfortunate accident. Thus, the only explanation for the loss is that the individual brought himself into the condition in time, by a free act. If, however, the individual has in fact cut himself off from the eternal by a free act then the pathos of his existential condition is accentuated to the utmost possible degree.

Now it just so happens that this is precisely how Christianity, with its doctrine of original sin, views the human condition. From the Christian standpoint a man is born in sin and as a sinner. Thus, in contradistinction to the Socratic man who has access to the eternal by way of recollection, the Christian is profoundly aware of his alienation from the eternal, a situation poignantly depicted in Hegel's analysis of the "Unhappy Conscience." Furthermore, Climacus reflects: "If it was paradoxical to posit the eternal truth in relationship to an existing individual, it is now absolutely paradoxical to posit it in relationship to such an individual as we have here defined" (p. 186).

However, this is exactly what Christianity proclaims to have taken place through the entrance of God into history as the Christ. Thus, if for Socrates the paradox is to be found in the relationship between the eternal truth and the existing individual, for the Christian the eternal truth itself is inherently paradoxical. This is because for the Christian the eternal (decisive truth) is precisely that the eternal truth (God) has come into being in time. Hence, what for Socrates remained an objective uncertainty is for the Christian an objective absurdity: "The absurd is that the eternal truth has come into being in time, that God has come into being, has been born, has grown up, and so forth, precisely like any other individual human being, quite indistinguishable from other individuals" (p. 188).

This absurdity is the content of the Christian faith, the "what" corresponding to the "how" of Christian inwardness. It is the absolute paradox, or the paradox *sensu eminentiori* to which the Socratic paradox and its corresponding inwardness bear only a remote analogy. Since the starting point of the whole discussion was the affirmation of the direct correlation between objective uncertainty and inwardness, "the less objective

security the more profound the possible inwardness,"
it would appear that it is only when the "what" becomes objectively absurd, and the more absurd the
better, that the maximum degree of inwardness is
attainable. Now since the requisite absurdity is found
in the content of Christian faith, we are led to the
conclusion that Christianity is the source of the maximum possible inwardness, and thus can be regarded as
the "true" religion (subjectively understood), not in
spite of, but precisely because of its objective absurdity!
For, in Climacus' own words: "The absurd is precisely
by its objective repulsion the measure of the intensity
of faith in inwardness" (p. 189).

Despite the protest of several recent commentators
this position must be regarded as radically irrationalistic.[3] The "argument" as it stands, with its explicit
correlation between objective absurdity and subjective
"truth" is clearly an expression of a consistent misologism or an "intellectualistic anti-intellectualism"[4]
which finds its closest historical antecedent in the
"credo quia absurdum" attributed to Tertullian. However, just as Hegel's panlogism differs from the pre-
Kantian rationalism of a Leibniz or Spinoza by virtue
of its dialectical structure, so Climacus' misologism can
be viewed as an irrationalistic revision of the Hegelian
schema. Thus, while Hegel rejects the absolute start-

[3] Cf. the essays of James Collins, Cornelio Falio and
N. H. Søe in *A Kierkegaard Critique*, ed. by Howard A.
Johnson and Niels Thustrup (New York, 1962) and Hey-
wood Thomas, *Subjectivity and Paradox* (New York, 1957).
The interpretation of these commentators is also attacked
along similar lines by H. M. Garelick in his *The Anti-
Christianity of Kierkegaard* (The Hague, 1965).

[4] This frequently reiterated charge seems to have been
most explicitly formulated in relation to the *Postscript*
by Thorsten Bohlen in *Kierkegaard's tro och Kierkegaard-
Studies* (Copenhagen, 1944). For a discussion of Bohlen's
position see Søe's "Kierkegaard's Doctrine of the Paradox"
in *A Kierkegaard Critique*, pp. 208–210. A similar position
is very forcibly argued by Richard Kroner in "Kierkegaard's
Hegelverstandnis," *Kant-Studien*, Bd. 46, Heft 1, 1954–55,
pp. 19–27.

ing point of his predecessors and begins instead with the immediate, viewing absolute knowledge as the goal to be obtained through the demonstration of the inadequacy of all finite forms ("Of the Absolute it must be said that it is essentially a result"), Climacus, in his endeavor "to make the necessity of the paradox evident" (p. 191), begins with an analysis of the inadequacy of all lower stages of inwardness. This analysis, which traces the spiritual life of the individual, rather than the life of Absolute Spirit, from the lowest level, aesthetic immediacy, to the highest non-Christian expression, infinite resignation, and the consciousness of guilt before God, occupies the bulk of the *Postscript*; but its main purpose, (suggested by the name Climacus) is to lead the individual up the dialectical ladder of inwardness to the point at which he can appreciate the uniqueness and absoluteness, as well as the absurdity of the Christian faith. Hence, one can say that for Hegel's conception of the necessary advance of the Spirit to absolute knowledge, Climacus substitutes the equally necessary (albeit in a different sense) advance of subjectivity to absolute paradox.

The necessity of this advance for the spiritual development of the individual is demonstrated by means of a further comparison of the Socratic and Christian forms of religiousness, here entitled A and B, or the "religiousness of immanence" and "paradoxical religiousness" respectively. The former is characterized by a "dying away from immediacy," the repudiation, or at least relativization of all one's finite concerns, and the devotion of all one's energies to the realization of one's "absolute telos," a phrase applied to both the individual's God-relationship and his eternal happiness, which seem to be identical for Climacus. Since the presupposition of this level of inwardness is the belief that the truth lies within, the individual is viewed as already potentially in possession of his God-relationship or eternal happiness, and his task is simply to transform his mode of existence so as to become in truth what he already is potentially. Hence, Climacus calls this level the "dialectic of inward transformation" (p. 494). The task of self-transformation, however, is soon shown to be far more difficult than it first appeared. Since this "dying away from immediacy" or "infinite resignation," cannot be accomplished once and for all, but must be undertaken at every instant, such a mode of existence essentially involves suffering. Moreover, since that which must be continually begun anew can never be completed, the decisive expression for this form of religiousness is the consciousness of guilt. This consciousness of guilt, the awareness of being in the wrong over and against God, is the highest development of the religiousness of inwardness, and we are thus led to the paradoxical conclusion that the deepest expression of the individual's God-relationship is to be found in the consciousness of the disrelationship.

It is at this point that the parallelism with Hegel once again becomes manifest. Just as the *Phenomenology of Mind* showed that one must traverse the "highway of despair" and experience the shipwreck of all finite forms of understanding before he is able to grasp the standpoint of the Absolute, so for Climacus, it is only the individual who has existentially striven to realize his God-relationship and has been shipwrecked upon the consciousness of guilt for whom the absolute paradox becomes meaningful. "Religiousness A," Climacus contends, "must be present in the individual before there can be any question of becoming aware of the dialectic of B" (p. 494). Only when existential pathos has reached its decisive expression in the consciousness of guilt can the venture into the absurd become an existential possibility. Just as it is the consciousness of the path which distinguishes the Hegelian conception of absolute knowledge from the dogmatic pretensions of his predecessors, for Climacus it is precisely the presence of this prior consciousness which distinguishes the venture into the absurd from superstition.

This implies that any speculative interpretation of the paradox involves a misunderstanding. The diffi-

culty involved in becoming a Christian is not the intellectual difficulty of understanding how the eternal
can be reconciled with the temporal, but the existential
difficulty of committing oneself to the belief that one's
eternal happiness is based upon something historical,
and moreover, something historical which by its very
nature cannot become historical. Such a commitment
involves the complete sacrifice of one's reason, both
theoretical and practical, for in addition to being inherently contradictory, the absolute paradox also vio-
lates the ethical integrity of the individual in that it
places the locus of his eternal destiny in something
external to him. The problem of the relationship between the ethical and the paradoxically religious modes
of existence is one of the most interesting, yet generally ignored aspects of Climacus' analysis. Nevertheless
he takes great pains to depict the proper relationship between them. The analogy, he argues, between
faith and the ethical mode of existence is to be found
in the "infinite interest" or "inwardness which distinguishes both from an aesthetic mode of existence." But
the believer differs from the ethicist in being infinitely
interested in the reality of another, i.e., in the fact that
God has existed in time" (p. 288).

This, Climacus asserts, can only be believed against
the understanding, so that the believer's task is not to
understand the paradox, but to understand that it
cannot be understood. However, in view of the elaborate dialectical analysis which prepares the way for
the apprehension of the paradox, it would seem that
this itself requires a good deal of understanding, and
is well beyond the ken of the "simple believer" whom
Climacus is always praising at the expense of the pretentious speculative philosopher. This is no doubt the
justification for those who regard the position of the
Postscript as an "intellectual anti-intellectualism," and
Climacus himself seems to admit as much when he
proclaims that it is after all necessary for the Christian
to make use of his understanding, "precisely in order
to believe against his understanding" (p. 504).

Thus, the dialectical ascent to faith culminates in the "crucifixion of the understanding" (p. 500). Here, at the highest level of the spiritual life we encounter a total break with immanence. The individual has gone through the process of "infinite resignation," and has come to the realization of the shipwreck of his own resources, both intellectual and moral. His consciousness of sin makes him fully aware of his alienation from God and the hopelessness of his situation. Yet he nevertheless clings passionately to the absurd, and, so Christianity tells us, finds therein his salvation.

Climacus' analysis of subjectivity has thus brought us to the point where we can indeed recognize "the necessity of the paradox" in that we can see that its acceptance through an act of faith is the only solution to the human predicament. Moreover, with this insight we are also able to apprehend the return of objectivity. The analysis of the "how" has led us inevitably to the "what" of Christianity as its only true correlate, as the only content capable of satisfying the "passion of the infinite." Objectivity and subjectivity are reconciled in the inwardness of faith in a manner strangely reminiscent of the speculative reconcilation of consciousness and its object at the end of the *Phenomenology of Mind*, and Climacus is rapidly emerging as a rather queer sort of Hegelian. The essence of Climacus' position is to be found in a passage near the end of the work where the relationship between the how and the what is explicitly formulated.

The thing of being a Christian is not determined by the what of Christianity but by the *how* of the Christian. This *how* can only correspond with one thing: the absolute paradox. There is therefore no vague talk to the effect that being a Christian is to accept, and to accept, and to accept quite differently, to appropriate, to believe, to appropriate by faith quite differently (all of them purely rhetorical and fictitious definitions); but to *believe* is specifically different from all other appropriation and inwardness. Faith is the objective uncertainty due to the repulsion of the absurd held fast by the

passion of inwardness, which in this instance is intensi-
fied to the utmost degree. This formula fits only the
believer, no one else, not a lover, not an enthusiast,
not a thinker, but simply and solely the believer who is
related to the absolute paradox [p. 540].

With this Climacus' conviction of the uniqueness and
incommensurability of the Christian faith with all other
levels of inwardness receives its decisive expression. It
thus is not true that it does not matter what one believes as long as one believes it with sufficient inwardness, for the only thing that can really be believed, i.e.,
truly appropriated with the "passion of the infinite" is
the absolute paradox. This aspect of Climacus' position
is clearly expressed by Kierkegaard himself, who in a
Journal entry for the year 1849, writes:

In all that is usually said about Johannes Climacus
being purely subjective and so on, people have for-
gotten, in addition to everything else concrete about
him, that in one of the last sections he shows that the
curious thing is: that there is a "how" which has this
quality, that if *it* is truly given, that the "what" is
also given; and that it is the "how" of "faith." Here,
quite certainly, we have inwardness at its maximum
proving to be objectivity once again. And this is an
aspect of the principle of subjectivity which, so far as
I know, has never before been presented or worked
out.[5]

III

Viewed in the usual manner as an argument for the
uniqueness, absoluteness and "subjective truth" of the
Christian faith, Climacus' "apologetic" must be regarded as an utter failure. In terms of his misologistic
orientation the "subjective truth" of Christianity is a

[5] *The Journals of Søren Kierkegaard,* ed. by Alexander
Dru (London, 1931), No. 528.

function of the absurdity of its objective content. It is only because of the "repulsion of the absurd" that Christianity is able to intensify inwardness to the "utmost degree," and it is thus its very absurdity which allegedly qualifies it as the only "what" corresponding to the ultimate "how." But at this point the question inevitably suggests itself to us in our misguided role as objective thinkers: why this particular absurdity? Granted, for the sake of argument, that the belief that our eternal happiness is based upon an objective absurdity is necessary to raise the passion of the religious individual to its highest level, but does that really serve to prove that Christianity is the only absurdity which can really be *believed* (in the strong Climacian sense)? At the most this would seem to show that the passionate acceptance of Jesus of Nazareth as the Christ requires the highest level of inwardness, but so, it seems, would the acceptance of the claim of any of an untold number of deluded fanatics who have believed that they were God. Moreover, if Christianity is really as absurd as Climacus contends, if becoming a Christian really does require a "crucifixion of the understanding," then it is hard to see what criteria we could find to distinguish between this saving absurdity, and plain "garden variety" nonsense. Once the understanding is crucified in the radical manner which Climacus suggests, it is clearly no easy task to resurrect it.

Yet perhaps we are jumping to conclusions. Climacus does in fact attempt to distinguish between the absurdity of the absolute paradox and mere nonsense. The problem is discussed in passing in the *Fragments*. There he distinguishes between the paradox, and the, to him, nonsensical belief that Christ's initial disciples stood in a special relationship to him, that they received the "condition," i.e., the inner witness of the Holy Spirit which makes faith possible, directly from him, and that they in turn were able to give this "condition" to the next generation of disciples. This view, which bears a curious analogy to the Roman Catholic and Grundtvigian conceptions of the Church as an objective authority and means of grace is distinguished from the paradox in that it is not only absurd, but self-contradictory, for it holds that "God is the God for the contemporary, but that the contemporary is God for the third party" (p. 27). Now, this would seem to suggest that the paradox differs from other absurdities in not containing a contradiction, but as we shall see, this hardly jibes with the analysis in the *Postscript*.

Again, in the *Postscript*, Climacus endeavors to distinguish between Christian faith and superstition or aestheticism, which may be regarded as a kind of nonsense. This is accomplished by means of an analysis of the dialectical structure of faith in its relationship to religiousness A:

> In case religiousness A does not come into the picture as *terminus a quo* for the paradoxical religiousness, religiousness A is higher than B, for then the paradox, the absurd etc., are not to be taken *sensu eminenti* (in the sense that they absolutely cannot be understood either by clever or by stupid people), but are used aesthetically of the marvelous among other marvelous things, which are indeed marvelous, but which after all can be comprehended [p. 496].

Thus, to base my hopes for eternity upon my red hair, believing that this color is particularly pleasing to the gods, is the lowest form of paganism, totally lacking in inwardness. It is a rather superficial application of the aesthetic category of fortune, something at which the subjective thinker who has striven with all his passion to realize his relationship to the eternal could only laugh (or perhaps cry?). Now this is quite true, but it is also the case, as Climacus points out, that Christianity itself bears "a certain resemblance" to aesthetics:

> Religiousness B is discriminative, selective and polemical: only upon a definite condition do I become blessed, and as I absolutely bind myself to this condition, so do I exclude every other man who does not thus bind himself. This is the incentive to particularism in universal pathos. Every Christian possesses the pathos of religiousness A, and then this pathos of discrimination.

This discrimination imports to the Christian a certain resemblance to one who is fortunate through favor, and when it is so conceived selfishly by a Christian we have the desperate presumption of predestination [p. 516].

This resemblance is, however, according to Climacus, misleading. The fact that his happiness is based upon something historical, he contends, "makes the Christian's happiness or good fortune recognizable by suffering," and as a consequence, "the religious determinant of being God's elect is as paradoxically contrary as possible to being a Pamphilius of fortune . . . (p. 516). But is it really? The essential difference between the Christian and the superstitious pagan is that the former believes "against his understanding" in full consciousness of its absurdity, and hence with suffering, while the latter (our red-headed Pamphilius of fortune) simply affirms his good fortune with a naive self-confidence. Now this certainly serves to distinguish between the "way" of believing or the levels of inwardness of the Christian and the pagan, but it hardly enables us to make any judgments concerning the *contents* of their respective beliefs. According to Climacus' analysis it would seem that they both believe absurdities, with the rather dubious advantage of the Christian being simply his awareness of the absurdity of his belief.

Finally, we must consider the passage in the *Postscript* where Climacus specifically endeavors to distinguish between the absurdity of Christianity and nonsense. As we have seen, Climacus argues that the proper use of understanding for a Christian is to make sure that he believes against his understanding. From this he concludes:

Nonsense therefore he cannot believe against the understanding, for precisely the understanding will discern that it is nonsense and will prevent him from believing it; but he makes so much use of the understanding that he becomes aware of the incomprehensible, and then he holds to this, believing against the understanding [p. 504].

This passage has been cited as evidence against the charge that Kierkegaard is an irrationalist, and it is suggested that Christianity is here distinguished from nonsense as being (in terms of the traditional distinction) above rather than contrary to reason.[6] It is clear, however, that such a contention hardly fits the argument of the *Postscript*. In addition to the fact that Climacus constantly emphasizes the need to believe against the understanding, rather than merely something which transcends it, the whole analysis of the *Postscript* is geared to showing the contradictory nature of the paradox. Traditionally, the realm of the *supra rationem* was held to be incomprehensible for the finite understanding, but not inherently contradictory. It was, for instance, precisely in terms of this distinction that Leibniz endeavored to reconcile faith and reason in the *Theodicée*. Climacus, however, maintains that the paradox contains not one, but two "dialectical contradictions": first the basing of one's eternal happiness upon the reality of something historical, the contradiction here being between the approximate nature of all historical knowledge, and the total commitment demanded by faith; and second, the "fact that this historical datum is compounded in a way contradictory to all thinking . . ." (p. 513).

It is true that these contradictions are called "dialectical," and the first instance at least this seems to suggest a juxtaposition of incongruous concepts, a kind of "category mistake," rather than a simple logical inconsistency. In the second instance, however, where the reference to the fact that the historical datum is one which by its very nature cannot become historical, is clearly a case of logical contradiction, and thus we are led once again to the recognition of the irrationality of the paradox.

With this we are back to our original question: If the paradox here viewed simply as "the incomprehensible" is indeed irrational and even contradictory, how is this peculiar kind of irrationality to be distinguished

[6] Søe in *A Kierkegaard Critique*, p. 290.

from mere nonsense? According to the cited passage this distinction is recognized by the understanding of the believer, but this raises two fundamental difficulties. The first is again the oft mentioned problem of criteria. Climacus has so strongly emphasized the absurdity of the paradox that it would seem that any effort to distinguish its objective content from mere nonsense is bound to fail. One could, of course, retort that these objective considerations are irrelevant, and that it is its subjective or existential significance for the believer which distinguishes the paradox from nonsense. This, however, gets us nowhere, for it amounts to the admission that *objectively* there are no criteria, and hence that the only difference between Christianity and nonsense is that the former happens to be taken seriously by some individuals while the latter is not. Moreover, we must remember that according to Climacus the distinction is recognized by the understanding. But if this is indeed the case, has not objectivity once again reared its ugly head in a decisive, albeit a perverse manner? From the standpoint of subjective reflection, with its direct correlation between subjective truth and objective uncertainty, would not the recognition, assuming it could be made, that "the incomprehensible" is not nonsense, actually serve as a check, rather than an inducement to inwardness? The only way to avoid this conclusion, and to distinguish between the paradox and mere nonsense, would be to suggest that the former is in some sense even more irrational than the latter. This would mean, however, that for the Hegelian demand to go beyond faith, Climacus is substituting the rather dubious demand to go beyond nonsense!

Secondly, and even more fundamental, Climacus' contention that the understanding will discern nonsense and *prevent* one from believing it, while a reasonable enough statement, stands in blatant contradiction to the distinction between will and intellect, subjectivity and objectivity, which is central to his whole "doctrine." In discussing the problem of historical knowledge in the *Fragments*, Climacus draws attention to the uncertainty involved in all statements about the past. Arguing against the Hegelian conception of history as the necessary process of Spirit in the world, he contends that since the past has come into existence it "has the elusiveness which is implicit in all coming into existence" and thus cannot be regarded as necessary. Now if this be the case, Climacus continues, "the organ for the historical must have an analogous structure. It must comprise a corresponding somewhat by which it may repeatedly negate in its certainty the uncertainty that corresponds to the uncertainty of coming into existence." This condition is met by faith or belief (*Tro*) because as an act of the will "there is always present a negated uncertainty, in every way corresponding to the uncertainty of coming into existence" (pp. 100–101). Furthermore, precisely the same reflection is applicable to doubt, the negative correlate of belief. According to Climacus the radical doubt of the Greek sceptics was not the result of cognition, but a free act of the will, and on this basis he argues against both Descartes and Hegel that doubt cannot be overcome by reflection but only "by a free act of the will" (p. 102). However, if belief and doubt are viewed as acts of will, and as such sharply distinguished from forms of knowledge, it seems rather difficult to see just how our understanding of anything, even nonsense, could "prevent" our belief.

Moreover, lest one suppose that our pseudonymous author has changed his position in the later work, we can readily see that the whole critique of the objective approach to Christianity in the *Postscript* is dependent upon the distinction between the decisiveness of will characteristic of Christian faith, and the disinterestedness of speculative understanding. It is on this basis that Climacus is able to argue that religious commitment (subjectivity) does not follow as a matter of course from objective considerations, but requires a "leap." But if an act of will, a religious commitment, necessarily involves a break with the understanding, how can one maintain that intellectual considerations, i.e., the recognition that something is nonsensical, can "prevent us from believing it"? If belief really is an act of the will, which by its very nature involves a "leap" beyond the understanding, then far from inhibiting belief, the recognition of the nonsensical character of a doctrine would seem to provide an inducement to inwardness, and hence be a potential source of "subjective truth." Thus, we are led to the conclusion that not only does Climacus' misologism fail to provide criteria in terms of which the understanding can distinguish between the Christian absurd and nonsense, but that even if such criteria were available they would be irrelevant to the "subjective thinker."

IV

We have attempted to find within the *Postscript* a relatively straightforward albeit bizarre argument for the "subjective truth" and uniqueness of the Christian faith, and we have come to the conclusion that viewed as such it is a colossal failure. Yet this conclusion raises more problems than it solves. The argument appears to be so bad that we can question whether it could have been seriously meant. Thus, we find ourselves confronted with a decision, which Kierkegaard would no doubt have found amusing: either we must dismiss him as an extremely muddleheaded thinker, who in opting for a subjectivist position, tried and failed to posit criteria in terms of which we can distinguish between Christianity and nonsense, or we shall have to make a new and more strenuous effort to come to grips with that enigma called Kierkegaard.

Now even apart from a consideration of Kierkegaard's frequent but not overly consistent treatment of the question of the precise status of the Christian absurd in his other writings, it is apparent from the structure of the work, its pseudonymous character, and the *First*

and Last Declaration which Kierkegaard appended to
it in his own name, that such a straightforward, un-
dialectical reading of the *Postscript* involves a serious
misunderstanding. As is well known, Kierkegaard proclaims in this "Declaration" that none of the teachings
of the pseudonymous are to be regarded as his.

So in the pseudonymous works there is not a single
word which is mine, I have no opinion about these
works except as a third person, no knowledge of their
meaning except as a reader, not the remotest private
relation to them, since such a thing is impossible in the
case of a doubly reflected communication.

This is no doubt somewhat of an overstatement, and
is to some extent contradicted by his analysis of his
authorship in *The Point of View*, but it does provide us
with an important clue for understanding the *Postscript.* Let us begin then with a consideration of the
character of the pseudonymous author. The name,
Johannes Climacus, is that of a sixth century monk of
the monastery at Sinai, and the surname was derived
from the title of his work: *Scala Paradisi.* Thus, Kierkegaard's use of the pseudonym clearly suggests the notion of climax, or ascent from purely human to
specifically Christian categories. It has been suggested
that the pseudonym represents Kierkegaard's own attitude during his student days at the University.[7] But
within the context of the *Postscript* he repeatedly describes himself as a non-Christian humorist who is concerned with the subjective problem of how to become
a Christian. This raises the question: to what extent
are Climacus' external, i.e., non-Christian perspective
and humoristic orientation reflected in the structure of
the work?

Climacus defines humor as a boundary stage between
the ethical and religious modes of existence, corresponding on a higher level to irony, which is the

---

[7] T. H. Croxall, *Assessment,* prefaced to his translation
of *Johannes Climacus,* or *De Omnibus Dubitandum Est*
(Stanford, California, 1958), pp. 18–19.

boundary between the aesthetic and the ethical. The
essential quality of the humorist is his ability to recognize contradiction, and specifically the contradiction
between the inwardness of the religious life and all its
outward manifestations. The humorist, Climacus contends,

> . . . sets the God-idea into conjunction with other things
> and evokes the contradiction—but he does not maintain
> a relationship to God in terms of religious passion
> *stricte sic dictus*, he transforms himself instead into a
> jesting and yet profound exchange-center for all these
> transactions, but he does not himself stand related to
> God [p. 451].

Thus, the humorist knows something about the existential difficulties of the God-relationship. He is able
to recognize objectivistic or superstitious perversions of
this relationship, but he comprehends in an intellectual,
i.e., objective, sort of way, what the believer appropri-
ates existentially. Since the God-relationship lies in
subjectivity, his very awareness of the difficulties of
such a relationship requires a certain degree of inwardness, but since he does not himself make the "leap,"
but rather withdraws into the realm of jest, he is obviously lacking the decisiveness of the truly committed
person. Now given Climacus' own description of the
stance of the humorist *vis-à-vis* Christianity, one would
expect to find this reflected in his own analysis of faith,
i.e., one would expect this analysis to be in its very
essence humorous, and therefore to some extent objective.

The humorous aspect of the argument is suggested
by the curious parallelism to Hegel, and this suggestion is further strengthened by a Journal entry wherein
Kierkegaard writes: "Hegel is a Johannes Climacus,
who did not, like the giants, storm the heavens by
setting mountain upon mountain, but entered by
means of his syllogisms."[8] Thus, both Hegel and

---

[8] Papier II A 335, Thulstrup's Commentary, *Philosophical
Fragments*, 2nd ed. (Princeton, 1962), p. 148.

Climacus are stormers of the heavens, searchers for the Absolute, and the main difference between them lies in their respective routes to this exalted goal. The one proceeds by way of speculative philosophy, the other by means of "the principle of subjectivity." Yet both attempts are equally futile, for despite the difference of their approaches, they both end up at the same place, viz., the identification of Christianity and nonsense. This follows for Hegel because the attempt to mediate between philosophy and Christianity destroys the decisiveness which is the very essence of the Christian faith, and it follows for Climacus because the attempt to locate the paradox on a scale of subjectivity, undercuts any possible means of determining the uniqueness of the Christian absurd.

In light of these considerations is it outlandish to view the whole "argument" of Climacus as a kind of perverse parody of Hegel? The dialectical structure of the analysis, and the "objective" concern for the ultimate reconciliation of the "how" and the "what" in Christian faith, which parallels the culmination of the *Phenomenology of Mind* in Spirit's consciousness of itself as Spirit, the reconciliation of subject and object in Absolute knowledge, certainly suggests such an interpretation. Moreover, this reading enables us to view the "argument" of the humorous Climacus as a jest, and thus, to overlook the philosophical absurdity of his position. But it naturally gives rise to the question: what is the point of the jest? Why should Kierkegaard's critique of Hegel take the form of a parody? Is he simply playing with us, or is he perhaps asking us to reconsider the possibility raised by the failure of Jacobi and Lavater to understand Lessing's earnestness: "unless it should happen to be the case that one cannot understand earnest without understanding jest" (p. 66)?

The answer, if it is to be found, may very well lie in Kierkegaard's conception of the problem of existential communication, and the recognition of the need for such communication to employ indirection and "double reflection." This possibility becomes very appealing when we recall that in his "Declaration" Kierkegaard characterized his pseudonymous works as examples of "doubly reflected communication," and that within the *Postscript* itself, Climacus begins his account of the "subjective problem" with an analysis of that very concept.

For Climacus, the problem of communication is grounded in the recognition of the different goals of objective and subjective reflection. Objective reflection, as we have seen, is concerned only with results, i.e., with the attainment of a body of authenticated truths. As results they can be directly communicated in a series of propositions. The subjective thinker, on the other hand, is not concerned with the acquisition of a given body of truths, with "finding something out," but with "existing in 'the truth,'" appropriating it existentially. This different goal demands a different type of reflection, "the reflection of inwardness or possession, by virtue of which it belongs to the thinking subject and no one else" (pp. 167–168). This uniquely personal quality of subjective reflection brings with it two consequences which determine the problem of existential communication. First, since the subjective thinker is concerned with the task of living in the truth he is constantly in the process of becoming. "Subjective truth," e.g., religion, faith, is not the sort of thing which one can simply acquire once and for all, but rather it requires a continual effort at re-appropriation. Thus, "subjective truth" can never be a permanent acquisition in the form of a result: "Subjective thought puts everything in process and omits the results." Second, the reflection of inwardness demands a "double reflection," both an intellectual reflection which leads to recognition, and an existential reflection which leads to appropriation. "In thinking," Climacus writes of the subjective thinker, "he thinks the universal; but as existing in his thought and as assimilating it in his inwardness, he becomes more and more subjectively isolated" (p. 68).

Thus, it is the very essence of subjective thought or existential reflection that it cannot be directly communicated, for to do so is to translate it into a result, and thus to contradict its "existential" character. Climacus offers several examples to illustrate this point, the most interesting of which is the analysis of the attempt to express the by now familiar conviction: "Truth is inwardness, there is no objective truth, but the truth consists in personal appropriation" (p. 71). How then is this "doctrine" to be proclaimed? An enthusiast, Climacus suggests, may expend great zeal in the propagation of this truth. He may make a special point of proclaiming it on every possible occasion. He may publish it in a learned treatise, and as a result gain many new adherents to his "doctrine," who in turn would strive to win others to the cause. However, as a consequence of such an endeavor, the champion of subjectivity succeeds only in rendering himself comical. In propagating the doctrine in this manner he has turned it into a result—an objective truth, a theory *about* the significance of subjectivity, and thus contradicted himself.

But how is this situation to be avoided? How is it possible for the subjective thinker, for one who really believes that the existential appropriation of the truth is the essential factor, to communicate this conviction without contradicting himself, without turning his conviction into a theory about subjectivity? According to Climacus the first requirement of such a communication is that it be expressed in such a way so as not to induce an immediate intellectual assent. Its goal is not the coercion of the recipient to a point of view, but his emancipation so that he may come to understand it inwardly, and as Climacus tells us: "The inwardness of understanding consists in each individual coming to understand it for himself" (p. 71). Such a goal, however, precisely because it is formulated in recognition of the freedom of the other cannot be achieved directly. Here Climacus is in thorough agreement with the Socratic contention that the only authentic relationship between individuals is the maieutic one, and it is because of this that he holds that any communication of a "personal" truth must be indirect, and that this indirection requires both artistry and self-control.[9]

The artistry is expressed in the form of the communication, and it consists in the elusiveness which forces the individual to reflect back upon himself. This elusiveness is the negative element in the process of communication, and it is decisive, for operating as a repellent factor, it prevents one from regarding such communication as a straightforward objective presentation of a doctrine. It is in terms of these considerations that we must understand "the subtle principle" of subjective thought: ". . . that the personalities must be held devoutly apart from one another, and not permitted to fuse or coagulate into objectivity. It is at this point that objectivity and subjectivity part from one another" (p. 73).

If this conception of the nature of existential communication is applied to the content of the *Postscript*, some interesting results follow. The book, as we have seen, points to the difficulties of becoming a Christian. It contends that in the ethical and religious spheres "truth is subjectivity," that subjectivity or passion stands in a direct correlation with objective uncertainty, and finally, that as an objective absurdity, Christianity is the objective correlate of the maximum degree of inwardness, and thus, can be regarded as the "true" or ultimate form of religiousness. We further saw that despite Climacus' protestations to the contrary, this view led to a consistent misologism, which ends with the identification of Christianity and nonsense. In proceeding in this way, however, it would seem that

[9] In this connection it is interesting to note that in the very year of the publication of the *Postscript* we find Kierkegaard commenting in his Journal: "The reason why several of Plato's dialogues end without results is more profound than I used to think. It is an expression of Socrates' maieutic art, which makes the reader or the hearer himself active, and so does not end in a result, but in a sting." *The Journals,* No. 528.

like the vast body of Kierkegaard's commentators, and "existential philosophers" in general, we have become "town criers of inwardness." We have attempted to treat as a philosophical proposition ("truth is subjectivity") what by its very nature cannot be regarded as such without contradiction. Is it any wonder then that qua philosophical proposition it reduces itself to an absurdity? The absurd consequences of this consistently misologistic position can now be seen to provide the repellent factor, the elusiveness necessary to indirection, which the author has artistically devised in order to avoid achieving a "result," and to throw his readers back upon themselves.

In light of these considerations let us return to Climacus' argument. The starting point of his trouble, the decisive passage which gives rise to the misologistic consequences is the assertion: "When subjectivity is the truth, the *conceptual determination* of the truth must include an expression of the antithesis to objectivity." The key words here are "conceptual determination" for they make clear that Climacus' misologism is a direct consequence of the conceptualization of the "principle of subjectivity"! But to conceptualize is to objectify, and, as we have seen, to speak objectively about inwardness (and Christianity, it will be remembered, is the highest form of inwardness) is stupidity. Thus, unless we are to view Kierkegaard as guilty of the very stupidity which he went to such great lengths to condemn, we must view the whole "argument" as a jest, as an expression of the author's artistry, the intent of which is not to "prove" the superiority of Christianity or even to show us in a theoretical way that the absolute paradox makes a kind of sense as *supra rationem* which is lacking in garden variety nonsense, but rather to help us realize existentially what it means to become a Christian, and to see that the only valid concept which we can form about Christianity is that it defies conceptualization. Moreover, it is only in light of these considerations that we can appreciate the significance of Kierkegaard's reflection: "Dialectically it is easy to see that Johannes Climacus' defense of Christianity is the most extreme that can be made and only a hair's breadth from an attack."[10] It is the most extreme that can be made because it consists essentially in pointing to its utter incommensurability with all human categories, and the "hair's breadth" which distinguishes this from an attack is nothing more than the double reflection of the subjective thinker. If this be omitted, and the *Postscript* viewed as an essay in existential apologetics, then it is indeed an attack for it leads to the ultimate identification of Christianity and nonsense.

Thus, as a genuine subjective thinker, for whom "everything is dialectical," and whose main work contains "not only a conclusion but a revocation" (p. 547), Kierkegaard remains perpetually elusive. Like Socrates, of whom he was a life long admirer, he believed that his task was not to expound but to sting, and hence any attempt to pin him down, to look for results in the form of an existential philosophy or Christian apologetic in his writings is, to use Climacus' analogy, "like trying to paint Mars in the armor that made him invisible," the supreme irony being, as Climacus points out and the whole history of Kierkegaard scholarship verifies, that such efforts seem to have "a partial success" (p. 73).

[10] *The Journals*, No. 994.

CHAPTER 6

THE TRANSFORMATION OF
HEIDEGGER'S THOUGHT

ALBERT BORGMANN*

•••━━◉━━•••

BETWEEN 1930 and 1940, a transformation took place
in Heidegger's thought.[1] It has a threefold significance.
First, it presents a problem in the philosophical biogra-
phy of Heidegger, for it is not readily visible precisely
when, how intentionally, and with what degree of
awareness this turn of thinking was taken by Heidegger.
Second, it is a touchstone in current philosophy, sepa-
rating those who grant that the early Heidegger gave
important impulses to the development of contemporary philosophy from those who see in the development of Heidegger's philosophy the realization of an
entirely new way of thinking.[2] Third and from Heidegger's point of view, it is the initial signal for the utterly
simple yet difficult task of essential thinking.

These questions are interrelated and can only be
discussed jointly. Our main concern, however, will be

* Albert Borgmann is Professor of Philosophy at Hawaii
University. This article was first published in *The Personalist*, Fall 1966, and appears here by permission of
both the editor and the author.

[1] This paper is a revised and expanded part of a lecture
read to the Philosophical Colloquium at the University of
Illinois on February 12, 1965, under the title "On the
Verifiability of Heidegger's Thought."

[2] I am setting aside here another even more radical distinction between the unconditional enemies of Heidegger
and the kind of philosophers mentioned above. A representative of the former school of thought is Julius Kraft,
Von Husserl zu Heidegger, 2nd ed. (Frankfurt am Main,
1957).

the third while we shall deal with the first two by way of introduction and exposition of the central problem.

The transformation of Heidegger's thought became manifest and received the term "reversal" (*Kehre*) when Heidegger, in the fall of 1946, wrote to Jean Beaufret in Paris: "The adequate rethinking of and participation in this other thought that has left subjectivity behind has been made more difficult, to be sure, by the fact that in the publication of *Being and Time*, the third section of the first part, 'Time and Being,' was held back (cf. *Being and Time*, p. 39 [pp. 63–64 in the English ed.]). Here the whole reverses itself. The respective section was held back because thinking failed in the adequate saying of this reversal. . . . The lecture *On the Nature of Truth* which was conceived and read in 1930, but not printed till 1943, gives a certain insight into the thinking of the reversal from 'Being and Time' to 'Time and Being.' "[3]

This passage gives the impression that the reversal was an elementary feature of an initial program which was carried out partly in *Being and Time*. But nowhere in that book, not even in the passages that mention the third section of the first part, does either the term occur nor is the radical transformation mentioned which that term signifies.[4] In *On the Nature of Truth*,

[3] Martin Heidegger, *Uber den Humanismus*, 2nd ed. (Frankfurt am Main, 1959), p. 17. As is evident from the introductory remark to the 7th and subsequent editions of *Sein und Zeit*, the missing parts will never be published by Heidegger (see p. [v] in the German ed., p. 17 in the English translation; cf. fn. 4 below). Heidegger did, however, give a lecture by the title of "Zeit und Sein" in 1962, a short account and discussion of which can be found in Heinrich Rombach, *Die Gegenwart der Philosophie*, Symposion, ed. Max Müller, Bernhard Welte, Erik Wolf, vol. 11, 2nd ed. (Freiburg, Munich, 1964), pp. 105–116.

[4] See *Sein und Zeit*, 9th ed. (Tübingen, 1960), pp. 39, 160 (*Being and Time*, tr. John Macquarrie and Edward Robinson [New York, 1962], pp. 63–64, 202). I have consulted the available translations, but I have made frequent alterations. After the initial reference, the page number of the translation is given in parentheses after the page number

we find, to be sure, the demand "that we be ready for a transformation of thought."[5] But this is no more than an incidental remark. The collection of lectures and treatises on Nietzsche has been published by Heidegger with the express intention of providing "a view of the path of thinking that I have taken since 1930 up to the *Letter on Humanism* (1947)."[6] In the criticisms of *Being and Time* that we find there, a change of thought is presupposed, though not discussed in its radical significance for Heidegger's development.[7] Finally, in his letter to William J. Richardson, Heidegger gives 1937 as the date of the first occurrence of the term "reversal" and at once emphasizes the continuity in this event and its unpredictable autonomous nature.[8]

A change in Heidegger's philosophy cannot be denied. But the question arises whether the reversal truly characterizes this change or whether it rather represents a reconstructive attempt at lending some meaning to a failure in intellectual growth. In trying to find an answer to this question, we are led to the second aspect of the transformation of Heidegger's thought.

The opinion that the reversal stands for a failure has been advanced repeatedly within the last few years. These writers generally agree that the early Heidegger

---

of the German original. Where no translations are mentioned, the English versions of the German texts are mine.

[5] *Vom Wesen der Wahrheit,* 4th ed. (Frankfurt am Main, 1961), p. 14 ("On the Essence of Truth," trans. R. F. C. Hull and Allan Crick in Martin Heidegger, *Existence and Being,* ed. Werner Brock [Chicago, 1949 (Gateway edition)], p. 305).

[6] *Nietzsche,* 2 vols. (Pfullingen, 1961), I, 10.

[7] Ib., I, 29; II, 194–195, 415. *Kehre* is used as a specific philosophical term with a different meaning in I, 24. Cf. also fn. 35 below.

[8] William J. Richardson, *Heidegger. Through Phenomenology to Thought.* Phaenomenologica, vol. 13 (The Hague, 1963), pp. xvii-xxi. Cf. also *Humanismus,* p. 17; *Unterwegs zur Sprache,* 2nd ed. (Pfullingen, 1960), pp. 98–99, 131.

successfully combatted shallow rationalism and academic sterility and gave new insight into human existence. It is likewise agreed that the reversal is a turn away from objectivity and clarity toward wilful and obscure speculation. For Jonas and Versényi, this turn is a dangerous evil, to be condemned and fought against.[9] For Magnus, it is the helpless aftermath that follows the early peak of achievement, for Wild a fall into confusion and error concerning the structure and significance of *world*.[10] For de Waelhens, it is an illegitimate and dangerous step beyond the limits of philosophy.[11]

The view that the reversal marks an important step forward in Heidegger's philosophy has also been frequently expressed in recent times. For Vincent Vycinas, this step is followed by the even more important turn to the foursome of earth and sky, gods and mortals.[12] Werner Marx sees in it a thesis and a task that calls for a discussion with the tradition of philosophy and for a confrontation with our own philosophical experiences.[13] Otto Pöggeler conceives it as a significant station of *Martin Heidegger's Path of Thought*, which can only be understood in faithfully contemplating and

[9] Hans Jonas, "Heidegger and Theology," *The Review of Metaphysics*, XVIII (1964), 218–233; Laszlo Versényi, *Heidegger, Being, and Truth* (New Haven, London, 1965), pp. 159–198. It must be noted that Jonas' appeal displays a forcible eloquence and a close acquaintance with the problems involved while Versényi's presentation is merely the repetition of a cliché.

[10] Bernd Magnus, "Heidegger and the Truth of Being," *International Philosophical Quarterly*, IV (1964), 245–264; John Wild, "The Philosophy of Martin Heidegger," *The Journal of Philosophy*, LX (1963), 664–677.

[11] Alphonse de Waelhens, "Reflections on Heidegger's Development. Apropos a Recent Book," *International Philosophical Quarterly*, V (1965), 475–502.

[12] Vincent Vycinas, *Earth and Gods. An Introduction to the Philosophy of Martin Heidegger* (The Hague, 1961).

[13] Werner Marx, *Heidegger und die Tradition. Eine problemgeschichtliche Einführung in die Grundbestimmungen des Seins* (Stuttgart, 1961), pp. 120–252.

following the course that Heidegger took in his philosophy.[14] In a more thorough and descriptive way, though less circumspectively and incisively than Pöggeler, Richardson presents the reversal in much the same light, distinguishing, however, more sharply between "Heidegger I" before and "Heidegger II" after the transformation of his thought.[15] For Max Müller, the reversal is the impetus to symphilosophize with Heidegger toward a renewal of metaphysics and a recovery of the Christian heritage.[16] Von Herrmann takes the reversal as a pivot and contrasts the later Heidegger's reflections on his own works with the original passages.[17] William Barrett, finally, approaches Heidegger's thought in a straightforward manner, seemingly unaware of the intricacies of Heidegger scholarship, yet, in the last analysis, bringing out the fundamental and at once simple nature of the reversal quite clearly.[18]

It would be vain simply to offer an additional interpretation of the transformation of Heidegger's thought. Yet it is equally unsatisfactory only to take the reversal as basis for an exercise in doxography. We deal here with a dispute concerning the validity of an event in the history of a thinker, an event, obviously, that challenges all commonly accepted standards of what is ultimately to be valid and true. If we mean to live up to this challenge, we can neither

[14] Otto Pöggeler, *Der Denkweg Martin Heideggers* (Pfullingen, 1963), pp. 163–188.

[15] Richardson, pp. 209–298.

[16] Max Müller, "Ende der Metaphysik?" *Philosophisches Jahrbuch*, LXXII (1964), 1–48; see also the third and enlarged edition of *Existenzphilosophie in geistigen Leben der Gegenwart* (Heidelberg, 1964) where this and other recent and related essays are reprinted.

[17] Friedrich Wilhelm von Herrmann, *Die Selbstinterpretation Martin Heideggers*. Monographien zur philosophischen Forschung, ed. Georgi Schischkoff, vol. 32 (Meisenheim am Glan, 1964.

[18] William Barrett, *What is Existentialism?* (New York, 1964), pp. 111–218.

ignore it nor hope to find a handy answer to it. Instead, we shall confine ourselves to an elucidation which tries to heed and complement what others have said and nonetheless remains preparatory toward a final answer.[19]

Such an investigation must do justice to the historical nature of the object in question and to its fundamental claim. Within the present limits, this can be achieved by investigating precisely the way in which this thought conceives its own communicability relative to its radical turn in the course of its development. We inquire, in other words, into the problem whether and how Heidegger himself attempts to demonstrate in the various stages of his philosophy that his thought is of general and vital concern.

The nature of a demonstration manifests itself in the principles to which it appeals and in the rules that it uses. Because of the rigor that is displayed by the exact sciences in that respect, these disciplines are widely regarded as the primary dispensers and guardians of truth. Heidegger, however, attempts to go far beyond their rigor and reliability by providing a foundation for all sciences. The first chapter of *Being and Time* gives an outline of the crises that the sciences and humanities underwent at the beginning of this century. These crises became apparent in a decay and subsequent transformation of the basic concepts of these disciplines. "Basic concepts," Heidegger writes, "determine the way in which we get an understanding beforehand of the area of subject-matter underlying all the objects a science takes as its theme, and all positive investigation is guided by this understanding. Only if this area has been similarly explored beforehand do these concepts become genuinely demonstrated and 'grounded.' But since every such area is itself obtained from the domain of entities [*sic*] themselves, this preliminary research, from which the basic concepts are drawn, signifies their basic state or

[19] I want to acknowledge here my debt to Max Müller, Werner Marx, and Otto Pöggeler.

Being. Such research must run ahead of the positive sciences, and it *can*."[20]

Being and Time proposes to undertake just that, though in a fundamental way, so fundamental, that it claims to sound the foundations of science more deeply and decisively than does what is commonly called philosophy of science. "Laying the foundations for the sciences in this way," Heidegger continues further below, "is different in principle from the kind of 'logic' which limps along after, investigating the status of some science as it chances to find it, in order to discover its 'method.' Laying the foundations, as we have described it, is rather a productive logic—in the sense that it leaps ahead, as it were, into some area of Being, discloses it for the first time in the constitution of its Being, and, after thus arriving at the structures within it, makes these available to the positive sciences as lucid assignments for their inquiry."[21]

To be sure, *Being and Time* is not exclusively devoted to providing a new foundation for the sciences. This is merely entailed by the pursuit of its primary object, that of "explicitly restating the question of Being."[22] It is the most fundamental question possible, where "fundamental" has a twofold meaning: the question is fundamental inasmuch as it is radical in its approach and attempts to reach beyond all previous sciences and even ontologies.[23] It is fundamental furthermore insofar as it poses *the* ontological question which in the order of significance precedes all ontal questions, i.e., those concerning individual entities, and hence it touches and possibly transforms the foundations of all there is. Heidegger consequently calls *Being and Time* again and again a *fundamental ontology.*[24]

This outlined procedure of *Being and Time* is ob-

[20] *Sein und Zeit*, p. 10 (30).
[21] *Ibid.*, pp. 10–11 (30–31).
[22] *Ibid.*, p. 2(21) (from the title of §1, pp. 2–4 [21–24]).
[23] *Ibid.*, p. 11 (31).
[24] See Hildegard Feick, *Index zu Heideggers "Sein und Zeit"* (Tübingen, 1961), p. 30; Macquarrie, p. 540.

viously circular. Entities are taken as guidelines for the investigation of Being; Being is the foundation and *raison d'être* of all entities. Heidegger took pains to show that this circle not only is unvicious but a necessary and essential characteristic of all human understanding.[25] More importantly for our investigation, this circular relationship between Being and the entities makes a respective mutual verification possible, since Being is fundamental for the entities, and the entities are symptomatic of Being. Being verifies the entities in the sense that only an explicit understanding of Being reveals *veritatem entium,* the true nature of the entities; Being is the origin and principle of ontal truth. The entities on the other hand verify *Being* insofar as they testify to its mode and agency and give access to ontological truth. "Verification" (*Bewährung, Beleg, Bezeugung*) and the respective verbs are therefore frequently occurring though generally overlooked terms.[26] They play a key part in *Being and Time,* where the relationship between the question of Being and verifiability is the procedural basis as is emphasized in the methodological chapter: "We can discuss such possibilities seriously and with positive results only if the question of Being has been reawakened and we have arrived at a field of controllable contentions and discussions."[27]

The concept of a fundamental ontology, which requires verification and simultaneously provides the grounds for it, still dominates the approach of *Kant*

[25] *Sein und Zeit,* pp. 148–153 (188–195), 314–315 (362–363).

[26] None of them is listed in Feick. Most occurrences are noted in Macquarrie's and Robinson's index; but some inconsistencies are to be found: *Bewährung* (*bewähren*) on pp. 17 (38) and 133 (172) is translated by "Interpretation" ("to Interpret") which (since capitalized) should stand for the quite different *Auslegung* (*auslegen*). *Beleg* on p. 188 (233) (cf. also p. 431 [483]) is rendered by "evidence" which is a simplifying overstatement. *Bewährung* is usually (and correctly) given as "confirmation" (cf. e.g. p. 183 [227]).

[27] *Sein und Zeit,* p. 27 (49).

and the Problem of Metaphysics, which appeared in 1929, two years after *Being and Time.*[28] The entire book was to be an elucidation and verification of fundamental ontology in the light of Kant's major work. In the introduction Heidegger says: "To explicate the idea of fundamental ontology means this: to demonstrate that the above mentioned ontological analytic of *Dasein* is a necessity and to clarify in doing so to what purpose and in what manner, within what limits and under what presuppositions it poses the concrete question: What is man? Inasmuch, however, as an idea chiefly manifests itself through its power of elucidation, the idea of fundamental ontology is to be verified and presented by means of an interpretation of the *Critique of Pure Reason* as a laying of the foundation of metaphysics."[29]

Heidegger's new concept of verification was as novel and fruitful as it was ambiguous. By reaching beyond all traditional ontology, it showed the limitations of commonly accepted objectivity, which necessarily distorts the true nature of man, history, and time by turning these phenomena into objects capable of being examined and described as are isolated physically present entities. The phenomenological analysis of these topics and the critique of their traditional interpretations compose the major part of *Being and Time.* Yet by applying the phenomenological method (in a reinterpreted form to be sure), the constitutional nature of this discipline, i.e., the search for the phenomenological constituents of things, had to be retained; and by adhering to the concept of fundamental research, a foundational order of results was inevitable. Both constitution and foundation are concepts that are meaningful only within the hierarchy of a philosophical system. But any true system is static and limited and

---

[28] In order of composition it was nearly simultaneous with *Sein und Zeit.* Cf. *Kant und das Problem der Metaphysik,* 2nd ed. (Frankfurt am Main, 1951), p. [7] (*Kant and the Problem of Metaphysics,* tr. James S. Churchill [Bloomington, 1962], p. xxiii).

[29] See *Kant,* p. 13 (4).

therefore has characteristics which run counter to the
original intent of *Being and Time*. The concept of
verification in *Being and Time* owes its novelty to
Heidegger's break with traditional ontology; it owes its
fruitfulness, i.e., its wide applicability, to the structural
kinship of *Being and Time* with systematic occidental
thought. Thus the *veritas* of the verification, the criterion of truth, remains hidden in *Being and Time*.

All of Heidegger's essays between the publication
of *Being and Time* and the end of the war are attempts
to turn away from foundational considerations. In
various trials, the element prior to any fundament is
presented and discussed as freedom in *The Essence
of Cause*, as Nothing in *What is Metaphysics?* and as
the Greek concept of truth, *aletheia*, in *On the Nature
of Truth* and *Plato's Teaching on Truth*.[30]

This last term proved to be the most consequential.
It is seen by Heidegger in contrast to the metaphysical
concept of truth, which is essentially a statement of
correlation between a standard and some entity.
Heidegger therefore calls it "correctness" (*Richtigkeit*)
and tries to show that it is derivative in relation to
the original concept of *aletheia*. *Aletheia* is that which
is contrary to *lethe,* i.e., darkness and forgetfulness,
that which *ou lanthanei,* i.e., not hidden; *aletheia* is
the appearance of the light and the opening of the
realm, within which only correctness and falsehood
are possible; *aletheia* is thus the very condition for
any correlation and verification (regardless of whether
the suggested etymology is philologically correct or
merely made up.)[31] It is consequently impossible to

[30] *Vom Wesen des Grundes*, 4th ed. (Frankfurt am Main,
1955); *Was ist Metaphysik?* 8th ed. (Frankfurt am Main,
1960) ("What is Metaphysics?" transl. by R. F. C. Hull
and Allan Crick in *Existence*, pp. 325-361); *Platons Lehre
von der Wahrheit*, 2nd ed. (Bern, 1954).

[31] To the extent that Paul Friedländer's refutation of
Heidegger's understanding of *aletheia* is based on philo-
logical arguments, it is therefore vacuous. See his *Plato.
An Introduction,* trans. Hans Meyerhoff (New York, Evans-

verify this concept of truth itself as it lies ever ahead of verification. And since we cannot verify it, we cannot get a firm grip on it. Truth, perceived as the primordial revelation of all entities, is therefore continually accompanied by essential obscurity, or to be more exact: truth as revelation is at once concealment.

These investigations are still subsidiary to the question of Being. Truth as revelation and concealment is to be an avenue to the meaning of Being or perhaps that meaning itself. The explication of truth probes the question of Being in a more incisive manner than *Being and Time* does, but its procedure nevertheless remains close to that of *Being and Time* because it still has not answered the decisive question: Is there a relationship of graduation and superiority between Being and the entities, so that Being is independent of entities yet the entities rest on Being? Is there such a relational order which would prescribe a corresponding procedure of investigation or is there not? And if not, what is the relationship between Being and entities? Can it be expressed in relational, that is metaphysical terms at all?

These questions have become manifest in a nutshell through the now famous change in the "Postscript" to *What is Metaphysics?* In the fourth edition of 1943, Heidegger said in discussing some objections to the supposedly nihilistic tendency of this treatise: "Without Being, whose unfathomable and still undiscovered essence Nothing imparts to us in essential anxiety, all entities would remain in Beinglessness. But this too, in its turn, is not a nugatory Nothing, assuming that it is of the truth of Being *that Being indeed prevails without entities, but never entities without Being.*"[32]

---

ton, 1964), pp. 221–229. Heidegger has pointed out himself how relatively unimportant this etymology is. See *Vorräge und Aufsätze*, 2nd ed. (Pfullingen, 1959), pp. 259, 262.

[32] *Was ist Metaphysik?*, 4th ed. (Frankfurt am Main, 1943), p. 26 (353–354). Italics mine. Max Müller was the first to point out this change. See his *Existenzphilosophie*, pp. 43–44.

In the fifth edition of 1949 the last part of this passage reads: "assuming that it is of the truth of Being *that Being never prevails without entities, that entities do not ever exist without Being.*"[33]

By way of interpreting the works of Nietzsche and Hölderlin, Heidegger sought to attain a clear view of the necessity and expressibility of this problem. Nietzsche stood for the last culmination of metaphysics which was to be overcome; from Hölderlin's, the poet's, insight, he hoped to receive advice and guidance in his attempt to put into words what he thought he had caught a glimpse of.[34]

The turn of thought, then, that becomes apparent in Heidegger's first publication after the war is nothing more than the final realization that in order to surpass metaphysics we must completely free ourselves of it and that any approach to the question of Being which proceeds from metaphysical starting points will always remain chained to them.[35] Heidegger, therefore, avoids any investigation that tries to explore Being by way of analyzing entities of whatever kind and rather seeks to be open for the advent of *Being* itself.

This new attitude is obviously different from a fundamental ontology and must be critical of it. In the introduction of 1949 to *What is Metaphysics?* Heidegger says of his earlier thought: "As long as this kind of thought calls itself fundamental ontology, it obstructs and obscures its own path with this term. For the title 'fundamental ontology' suggests that this

[33] *Was ist Metaphysik?*, 8th ed., p. 46. Italics mine.

[34] Cf. *inter alia Nietzsche*, 2 vols. (Pfullingen, 1961) and *Erläuterungen zu Hölderlins Dichtung*, 2nd ed. (Frankfurt am Main, 1951) (the first two of these interpretations are translated in *Existence*, pp. 233-291).

[35] For Heidegger himself, "reversal" is therefore nothing but the term for a task as is obvious from the way he uses it in "Die Kehre" in *Die Technik und die Kehre* (Pfullingen, 1962), pp. 37-47. The tenor of his answer to Richardson (cf. fn. 8 above) indicates that our first aspect of the reversal is utterly insignificant to him.

kind of thought, which attempts to think the truth of Being and not, as all other ontologies do, the truth of the entities, was, in being fundamental ontology, nonetheless some sort of ontology."[36] And in the *Letter on Humanism* he says of *Being and Time*: "Thought which attempts to think ahead into the truth of Being accomplishes but little in this entirely different dimension, due to the distress of the first breakthrough. The thought of this new dimension furthermore distorts itself inasmuch as it does not succeed in retaining the essential support of the phenomenological approach and in nevertheless dropping its inappropriate leaning towards 'science' and 'research.'"[37]

The renunciation of fundamental ontology quite apparently deprives this new thought of the possibility of verification described earlier. It abandons the wealth of observations and insights that is gained from the analysis of entities. Now thought becomes severe and simple in turning to Being directly.[38]

All of Heidegger's publications after the war (except of course those containing lectures read in the thirties) are devoted to the experience of Being itself and to the attempt of rendering account of this experience. If Being is prior to and incommensurable with any entity, how then is it possible to experience it at all? There are five ways in which Heidegger reaches out for this experience. The first is a contemplation and interpretation of poetry, for Heidegger holds that certain poets have given testimony of the primordial encounter with Being.[39] The second ap-

---

[36] *Was ist Metaphysik?* 8th. ed., p. 21 (Walter Kaufmann, ed., *Existentialism from Dostoevsky to Sarte* [New York, 1956], p. 219).

[37] *Humanismus*, p. 41–42; cf. also fn. 7 above.

[38] Cf. *Vorträge*, pp. 69–70, 183–184; letter to Richardson, p. xxiii; *Aus der Erfahrung des Denkens* (Pfullingen, 1954), pp. 7, 19.

[39] See *Hölderlin* and *Unterwegs zur Sprache*, 2nd ed. (Pfullingen, 1960), pp. 9–33, 35–82. In *Holzwege*, 3rd ed. (Frankfurt am Main, 1957), a painting of van Gogh is interpreted with the same intention (pp. 22–26).

proach consists in a discussion of some of the fragments of the Pre-Socratics. According to Heidegger
their insight into the meaning of Being found expression in terms such as *logos, moira, aletheia,* and
others.[40] Their thought precedes the establishment of
metaphysics, whose basic question is not that of Being
but rather: What is the nature of entities? Hence
metaphysics is said to have obscured the Pre-Socratics'
vision, and any criticisms on a metaphysical basis,
such as the accusations of primitivism, mythicism, and
irrationalism, are therefore metaphysically correct but
basically inadequate. Yet another approach proceeds
from some common metaphysical teaching such as the
principle of identity or from some thesis of a metaphysical thinker, e.g., Hegel's concept of experience,
and the discussion of these philosophemes yields the
initial steps towards the experience of Being.[41] A
typical example is the treatise *Der Satz vom Grund,*
i.e., "The Principle of Causality," where in the course
of the lectures the title changes its meaning to "The
Leap away from the Ground" (i.e., the ground of
metaphysics) which in German is homonymous with
the former.[42] A fourth method takes as its starting
point an analysis of the essential traits of the present
time, namely technology and nihilism.[43] Heidegger in-
terprets both of these characteristics as the inheritance
of metaphysics, and hence this approach is akin to
the one just mentioned. The last attempt of gaining insight into Being is the most direct. It tries to show how
Being prevails in the simple things and events of

[40] See *Vorträge,* pp. 207–282; *Holzwege,* pp. 296–343;
Was heißt Denken?, 2nd ed. (Tübingen, 1961), pp. 105–
149.

[41] See "Hegels Begriff der Erfahrung" in *Holzwege,* pp.
105–192; "Nietzsches Wort 'Gott ist tot'," ibd., pp. 193–
247; *Kants These über das Sein* (Frankfurt am Main,
1963), *et alia.*

[42] See *Der Satz vom Grund,* ed. (Pfullingen, 1958).

[43] See *Vorträge,* pp. 13–70; *Holzwege,* pp. 69–104; *Zur
Seinsfrage,* 2nd ed. (Frankfurt am Main, 1959) (*The Ques-
tion of Being,* tr. William Kluback and Jean T. Wilde
[New York, 1958]).

everyday life, such as a bridge, a pitcher, building and living in houses, a dialogue of friends. In all these cases Being is not rigorously deducible from these phenomena; quite on the contrary, the prevalence of Being is a gift and a favor that happens to come to light in these things and events.

In the quotation from the *Letter on Humanism* cited earlier, Heidegger pointed out the cautious and weary way in which the thought of Being proceeds. "It must therefore limit itself to tentative steps," Heidegger says furthermore in a letter to Ernst Jünger.[44] And in the conversation between Heidegger and a Japanese scholar in *On the Way toward Language* Heidegger says: "In the summer semester of 1934 I gave a lecture entitled 'Logic.' It was, however, concerned with the *logos* wherein I sought the nature of language. Yet it almost took another decade till I was able to say what I thought—the adequate words are lacking even today."[45]

Since language fails the philosopher, what is being left unsaid may be more significant in some contexts than what is expressed. Thus, keeping silent is repeatedly presented as a last possibility of preparing for the elucidation of Being.[46] In the conversation just mentioned we read: "*Japanese* [i.e., the scholar from Japan]. The course of such a conversation would have to be of a singular nature according to which there would be more silence than speaking. *One who is asking* [i.e., Heidegger]. Silence especially as to what silence is . . . *J.* since speaking and writing about silence causes the most pernicious talk. . . . *O.* Who would be capable of simply keeping silent about silence? *J.* This ought to be true speaking . . . *O.* and would always be the constant prelude to the true conversa-

[44] *Seinsfrage*, pp. 43–44 (106–108).

[45] *Sprache*, p. 93.

[46] See *Sprache*, p. 152; *Vorträge*, pp. 243, 249, 279. *Was heißt Denken?*, p. 165. Nietzsche I, 264–266, 471–472. Cf. also Pöggeler, p. 276 who refers to an unpublished ms. of Heidegger's where this approach is explicitly considered under the title of *sigetic* as opposed to *logic*.

tion on language. *J.* Are we not thus attempting the impossible?"[47]

This is certainly far removed from the maxim in *Being and Time,* calling for "a field of controllable contentions and discussions."[48] Thinking has now left behind the field on which it is possible to exchange arguments, to demonstrate and "to be right." It is thus more vulnerable *and* less accessible. There is no longer any place for enemies (*Gegner*) who fight against this thinking in an arena that it has left. But there must be adversaries (*Widersacher*), that is thinkers who turn to the same task (*advertunt*) and then give contrary testimony (*adversum testimonium*) of their experience.[49]

In conclusion, we must therefore briefly sketch once more the experiences by which Heidegger's thought has been transformed and which have to be attained and contemplated if this thought is to be understood, especially in its hints as to where our thought may have to proceed from these experiences.

The first experience is that of metaphysics as the fate and essence first of Europe and now, with the steady expansion of Western civilization, of the globe. Metaphysics in this general sense has its beginning with Plato and Aristotle and culminates with Nietzsche. In metaphysics the basic mode of Being is presence (*Anwesenheit*), presence of entities, that is, and the metaphysical preoccupation with the nature of entities goes hand in hand with an obscuration of Being itself, an event which is not the work of men but the history and fate (*Geschick*) of Being itself.

---

[47] *Sprache,* p. 152.
[48] *Sein und Zeit,* p. 27 (49).
[49] This explication is based on *Erfahrung,* p. 9. The etymological suggestions are possible in German too if we say that a *Widersacher* stands over against (*wider*) Heidegger's thought, devoted to the same task of thinking (*Sache des Denkens*). In different words, Heidegger discusses the same problem in connection with the understanding of Nietzsche's works in *Nietzsche,* I, 33.

The documents of this history are the teachings of the great philosophers.

Heidegger's second basic experience is that of our present time, which is said to be characterized by technology.[50] This characteristic is not taken as one aspect of our culture, which is symptomatic for the latter; it is rather the very nature of our age, pervading everything there is: the sciences first of all and of course industry and commerce, but also the humanities, art, and religion. The universal action of technology is this: to challenge everything, to make it come out into the open, and then to get hold of it and control it. This process, according to Heidegger, is steadily gaining momentum and threatens to destroy mankind. The possibility of a nuclear holocaust is only a subordinate factual aspect of this phenomenon. Its innermost danger is its tendency to hide its very nature and to pervert the humanity of humankind while more and more people live in prosperity and free of care. Again this state of affairs is not due to any tangible failure on the part of man, but it is the concealment of Being. In metaphysics, Being prevails as presence; in technology, Being presents the entities in such a singular and prominent manner as to hide *itself* entirely, so completely indeed that we are all but unable to feel its absence. Technology as the presence of Being in hiddenness is the ultimate phase of metaphysics.

Thus these two basic experiences of Heidegger's thought turn out to be one and the same: It is the historicity of Being to put it formally; or stated materially: The prevalence of Being as presence is, in the historic mode of metaphysics, the fate of the world; the culmination of this fate is the hiddenness of Being in technology.

We have to take yet one step further to see the

[50] Nihilism was mentioned earlier as a second characteristic. Since it is but another manifestation of what the term technology stands for, it is not discussed explicitly.

whole of Heidegger's experience. It claims to listen to Being itself, an experience that has perceived the onesidedness of Being in metaphysics and tries to overcome the blindness towards Being in technology. It suggests that from these attempts alone salvation can result. Heidegger does not claim that he has succeeded in these attempts nor even that he has advanced any farther than others in what he calls "essential thinking." In the lecture series *What Does Thinking Mean?* he says: "A haze still hides the essence of modern science and scholarship. This haze, however, is not produced within science and scholarship by the individual scientists and scholars. It is not made by man at all. It arises from the region of what has to be thought most urgently, namely that we do not think yet, none of us, including the speaker, he least of all."[51] The question arises: What are we to do to dispel this haze?

Heidegger would answer that posing the question of Being earnestly and devotedly is in itself the first step towards salvation. Yet he went beyond that and attempted to delineate the new experience of Being in showing how in some simple things such as pitcher, bridge, plow, creek, mountain, doe, and steer the foursome of earth and sky, gods and mortals shines forth.[52] But these tentative sketches are to be taken as hints rather than definite teachings; they certainly pose more questions than they answer, perhaps intentionally.[53] We have to be patient and humble in our striving for essential thinking. In the dialogue *On the Discussion of Detachment* we read the following: "*Researcher.* As hard as I try, I just cannot grasp

[51] *Was heißt Denken?*, p. 49; cf. *Vorträge*, pp. 182–185.
[52] See *Vorträge*, p. 163–181.
[53] To take these sketches and their term as literally as Vycinas does, certainly goes against their innermost intent and ignores their difficult origin and background as they are to be found in *Hölderlin*, in "Der Ursprung des Kunstwerkes" (in *Holzwege*, pp. 7–68), in *Nietzsche*, I, 352–353, in *Humanismus*, pp. 36–37, and in *Hebel—der Hausfreund*, 2nd ed. (Pfullingen, 1958), pp. 17–18, 37–38.

this essential kind of thinking. *Teacher.* Because this sort of trying hard and your kind of thinking, conceived as grasping, is precisely what keeps you from doing so. *R.* What in the world am I supposed to do? *Scholar.* I have been asking myself that same question. *T.* We are not to do anything; we have to wait. *S.* That is a poor consolation. *T.* Whether poor or not is unimportant; nor are we supposed to expect consolation, which we do even if we simply fall into despair. *R.* Well, what are we supposed to wait for? And where? I hardly know by now where I am and who I am. *T.* None of us knows, as soon as we stop deceiving ourselves. *S.* Yet we do have our path of thought, do we not? *T.* Indeed. And by forgetting it too soon, we abandon thinking."[54]

Here, then, is the point where we must try to become Heidegger's adversaries and find our answer.

[54] *Gelassenheit*, 2nd ed. (Pfullingen, 1959), pp. 36–37; cf. also *Vorträge*, pp. 139–140.

CHAPTER 7

MARXIST EXISTENTIALISM

ARTHUR LESSING*

I

THE *rapprochement* of existential and Marxist philosophy has received a good deal of attention since Sartre published in 1960 his *Critique de la raison dialectique*.[1] Its introduction, *Question de méthode*, has been translated into English by Hazel Barnes.[2] At least two major explications of the work have appeared in the last two years.[3] Extensive reviews have appeared in philosophical journals in this country and aboard.[4] Finally, at least one critical study devoted explicitly to

---

* Arthur Lessing is Assistant Professor of Philosophy at Lake Forest College. His article originally appeared in *The Review of Metaphysics*, Vol. 20, No. 3 (March 1967), and is printed here by permission of the editor and the author.

[1] Jean-Paul Sartre, *Critique de la raison dialectique, précédé de Question de méthode, Tome I: Théorie des ensembles pratiques* (Paris, 1960).

[2] *Search for Method* (New York, 1963).

[3] Wilfrid Desan, *The Marxism of Jean-Paul Sartre* (New York, 1965); Laing and Cooper, *Reason and Violence: A Decade of Sartre's Philosophy, 1950–1960* (New York, 1964).

[4] Burkle, "Schaff and Sartre on the Grounds of Individual Freedom," *International Philosophical Quarterly*, Vol. V, no. 4 (December, 1965); Burkle, "'The Marxism of Jean-Paul Sartre' by Wilfrid Desan: A Book Review," *International Philosophical Quarterly*, Vol. VI, no. 1 (March, 1966); Javey, "Sartre from Being and Nothingness to a Critique of Dialectic Reason," *Philosophy Today* (Fall, 1961); Kaelin, "Three Stages on Sartre's Way," *European Philosophy Today*, ed. by G. Kline (Chicago, 1965); Morot-

the problems such a marriage entails was published last year in paperback format.[5] Another publication which brings together a collection of essays and excerpts is titled *Existentialism Versus Marxism* and has already decided the future of the marriage by its subtitle: "Conflicting Views on Humanism."[6]

The purpose of this essay cannot be the evaluation of this considerable body of critical study. Wilfrid Desan's critical *explication du texte* and Laing's sympathetic reading of the *Critique* present an excellent starting-point for those who want to join the controversy.

It seems evident, however, that some of the controversy generated by this union of "existentialism" and "Marxism" is proceeding on ideological rather than philosophical grounds. "Existentialism," one despairing critic writes, "has retained a meaning in American usage which it has practically ceased to have in Western Europe; it is associated with certain beatnik-like phenomena with clichés about the absurdity of life and despair."[7] "Marxism," on the other hand, is still commonly defined in this country as a materialist doctrine which reduces all human life to historical determinism and class conflict. The ideology of the absurd individual, on the one hand, has therefore obviously nothing to say, least of all propose marriage, to an ideology, on the other hand, which considers the obsession with the individual and his idiosyncratic *Angst* typical of corrupt bourgeois experience.

Sir, "Sartre's Critique of Dialectic Reason," *Journal of the History of Ideas*, Vol. XXII, no. 4 (October, 1961); Waelhens, "Sartre et la critique de la raison dialectique," *Revue Philosophique de Louvain* (February, 1962); G. Lichtheim, "Sartre, Marxism and History," *History and Theory*, Vol. III, no. 2 (1963); Kwant, "Het Marxisme van Sartre," *Tijdschrift voor Philosophie* (December, 1960).

[5] Odajnyk, *Marxism and Existentialism* (New York, 1965).

[6] Edited by George Novack (New York, 1966).

[7] James Edie, "Recent Work in Phenomenology," *American Philosophical Quarterly*, Vol. I, no. 2 (April, 1964).

For us the problem does not lie in welding together two "historical" movements, "movements" which have been characterized and formulated by intellectual historians. It may well be that future historians can locate two strains of thought which can be labeled "existentialism" and "Marxism" and recount how some sort of ideological union was attempted in the 1960's, and either failed or succeeded. Such success or failure indicates little to the philosopher who continues to be concerned not with ideology or social attitude but *what truly is,* in other words, truth.

The problem at hand must deal with the philosophical structures themselves, in this case those of Sartre and, to a limited extent, Merleau-Ponty. To blandly identify their efforts to develop in their existential philosophy certain conceptual formulations which seek to do justice to current socio-economic and historical conditions with broad terms like "existentialism" and "Marxism" is to lose sight of the specific issues from the start. Both have developed full-fledged ontological systems which claim to do full justice to the definition of man, world, history, and thought. At the same time, both seek to return ontological realizations to the realm of historic and personal concreteness. Neither thinker is merely an ideologist, i.e., a "representative" of a socio-political movement; neither is merely an intellectual apologist for a political position. This does not mean, however, that Sartre and Merleau-Ponty have ever chosen the option of political neutrality; witness the pages of *Les Temps Modernes* since its birth in 1945. Their explicit and often controversial commitment to particular socio-political issues and causes emerges from their strong philosophical arguments for commitment and liberty. Their role in French political life is well-known and now well-documented in this country.[8]

It may well be the case that Sartre is responsible

---

[8] David Caute, *Communism and the French Intellectuals, 1914–1960* (New York, 1964); George Lichtheim, *Marxism in Modern France* (New York, 1966).

for the growth of what may be called existentialist ideology because his rich intellect continues up to today to serve literature, philosophy, and polemic as well as the critique of politics. He himself, however, has indicated more than once that he stands alone as thinker, disassociated from all ideology and party-membership. Philosophy for him has two functions: (a) to develop a comprehensive metaphysics of human reality, and (b) to actualize such a metaphysics in history. The revolutionary, critical, and therefore negative role of the philosopher in society distinguishes Sartre and Merleau-Ponty today from those who still believe that philosophy primarily addresses itself only to other philosophers. Sartre long ago left the ivory tower; the world is not to be reduced to the university.

If Sartre refuses to identify his later thought (embodied in the *Critique*) with the notion of *existentialisme*, it is equally true that his conception of *marxisme* can hardly be equated with Soviet or French Marxism. We must examine the meanings of these terms for Sartre. The same goes for Merleau-Ponty. This is the task of this paper.

The importance of this endeavor lies in the programmatic nature of their philosophies. Their attempt to extend their philosophies of individual existence to include the facts of social reality in history have important programmatic import for those who have not despaired of either metaphysics or contemporary historical crises. With this hope expressed, we can conclude these general remarks and turn toward the specific features of this expansion of their philosophic contexts.

II

Both Sartre and Merleau-Ponty dealt with Marxism from the very start of their philosophic careers. Neither Sartre's *L'être et le néant* (1943) nor Merleau-Ponty's

La phénoménologie de la perception (1945) takes up
in any extensive fashion Marxism either as philosophy
or ideology, although interesting comments are
scattered throughout the pages of these principle works.
Merleau-Ponty appends a long footnote to the chapter
"The Body in its Sexual Being" in which he defends
Marx's historical materialism:

If existence is the permanent act by which man takes
up for his own purpose, and makes his own certain *de
facto* situation, none of his thoughts will be able to be
quite detached from the historical context in which he
lives, and particularly from his economic situation. Precisely because economics is not a closed world, and
because all motivations intermingle at the core of
history, the external becomes internal, and the internal
external, and no constituent of our existence can ever
be outrun.[9]

A philosophy of subjectivity can hardly afford to
minimize history and historical situation. At the same
time, Merleau-Ponty is already critical of those French
Marxists who reduce subjectivity to nothing else but
economic relations. The question whether history is
made significant in predominantly economic terms,
Merleau-Ponty feels, is to be decided in the future
by politics.[10] In a lengthy review of Sartre's *L'être et
le néant,* Merleau-Ponty argues persuasively against the
Marxists who accuse Sartre of "residual idealism." He
warns Marxists that the denial of subjectivity leads to
a theoretical treatment of consciousness which cannot
make sense of reflection and consequently knowledge.
If interior lucidity is denied, how can consciousness
ever recognize that it knows anything whatsoever?
"No in-itself would be accessible to us, if it were not at
the very same time *for us,* and the meaning we find in
it depends on our consent."[11] He concludes that no

[9] *Phenomenology of Perception,* trans. by Colin Smith
(New York, 1962), p. 172.

[10] *Ibid.,* p. 173.

[11] "The Battle over Existentialism," *Sense and Non-Sense,*
trans. by Hubert and Patricia Dreyfus (Evanston, 1964),
p. 79.

man can theoretically reject the Cartesian *cogito* since he can ultimately no longer know what he is saying, affirming, or renouncing.[12]

Merleau-Ponty's review appeared in November, 1945, but already it was clear that (a) Sartre and Merleau-Ponty both seek to incorporate in their philosophic position a theory of history; that (b) such a theory must follow from rather than precede a theory of consciousness; and, finally (c) that this can be accomplished by an existential critique rather than bland acceptance of the most pertinent theory of history available, namely Marxism.

Both agree that the Hegelian theory of history is unacceptable because it is essentially a quietism which conservatively encompasses the facts of history without submitting them to a thoroughgoing critique.[13] This becomes particularly clear after World War II. Hegel can say nothing about Auschwitz and Bergen-Belsen.

Dismissing Hegel's conservative theory of history does not necessarily entail rejecting Hegel's *Phenomenology of Mind*. Sartre and Merleau-Ponty have learned too much from it. In it, Hegel aims for that consciousness which seeks to re-appropriate itself in historical temporality. The restless and contradictory *Bewußtsein* of Hegel serves as model for Sartre's and Merleau-Ponty's Cartesian *cogito*, paradoxically enough. All three agree that consciousness seeks to come to its own "worldliness" (*Weltlichkeit*), that is to say, its *central place in the world as genuine subject*.[14]

To treat consciousness as an object alongside other objects within the objective multiplicity of the world fails to define man's intentionality. Consciousness is placed in the world, but placed in the center if that world is to be intelligible and human. Only from this

[12] *Ibid.*, pp. 79–80.
[13] *Ibid.*, p. 82.
[14] Introduction to Hegel's *Phenomenology*, trans. by Walter Kaufmann in his *Hegel* (New York, 1966), p. 410.

central position, in which consciousness always is subject, can it make sense to talk of dialectic movement in history and genuine freedom.

Such claims about dialectic movement and freedom need to be clarified if Marxism is to be treated as both enemy *and* friend of Sartre and Merleau-Ponty. We can conclude at this point that a simple acceptance of Marxism is ruled out by both. If we can honestly speak of a Marxism in either Sartre or Merleau-Ponty, we must realize that the friend and enemy is given a new appearance. The reinterpretation of Marx by both constitutes at the same time their critique of Marx, Marxism, and contemporary Marxism in France.

In 1946, Sartre published in *Les Temps Modernes* a long essay titled "Materialism and Revolution." It spells out in detail his critique of Soviet and French Marxism. Again the problem is subjectivity and the Marxist attempt to eliminate it from his theoretical vocabulary:

The materialist thinks that by denying his subjectivity he has made it disappear. But the trick is easy to expose. *In order* to eliminate subjectivity, the materialist declares that he is an *object*, that is, the subject-matter of science. But once he has eliminated subjectivity in favor of the object, instead of seeing himself as a thing among other things, buffeted about by the physical universe, he makes of himself an *objective beholder* and claims to contemplate nature as it is, in the absolute.[15]

If observation is to be objective, what is the basis of certainty which allows the materialist to claim objectivity in the first place? It cannot simply be the fact of being an object in the world, because that fact itself is wholly contingent and even irrational. Certainty could claim itself on the basis of reason. But if reason itself is a contingent product of material and biological evolution, what stature *as truth* or certainty can it possibly possess? "How could a captive reason, gov-

[15] Trans. by Annette Michelson, *Literary and Philosophical Essays* (New York, 1962), p. 202.

erned from without and maneuvered by a series of blind causes, still be reason?" asks Sartre.[16]

Materialism cannot claim a rational basis because it cannot defend the absolute nature of rational truth on the basis of the existence of matter. Sartre, on the other hand, explains the absolute nature of reason by locating it in the consciousness with the aid of a theory which argues for the absolute autonomy of consciousness. If, as he declares in *L'être et le néant*, consciousness has no source other than itself, then its rationality too is absolute and not reducible to natural and material causes. This philosophic argument Sartre shares with Merleau-Ponty but ultimately derives from Hegel's *Phenomenology*. (Taking cognizance of these particular conclusions, it appears strange indeed that Sartre continues to be identified as an

[16] *Ibid.*, p. 203. Sartre goes on to argue against Engels rather than Marx that a dialectic conception of nature is impossible. Natural history is an absurdity because all history demands the notion of intention. "History cannot be characterized by change nor by the pure and simple action of the part. It is defined by the deliberate resumption of the past by the present; only human history is possible (*Ibid.*, p. 206). In fact, the notion of a dialectic of exteriority contradicts the very concept of dialectic as Hegel held it, since dialectic aims for absolute interiority. The materialist is operating with a vulgar definition of dialectic in trying to bend Hegel's dialectic toward a materialist direction. Dialectic is movement toward cumulative totality in which each advanced stage incorporates past stages. To superimpose this onto material and biological phenomena strains our credulity in the face of the scientific evidence itself. This Sartrean argument would however operate against Sartre's own philosophy. Hegel's dialectic does not only aim for interiority but for a transcendence of the dichotomy of interiority *and* exteriority. Sartre's own commitment to dialectic depends on (a) the contention that consciousness gives itself to itself only exterior of subjectivity, and (b) exteriority is dialectically the negation of consciousness; hence (c) the irreducible conflict between *pour-soi* and *en-soi* in *L'être et le néant*. The argument against a dialectic of nature, however, appears convincing. Generally, Sartre disassociates Engels from Marx in discussing his own brand of Marxism.

irrationalist or as a philosopher of the irrational by
critics of his philosophy.)

The new position which Sartre seeks is clearly beyond naive idealism and materialism. Sartre's concept of "situation" replaces the notion of brute material
existence. Only consciousness can posit the material
world, and then only when it finds itself to be an
adversary of it. The facticity of matter is defined thus
as a "coefficient of adversity"[17] (Bachelard), i.e., relative to the intent of consciousness. "In order for a hill
to be easy or hard to ascend, one must have planned
to climb it to its summit." [18] This position Sartre calls
"revolutionary realism." It can be summarized by saying that reality appears real only when man struggles
against it.[19]

Sartre does not disagree with Marx's contention that
the task of consciousness is to transform the world.
Precisely by interacting and changing the natural and
material world, we come to know it, and not the other
way around.[20] In the encounter between consciousness and material reality (an encounter defined in
terms now of struggle, action, and labor rather than
comprehension) the *cogito* becomes worldly and the
world appears for the first time as totality in process.
Sartre never changed his mind that the only way to
make sense of Marx is therefore to drop the notion
of dialectic materialism and replace it with historical
materialism. With Marx, he holds that history is the
account of how man transforms his material world
and is oppressed by the very processes of transformation.

For that reason, as Sartre recognizes, his philosophy
addresses itself first to revolution and revolutionaries
because his intent is to reintroduce the free consciousness in historical reality, not to simply abide with his-

[17] *Being and Nothingness*, trans. by Hazel Barnes (New
York, 1956), p. 482 ff.
[18] *Ibid.*, p. 247.
[19] *Ibid.*
[20] *Ibid.*, p. 252.

torical circumstance, but to struggle and realize a new authentic history. What does this mean?

The truth of man lies in his self-consciousness. But this consciousness is both *in* the world and *to* the world by the very nature of consciousness. Hence consciousness has no choice but to bring to the world its own freedom. If historical circumstances deny freedom to certain men, then in order for consciousness *to be itself*, it must liberate them. The oppressed are the subject matter of philosophy. A strict materialism, on the other hand, could stifle any hope of revolution because it cannot make a genuine case for freedom.[21]

Sartre made the above arguments in 1946. The *Critique de la raison dialectique* (1961) represents nothing else but a continuation of these arguments. No radical conflict appears here between it and *L'être et le néant*.

III

Critics of Sartre describe his *Critique de la raison dialectique* as the dissolution of his existentialism into Marxism. At least four critics (Desan, Morot-Sir, Odajnyk, and Novack) believe the transformation may well be doomed. Burkle and Lichtheim appear to be more optimistic.[22]

Sartre himself is responsible for this formulation of the problem. In *Question de méthode*, the introduction to the *Critique*, he typifies existentialism, including his own, as a temporary stage of the philosophy of dialectical reason expressed by Hegel and Marx. Existentialism is now recognized as an "ideological" reaction to a more pervasive world view which it at first criticized but in which it now seeks to be integrated.[23] Kierkegaard's human outcry against the Hegelian sys-

21 *Ibid.*, p. 256.
22 Cf. footnotes 3–6.
23 *Critique*, p. 18.

tem was already incorporated in the Hegelian structure six years before Kierkegaard was born.[24] Kierkegaard's insistence on pathos versus reason, subjectivity versus The System, individual despair versus abstraction is itself characteristic of so-called Unhappy Consciousness, a philosophical pose transcended quite early in the pages of Hegel's *Phenomenology*. Does this dispose of Kierkegaard's stand? Not really, as Sartre shows. The essence of Kierkegaard's stand against Hegel lies in his insistence that a concrete life cannot be reduced to a conceptual stage of theory.[25] The immediate reality of an individual existence cannot be surpassed by philosophic dialectics. Kierkegaard appears to Sartre as a revolutionary critic who will not obey the rules of Hegelian philosophy by which he must agree upon his own disappearance as individual into the totality of metaphysical history.

Sartre views Marx's protest against Hegel in much the same way. Marx, like Kierkegaard, insists upon the concrete individual who works, must eat and live, an individual who hopes, but almost always fails, to actualize his possibilities in history, not through logically successive stages of cognition, but through hard labor. Hegel wrongly believes that alienation is a necessary condition of all cultural objectification.[26] Estrangement, frustration, and homelessness are not products of a logic of historical motion but of particular socio-economic conditions. These conditions must be overcome. And this cannot be achieved by pure thought.

Marx, for Sartre, affirms *"la spécifité de l'existence humaine . . . l'homme concret dans sa réalité objective."*[27] Marxism is *"la philosophie de notre temps"* because the very character of contemporary times is defined in economic and material terms, i.e., scarcity,

---

[24] Cf. Lessing, "Hegel and Existentialism: An Essay on Unhappiness," *The Personalist* (1967).

[25] *Critique*, p. 22.

[26] *Ibid.*, p. 20.

[27] *Ibid.*, p. 21.

labor, and production. Marxism cannot be surpassed because the very conditions which have given rise to it are not yet surpassed.[28]

A number of critical observations must be made at this point of our inquiry. If economic oppression does characterize man in modern times, then Marxism united with existentialism speaks for the individual by preparing him at the same time for his revolt against oppressing economic conditions and institutions. The aim of philosophy is liberation. With the end of oppression, however, would come the end of Marxism, as Sartre admits. Sartre seems to suggest that philosophies are either *passable* or *indépassable*, depending on the times in and for which they appear. This means that just as existentialism is a passing phase of Marxism, so Marxism must ultimately become a passing phase of dialectic reason. Sartre's conception of philosophy therefore seems now to include the historicity of all philosophy, including his own. Such a view seriously weakens the absolute basis on which he earlier developed his concept of consciousness. In *L'être et le néant*, Sartre argues persuasively that the synthesis of *pour-soi* and *en-soi*, nothingness and being, cannot dialectically develop. Man is therefore a useless passion. If this conclusion is now understood as a historical comment, or a philosophic realization which attains and consequently loses its truth in passage, then the basis of truth itself is no longer the *cogito* but history. Truth as the ontological condition of negative consciousness is replaced by the so-called truth of history.[29] Precisely for that reason, existentialism will be understood to have been a passing phase of Marxism.

Here we take issue with Sartre's interpretation of his own past work. First, the proposition that Marxism is

[28] *Ibid.*, p. 29. Marxism *"reste donc la philosophie de notre temps; il est indépassable parce que les circonstances qui l'ont engendré ne sont pas encore dépassées."*

[29] Sartre suggests along Hegelian lines that the *cogito* will realize itself completely in history and establish a new synthetic reality which he calls "La Vérité de l'histoire" (*Critique*, p. 142).

indépassable, unsurpassed, because the circumstances
it addresses are unsurpassed, establishes that any philosophy is viable and significant, even attains its truth
insofar as it addresses a set of peculiar and particular
socio-economic circumstances. Sartre's contention, moreover, is that reality today is Marxist reality (exploitation, oppression, and alienation through economic
means). This contention is neither argued nor proven
in the *Critique.*[30] It is in fact its assumption. If it is
not merely an assumption, granting Sartre's point
more truth than it deserves, the assertion "contemporary reality is Marxist reality" can only be an historical, i.e., empirical, observation generalized from
interpreting socio-economic and historical phenomena.
In any case, the proposition is not a metaphysical one.
Why, if this is the case, should we therefore exchange
and subsume one metaphysics (i.e., existentialism) into
another (Marxism) on the basis of what is ultimately
nothing more than an empirical generalization about
what goes on in the world? If our choice of metaphysical contexts is decided upon by historical and
socio-economic considerations, how can we ever bring
a viable metaphysical critique *toward* such conditions?

Let us develop the implications of this argument a
bit further. Sartre proclaims in *L'être et le néant* the
absolute autonomy of the individual. This proclama-
tion is the conclusion of a series of ontological arguments which point toward the irreducible character of
nihilation and its need to-be and to-be-in-the-world.
To be "worldly" is both (a) the projective destiny of
consciousness because it is always intentionally directed
toward the world, and (b) the condition of "facticity,"
being-a-body in the world.[31] Now Sartre argues in the

---

[30] This becomes quite clear in such statements as the
following: "The essential discovery of Marxism is that
labor, as historical reality and as the utilization of determined tools is an already determined social and material
sphere, is the real basis of the organization of social
relation. This discovery *can no longer* be challenged"
(*Critique,* pp. 224–225n).

[31] Cf. *Being and Nothingness,* p. 308 ff.

Critique that this philosophical position *in toto* is to be subsumed by another in which the individual is now seen to be a socio-economic product defined by labor and production first, consciousness second. On the grounds established in *L'être et le néant* such a subsumption is not an expansion of the notion of man, but obviously a contraction. We have contracted a metaphysical definition of the individual to an empirical definition. More seriously, we have exchanged phenomenological descriptions of the necessary conditions of human existence (negation, time, body) for sociopolitical descriptions of certain contingent "facts" which shape contemporary man and society (the group, labor, authority). Yet Sartre maintains that this marks a philosophical advance.

From the point of view of the free *cogito*, sociopolitical life with its own demands and characterizations appears as one choice among a great many life-styles available to the individual. From the point of view of Marxism, this fact is historically untrue. Man is defined by *praxis* first, free-choosing consciousness later. Historically speaking, the latter position may well be more relevant and true to the facts of our times. However, to assert that man is laborer, producer, oppressed or oppressor is not to say anything which metaphysically appears self-evidently true, particularly if we continue to maintain, and rightfully so, that production, labor, economic life in general *is chosen* and therefore a contingent rather than necessary form of behavior—a particular structure of freely chosen projects rather than any essential definition of human reality as such.

Even if we grant Sartre's empirical contention that man is oppressed, that he does find himself caught in an economic prison which degrades all else in life, we fail to see why these facts of history force us to abandon the metaphysical position of the free *cogito* in favor of what appears to be a series of historical observations. How can historical circumstance determine the validity of metaphysical theory, particularly if the metaphysics in question (Sartre's earlier existentialism) defines history as a construct of the individual?

In short, if Sartre is intent upon subsuming existentialism into Marxism, he is running the clear chance that he will exchange rather than incorporate metaphysical for empirical theory, particularly if Marxism itself is only viable because it presently reflects the facts of modern life. There is no question that Sartre has the right to shift from metaphysical to sociological and economic theory. He does not, however, have the right to claim that such a shift actually expands the perspective of his earlier metaphysical position. In fact, as we have argued above, the result is the opposite.

If Sartre is to escape these criticisms, he must maintain that Marxism is not merely a product of a particular time, but establishes its validity beyond it as well. In short, Sartre must claim Marxism as a metaphysics. This is precisely what Sartre tries to accomplish in the *Critique*. Sartre's Marxism turns out to be another variety of Hegelian philosophy.

Dialecticity. Dialectical Reason is both the subject under discussion and the method by which the discussion is proceeding. Sartre accepts Hegel's general theory of dialectic but disagrees that all dialectic movement culminates in an absolute which lies beyond individual consciousness. With Hegel, Sartre holds that history and institutions show a dialectic development, that is to say, a growth ("totalization") governed by the action and reaction of consciousness. The dialectic, therefore, always has for its subject the self which seeks to place itself in the world through presenting, representing, and recreating itself in cultural institutions and projects. Dialectic is never merely logical but always "worldly" as well. The creative effort of man to objectify himself in order to existentially recapture his soul in concrete universality is the task of consciousness. Sartre modifies Hegel's notion of universality somewhat. For Hegel, the concrete universal is essentially a religious achievement, God-in-process. For Sartre, the concrete universal is Man or Humanity.[32] And this concrete universal remains historical, i.e., temporal. It does not transcend time for the sake of attaining eternity. Sartre's world remains finite.

Although the dialectic can be understood abstractly by thought, its motion is most concretely found in *praxis. Praxis* is performed by individual consciousness through the use of the body, but its meaning is embodied in the processes themselves in labor and production rather than pure (intentional) consciousness.

Our difficulty in grasping Sartre's appropriation of Hegel's dialectic must focus again on how Sartre can locate nihilating consciousness in real history. First consciousness for itself, *pour soi,* has only one activity, nihilation. It is difficult to believe that Sartre can locate any dialectic intention in nihilating consciousness, because by its very nature Sartrean consciousness is incapable of giving itself over to material being without falsifying itself.[33] Sartre defines self-deception and bad faith (*mauvaise foi*) as any and all attempts on the part of the *cogito* to define itself in any medium other than its own nihilations. How then can any authentic dialectic ever begin between mind and matter? If the *cogito* is nothing else but itself, i.e., thinking, how can it ever present itself as laborer and producer? The problem lies in the fact that Hegel believes that

[32] *Critique,* pp. 141, 143.
[33] Even the incarnation of consciousness in a material body is an extremely uncomfortable situation for Sartre. The body is factually there, in the world, but consciousness does its best to either evade it or transcend it altogether. Nowhere in *L'être et le néant* does Sartre make out any kind of positive case for a positive relationship between *cogito* and body. The *cogito* fundamentally must negate its own incarnation. How then in the *Critique* can the body's labor be intentional, i.e., conscious? Cf. my papers "Immediacy, Eros and Freedom," *Review of Existential Psychology and Psychiatry,* Vol. V, no. 1 (Winter, 1965); "Eros, Dionysus and Ontology," *Existential Psychiatry,* Vol. I, no. 3 (Winter, 1966).

both positing and negating are authentic acts; Sartre in *L'être et le néant* denies any positivity for consciousness and, consequently, man.

While earlier Sartre maintained that each man by his choices constructs his own projects, in the *Critique* it appears that history and the construction of authentic collective history is the primary project for all. *Must* consciousness be historical? *Must* the individual who seeks a life-style submit himself to the political projects of history? Finally, what is the status of "history"? If there are irreducible free human beings, what can historical circumstance be except the limitations which these free beings face in their attempt to be individuals? If the ultimate project is to construct a dialectic totality called "history," will history still be inhabited by individuals? Is there no possibility to choose to be unhistorical?

Totality and Totalizing. What is "totality" for Hegel and what is it for Sartre? For Hegel, totality is the coming-to-be of some concrete whole which is permeated by rational consciousness. Such a totality could be a symphony, panorama, Greek sculpture, feudal society, mathematical theory, social class. For Hegel, all totalities by coming to terms with their own relative incompleteness and contradictoriness are taken up into more comprehensive totalities (symphony into music, panorama into perception, sculpture into art, etc.). Sartre here agrees with Hegel, but actively pursues social totalities which, he maintains, are the basis for all other totalities. With Hegel, he believes that all human productivity aims for its totalization within rational wholes. With Hegel's *Phenomenology*, Sartre holds that the reflective awareness of the totalizing process by which parts enter into social wholes is itself included in such wholes. The viewer cannot have a privileged standpoint. On the contrary, he is existentially placed within the very totalities which he seeks to comprehend. Critical experience "goes on inside the totalization, and cannot be a contemplative grasp of the totalizing movement. . . . Rather, it is a real moment of the totalization in process."[34] The upshot of this important Sartrean point is that the individual consciousness is always and already enclosed within historical totalities. These it can either reject, accept or change. No one can step out of history within this view. The point of human existence is therefore no longer the affirmation of one's own singular distance from the world through negation; but rather the opposite: one aims for intelligible inclusion in the processes within society, keeping in mind that society is itself a totality coming-to-be. The singular critic (every consciousness, insofar as consciousness is negative, is always critical) must go so far as "to deny his own singular determination in order to seek his dialectical intelligibility in the whole of the human adventure," writes Sartre.[35] In this manner does the individual discover through work that he *is* history personified, in fact, the truth of history itself.[36]

The truth of history is ultimately a network of relations which holds the individual within his totalities and makes his own totalizations meaningful: this is consciousness of "the totality of his practical links with others, and thereby the structure of the diverse practical multiplicities with others, and through the contradictions and struggles among these, the concrete absolute: historical man."[37]

The emphasis on *praxis* to the exclusion of everything else is disturbing. Why is there no mention here of all those impractical links with others which effect, even within their tension and release, concrete totalities of their own? Examples would be friendship, love, and playfulness. Are these totalities to be reduced to *praxis*?

Sartre seems to believe that the ultimate totality is history, but we have already posed the problem of the

[34] *Critique*, p. 140.
[35] *Ibid.*, p. 141.
[36] Cf. pp. 168–170 of this paper.
[37] *Critique*, p. 143.

individual who demands to be unhistorical. Is this not
the cry of Kierkegaard? With Marx, Sartre affirms that
individuals collectively make history. With Marx,
Sartre believes that the individual is already in history,
but must rationally create new history. The aim of all
consciousness, in any case, lies now beyond its immediate negative freedom. Negation serves history (but,
curiously enough, is not free to deny historicity as
such). This marks a questionable advance in Sartre's
thinking. If structures of totality exist in which a
multiplicity of totalizing processes find themselves
intertwined and interdetermined, the aim of negative
consciousness is to seek out a total rational structure
in which all totalizing processes will themselves be
totalized, i.e., subsumed. Dialectic tension will keep
the whole machine running and growing. But where
will the individual make his home? In which totality
will he pursue his *own* life?

Has Sartre, like Hegel, built another castle in which
no human being can live? Hegel's castle is Absolute
Mind. Sartre's, Absolute History. In a frightening way,
they resemble Kafka's castle. (Totality combined with
reason, as we now know only too well, can give us
Stalinism as well as Berkeley's bureaucracies.[38])

In fairness to Sartre's position, his final totality
cannot complete itself since it is history itself. History
can neither freeze nor end; in fact, Sartre depends
heavily upon the negative consciousness of the individual to keep history going. At least the open and
fluid character of institutions will make possible the
possibility of freedom. Here Sartre must be distinguished from Hegel, for whom the last dialectic step
effects a unity between freedom and necessity so that
all protest ends.

Nevertheless, Sartre is overly optimistic about the
individual's revolutionary role in history. The existence
of totalities which seek inclusion in the final totality
present a massive wall against which the revolutionary

[38] Cf. Lionel Abel, "Metaphysical Stalinism," *Dissent*
(Spring, 1961).

may well fail. Even the totalization of the individual into a revolutionary group may find itself powerless.

Freedom. Sartre's philosophy is a philosophy of human freedom. In *L'être et le néant,* Sartre presents the most absolute and radical theory of freedom in the history of Western philosophy. This is not the place to delineate the intricacies of his arguments; elsewhere I have done this.[39] Suffice it to say that the *radical* nature of Sartre's theory of freedom lies with his conclusions. These can be summarized as follows:

1. The nature of consciousness is such that (a) it can not be reduced to any source or cause other than itself; and (b) it is radically other than and excluded from all other beings which appear. Thirdly, consciousness is therefore through and through negative. To be conscious is to nihilate.

2. Negation is freedom. Consciousness is nothing else but freedom itself, i.e., the process by which consciousness establishes itself as for itself. All determinist arguments rest either upon self-deception or mistaken argument.

3. Man is not merely free, but the principle of freedom incarnate. Human reality is contingent. The individual through projects builds up life-styles and structures within historical situations which in themselves have no final efficacy or justification.

4. Freedom cannot be taken away except by death. Freedom can be degraded but only through the degradation of the body. Negative consciousness as an ontological condition of all concrete human existence can only be evaded. In order for man to be himself, he must be free. Freedom is the necessary condition of his contingency. *All else* follows from this ontological condition, including meaning.

The six-hundred pages of *L'être et le néant* explicate the implications of this argument. These emphasize the individual who, although free, either deceives himself

[39] Arthur Lessing, *Man Is Freedom: A Critical Study of the Conception of Human Freedom in the Philosophies of Martin Heidegger and Jean-Paul Sartre.* A Ph. D. dissertation. Tulane University (May, 1966).

or attempts to construct an authentic life. Either one
contradicts freedom itself. The arguments for the radical freedom of the individual are ontological ones,
based upon certain phenomenological descriptions.
Sartre's position is essentially a metaphysical one. Historical circumstance might deny metaphysical freedom,
but in fact become occasions to put freedom to work,
to overcome these circumstances, in other words, *revolt*.
In an essay written immediately after World War II,
Sartre points out:

We were never more free than during the German
occupation. We had lost all our rights, beginning with
the right to talk. Every day we were insulted to our
faces and had to take it in silence. Under one pretext
or another, we were deported *en masse*. Everywhere,
on billboards, in the newspapers, on the screen, we
encountered the revolting and insipid picture of ourselves that our oppressors wanted us to accept. And
because of all this we were free.[40]

For the early Sartre freedom is secure from history.
The success of revolt is irrelevant to the definition of
revolt itself. Historical facts never deny freedom, but,
instead, provide a stage upon which the individual
acts out his freedom, even if the only action left must
be the destruction of the stage itself. Witness the events
of Watts in 1965. To be free one must revolt. All else is
the hypocrisy of *salauds*.

This view has been modified in the *Critique*, modifi-
cations which Merleau-Ponty anticipated sixteen years
earlier.[41] Freedom in the *Critique* is still founded on
the nature of the *cogito*, but now is more and more
located in the group and class.[42] Revolt is still stressed,
but it is the revolution of the group, not the individual
alone. The individual must (freely) join others if his
freedom is to mean anything in social action. Individual
freedom is now too "abstract" for Sartre because it

[40] "The Republic of Silence" (New York, 1947), p. 498.
[41] Cf. Merleau-Ponty's treatment of freedom in his
Phenomenology of Perception, Part III, ch. 3.
[42] *Critique*, p. 425.

cannot possibly succeed alone. Only the group can grasp power and use it, and consequently has concrete freedom.

In rejecting the Nobel Prize in 1964, Sartre said:

In the citation[43] of the Swedish Academy, freedom is spoken of. This is a word that lends itself to numerous interpretations. In the West, it is taken to mean abstract freedom. But to me it means a more concrete freedom—the right to have more than one pair of shoes and to eat when hungry.[44]

It need not be mentioned that food and shoes are the products of a society and not an individual. Negative consciousness appears irrelevant here. The argument is typically Marxian: thought fails to bring about true freedom; only the action of an authentic society can accomplish this task. For the existentialist, freedom *is* the individual; for the Marxist, it is the blessing of an authentic society. Sartre seems to be trying to maintain both in the *Critique*.

Sartre closes the introduction to the *Critique* with a reference to a few sentences of Marx taken from the third volume of *Das Kapital*:

We all know the passage of Marx which makes an allusion to a distant epoch: "The reign of freedom actually begins only where labor imposed by necessity and mundane considerations ceases; it will find itself henceforth beyond the sphere of material production as such." As soon as there will exist for everyone a margin of real freedom beyond the production of life, Marxism will have lived out its span; a philosophy of freedom will take its place. But we have no means, no intellectual instrument, no concrete experience which allows us to conceive of this freedom or of this philosophy.[45]

---

[43] The citation says that Sartre's authorship "has always been rich in ideas and has had a vast influence on our times, mainly through its spirit of liberty and quest for truth" (*New York Times*, Friday, October 23, 1964, p. 1).

[44] Cited on the dust-jacket of *The Philosophy of Jean-Paul Sartre*, ed. by Robert D. Cumming (New York, 1965).

[45] *Critique*, p. 32. The Marx passage can be found in *Capital*, Vol. III, (Moscow, 1959), pp. 779–780.

Several points need to be made about this new notion of freedom:

1. Freedom must address itself to those economic conditions (exploitation, poverty, scarcity, etc.) if it is to be "concrete" rather than "abstract."[46] Real freedom is real by virtue of the philosophy's social relevance.

2. With a new reign of freedom, Marxism will be replaced by a philosophy of freedom which at this point in history has not yet any relevance. In fact, given our place, Sartre claims we cannot even conceive of such a philosophy. Does this really make sense? If we admittedly recognize oppression, on what basis do we recognize it? Oppression does not merely present itself; we interpret oppression to be the case if historical and socio-economic conditions do not live up to what we conceive to be human freedom. But we are not yet in a position to know what we conceive to be freedom, Sartre asserts above. How then can we judge that contemporary life is deficient in freedom? Is not an implicit commitment to Sartre's earlier theory of freedom precisely the basis of our judgment? But this basis is the one that Sartre wants to dissolve in Marxism. Presumably, the radical freedom of the individual is only a reactionary ideology rather than true philosophy.

3. We are therefore puzzled by Sartre's inability to conceive of a philosophy of freedom beyond the sphere of material production. Sartre developed such a philosophy eighteen years earlier in his *L'être et le néant*. We are puzzled by Sartre's inability to point to any concrete experience for such a philosophy because in *L'être et le néant*, he provides us with many rich phenomenological descriptions of such experiences, from nausea, despair, flight to sexuality, action, and even skiing. Is not *L'être et le néant* the answer to

---

[46] We must keep in mind that Sartre uses "abstract" and "concrete" as relative descriptive terms applied to relative stages of totalization (*Critique*, p. 143n).

the problem of the *Critique*? If it is, however, we have
turned Sartre on his head because he argues for the
opposite.

This is not merely a quibble about relative emphases.
Sartre's claim is that the framework of a theory of
free consciousness is to be subsumed and therefore
replaced by the framework of Marxist theory. The
problem is that Sartre has kept it as (a) the basis for
a critique of material and economic life which deprives
us of freedom, and (b) as the philosophy which ultimately Marxism aims for in overthrowing economic
oppression.

It seems clear that the rock-bottom foundation of
Sartre's Marxism is his earlier existentialism rather than
the other way around. What Sartre is aiming for is not
a new Marxism but a new existentialism, in fact, a
Marxist existentialism.

IV

What is entailed in a Marxist existentialism? The
basis of all existential thought is a metaphysics of
freedom. Freedom is the foundation of existence. History is made up of the contingent structures which are
both products and expressions of that freedom. Freedom is not a value associated with particular historical
periods or specific economic institutions such as capitalism. All history and politics presupposes human
freedom as their origin and their future. The individual
does not have freedom the way he has "rights" which
entail "responsibility" and "citizenship." Man is freedom. Hence, his human task is to be free, to be conscious because only as consciousness does freedom
appear as itself.

The oppression of social and economic institutions
can therefore be measured in terms of their attack on

and destruction of the *cogito*. To liberate man from his obsession with material goods, material wants, profit, and the quantitative life of economic transaction means to liberate his very consciousness. The quantification of all human life which accompanies capitalism as well as communism degrades consciousness. The problem of the individual in society must be reformulated in terms of the problem of qualitative existence within a quantified society. A society reduces and degrades human freedom when it quantifies the very qualitative awareness which gives us a measure of self-consciousness.

The achievement of existentialism (I speak of Kierkegaard, Nietzsche, Heidegger, and Sartre) lies in its recognition that the qualitative existence of human beings constitutes the foundation of all human life.

Capitalism claims, of course, that the life of quantity makes possible increased leisure which is to be used qualitatively. Increasingly, however, qualitative life is only possible after work in an industrial society such as ours. Strangely enough this would clearly seem to imply that only in leisure are we thus allowed to be human. This is intolerable.

On the other hand, it would seem that the solution does not lie in a new relationship between labor, capital, and means of production, as Marx suggests. The real problem lies in moving beyond material and economic life altogether, as Marx also suggests. Paradoxically, the increased quantification of production (through the immense development of automation and computer theory) may well make this a practical reality. I say "paradoxically," because increased automation of a socio-economic system does not necessarily lead to a great qualitative life for the leisured individual. The phenomenon of self-deception, so ably exposed by Sartre, is much in evidence in modern society. In creating machines, we are capable in the process of turning ourselves into machines as well. The negativity of freedom has always been a burden for the majority of us; we willingly give up our liberties for the sake of authorities which promise security and peace. What better way to give up the burden of freedom than to objectify our most precious possession, lucid awareness, in the machines of tomorrow? We cannot remain free and cowards at the same time.

CHAPTER 8

EXISTENTIAL
PHENOMENOLOGY

ASHER MOORE AND
ROLLO HANDY*

THE Association for Phenomenology and Existential
Philosophy now has 250 members. It also has a journal.
Responsible departments have included courses in these
areas, and one department makes something of a spe-
cialty of supplying instructors for them. Phenomenology
and existentialism, in short, are not only growing
rapidly in importance but are undergoing the universal
concomitant of such growth, institutionalization.

My remarks concern the relation between these two
lines of thought. Admittedly, discussions of *isms* and
ologies can be exceedingly unprofitable. Such questions
are in part verbal, requiring not inquiry but decision;
they are partly matters of historical record, needing
careful scholarship; and there are those who doubt that
they are anything else. But when philosophies are in
the process of institutionalization in the world of de-
grees, budgets, movable type, and, above all of course,
foundations, it seems to me there is more than a verbal
importance to assuring that the institutional embodi-
ments reflect genuinely philosophic relationships and
not transitory misapprehensions. Some of our colleagues,

* Asher Moore is Professor of Philosophy at the University of New Hampshire and Rollo Handy is in the Philosophy Department at the State University of New York at
Buffalo. These papers first appeared in *Philosophy and
Phenomenological Research*, March 1967, and they are
printed here by permission of the editors and the authors.

especially younger ones, no longer speak of phenomenology *and* existentialism, but of existential phenomenology. The disturbing thing is not that they see a single idea where others thought they saw two ideas, but that their training apparently did not so much as raise in their minds the question. Instead, by passing along the term existential phenomenology, it passed along also a dogma. In such circumstances, I think we should seek to determine whether the cohabitation of phenomenology and existentialism is a valid sacrament, a marriage of convenience, or miscegenation pure and simple. My own view is that the alliance is unholy.

Those who speak of existential phenomenology as a single philosophy take phenomenology to be the method of that philosophy and existentialism its content. Through the phenomenological method, existentialism seizes upon and clarifies that which is in the focus of its substantive concern, human existence. Conversely, when phenomenological insight is turned upon human existence, what it discloses are those structures of choice, care, ekstasis, and so on, which are the substance of existentialist thought. The issue then, is whether phenomenology must be, or is, or could be, the method of existentialism, or whether existentialism is a self-sufficient philosophy with a distinctive method of its own. I propose to touch upon four features of phenomenological method which in my opinion unfit it for existential inquiry and upon four corresponding features of the existentialist's concern which require him to philosophize from that natural standpoint which Husserl thought it necessary to bracket. I shall touch these points two by two.

Precisely because it is insight into structures, phenomenology discloses exclusively the universal. Secondly, since the contingent is associated by phenomenology with the natural standpoint and with the empirical science which stands at that point, phenomenological insight extends no further than the necessary. The existentialist, however, is interested in human beings and human life. And human beings are not universal and human life is not necessary—not, anyway, on the level at which philosophy is interested.

A human being is not a universal structure or a set of universal structures. Whatever may be true of other things, the identity of human persons is not defined by Leibniz' principle. A human being is unique, unrepeatable, and entirely particular. Or rather, since of course human beings *may* participate in or illustrate common structures, let us say that whether or not a particular person illustrates a certain structure is always a question of fact, to be determined by consulting him, never a question about man, to be settled by essential insight into man-ness, or a question about men, to be settled by inductive inference from other men. A human being who lacked all common structures would doubtless be literally incommunicado, but he would still be himself. *What* a human being is, in the sense of what universals he exemplifies, does not determine, but is determined by, *who* he is.

A human being is free, and his life is not necessary but contingent. There are no patterns or laws to which a human being's life must conform, no channels it must follow. A particular life may be in large part, or even entirely, necessitated—habitual, predictable, compulsive. But whether this is so or not is a contingent matter. As it is contingent that there is something rather than nothing, so a thing is necessary only if it happens to be. A person can be un-free, but whether he is lies within the scope of his freedom. The neurotic is genuinely compelled, but in the end the only way for him to stop being compelled is to stop. Existential psychoanalysis may succeed in uncovering an individual's basic project, but there can be no guarantee of success, since some of us may have no basic project. It lies within a human being's freedom to choose chaos: in some sense, dissociation is exactly that choice. Since there is nothing which a human being must inevitably be, or become, or do, one must wait to see what he will do, wait to see what will happen. Temporarily is a timeless structure but human life is not timeless, but open to a future.

It will be objected that we have misunderstood the nature of those structures which universally and necessarily characterize human existence by mistakenly identifying them with the sort of universal structure which constitutes the determinate *nature* of a *thing*, determining *what* the thing is. A human being is not a *what* but a *who*. The structures involved in being a human being are therefore not *what* a human being is; they do not make up his nature. A human being is not determinate, but self-determining. He will have been what he chooses to be. But the fact that human beings do not embody the same structures as things, or embody them in the same way, does not mean that human beings embody no structures. On the contrary, they embody those structures which apply to a free *who*, those structures which are conditions of the possibility of a free life. These structures are ontological, not ontic; they are not categories or essences, but existentials.

Furthermore, it will be pointed out, we have throughout our own discussion freely availed ourselves of exactly such structures. A human being, we said, is not a universal or a set of universals, because he is a unique individual. But what does that mean if not that human existence universally and necessarily involves the existential structures of individuality, and uniqueness, and everything implicated in them? After all, particularity is a universal structure. Similarly, in the sense of the term necessary which is applicable to things, human acts are not necessary, but contingent, since human existence is free. Nonetheless, it is a necessary truth that human existence is free. Man is condemned to freedom. And it is a necessary truth that freedom is just the sort of thing it is. That we ourselves, in the act of denying that universal and necessary structures can be ascribed to human beings, ascribed to them the structures of freedom and individuality, was no avoidable slip, but illustrates the fact that without such structures nothing at all can be said about human existence, even that it is human existence. It is these structures, it is contended, which are open to, and open only to, phenomenological insight.

Evidently, there is something here which must be admitted. Nothing can be said about human existence, or about anything else, except in terms of universal structures which can be predicated of it. Even raising the question whether I am a free individual involves knowing what freedom is and what individuality is. Existentialism thus does presuppose general terms of thought—especially, although by no means exclusively, those regional terms which, because their domain is human existence, may be called existentials. The clearer such terms of thought are, the better, of course, and while phenomenology is not the only theory of how we come by general ideas and achieve a passable clarity about them, it is certainly a possible view.

Phenomenology, however, is interested in these universal, necessary terms of thought for their own sake: in the general nature of uniqueness, the necessary structure of freedom, the eternal character of time, and the changeless being of change. It does not permit itself to be interested in whether these structures are incorporated in existing things. The existent thing is bracketed in favor of eidetic structures and is resurrected only in the form of exist*ence*, another structure. For the existentialist, on the contrary, these general terms of thought are only predicables to be employed in characterizing human beings. Whereas the phenomenologist focuses upon the structure and asks what more precisely it is, the existentialist begins with the particular and asks what structures it embodies, which is another way of saying that phenomenology is an essentialism whereas existentialism is an existentialism, and that that fact is not altered when the essence in question is the essence of existence. It may of course be that human being necessarily involves individuality and freedom. But it is the phenomenologist, not the existentialist, who is interested in such eidetic truths. There are also well-founded empirical generalizations about such beings. The existentialist is not concerned with them, either. Strictly speaking, and contrary to what our own earlier usage may have implied, the existentialist is not interested in "human beings."

As an existentialist, I am directly and immediately concerned with myself—which, be it noted, is not the same as being concerned with myself-ness, *Jemeinigkeit.* Then I am concerned with you, and with him, and her, and with them, and possibly with thee. I am concerned with we, and with us, and with what *it* means to us. The subjects of my thought and the objects of my concern are existing individuals. I begin with proper names, with ostension, with encounters. I take thought of structures such as existence and human being only as things which may be predicable of me, or you, or somebody else. And "may" is the proper word here, for it is always contingent what structures I embody. It may be an eidetic truth that anything that exists is individual, but whether I am an individual and therefore perhaps exist is an empirical question. If I am an anonymous one, then I am not an individual but a conglomeration of universal structures. If I am completely overwhelmed by compulsions, then I am not free. But I am still I. Neither Sartre nor anyone else is condemned to freedom. To call me inauthentic because I deny that I am free and responsible is simply a remnant of moralism. Like all taunts, it lacks the power of sticks and stones, and leaves me very much myself. I can be deprived of freedom and individuality, of humanity and of existence, of any existential structure whatever, and at the end of it all—here I am. And here you are. And all the others. Existentialism, like the empirical sciences, is concerned with particular "this's." Most of the "this's" have by now an appropriate science devoted to them. Even the 1,000,000 divided by 1,000,000 has its science—psychology. Existentialism is the empirical science of you and me and the others.

In important ways, to be sure, as we shall shortly urge, it is seriously misleading to call existentialism a science. Mr. Earle has suggested the term "ontological autobiography," but he has subsequently begun to have doubts about the "ontological." However we may name the distinctive method of existentialism, the point is that it is not eidetic but empirical, an empirical search into myself and such others as I happen to meet. Nor do I, for one, feel bound to draw from this the conclusion that since existential reflection is empirical it is therefore not philosophical. If philosophy nowhere confronts the existent, it is limited to the *a priori* elaboration of possibilities—a life I am prepared to accept if I must but which I cannot be expected to rush forth to embrace. Nor does the argument which has rightly driven us philosophers from one area after another of empirical inquiry—the argument that we lack special information and special training—apply to existential reflection. It would be not modest, but grotesque, for me to insist on handing over reflection upon myself to someone better qualified.

Phenomenology is a science, an impersonal and objective inquiry into independent objects. Existentialism is not a science at all, but personal existence become reflective. My third and fourth points are only different emphases, bearing the one on the object and the other on the subject of this fundamental incompatability.

The objects of phenomenological insight are independent of the thinker's encounter with them. Granted, the phenomenological reduction is precisely a recognition that the noematic essentially involves the noetic, so that in this sense thought is active and constitutive, not a passive recording of what is given. But it is thought which is active and constitutive, not the thinking of an actual person. The objects of phenomenological insight are dependent upon transcendental consciousness, to be sure, but they are entirely independent of the actual process of inquiry as this is concretely lived by an actual person. Inde-

pendent of everything which is personal about persons
—action, faith, passion, error, ignorance, openness, and
closedness—they are relative only to that in the thinker
which is his nearest approach to impersonality, transcendental subjectivity, transcendental unity of thought.

As an existentialist, on the other hand, my primary
object is myself and my own life. And if there is anything which is clearly not independent of my reflection
upon it, it is myself. While this is not of course the
whole truth, it is half true that I am what I think about
myself and what I do to myself and suffer from myself
and what care I give myself. Existential reflection is
truly reflection: its object is the very being who reflects.
Clearly, that being changes as its reflections change.
Any plausible philosophy must allow for my being
mistaken about myself. But equally, any plausible philosophy must allow that "me" is not an independent
object, unaffected by the decisions of "I." As for you
and the others, and the world around us, I am concerned with these insofar as I encounter them in my
life. You are no more independent of my existential decisions than I am. If you were more than your impinge-
ment upon me, more than what I experience you as,
you would to that extent not be *you*. I do, to be sure,
experience you as another subject, another I. But it is
you who are an I.

The same fact can be seen from the perspective of
the thinker, the subject. Phenomenological insight is
something independent of the actual existence of the
particular person whose insight it is. Indeed, while it is
not at all peculiar to call a discovery or a quest mine,
it is very odd to call an insight mine. The phenomenological subject is transcendental thought, not an existing, willing, acting, choosing human being. Or, more
accurately, the phenomenological subject is not "I."
Phenomenological inquiry, like much of traditional
philosophical thought, remains irrelevant to and divorced from the life of the inquirer, something one
does in one's office, during working hours, a task one

works at along with others, even subcontracts to others, in the expectation that one's work will eventually produce "solutions" to "problems."

Existential reflection, on the other hand, is a free and personal act, my act. A coward cannot do it, a glutton cannot do it, a defeated man cannot do it, a detached observer cannot do it. Each must do it for himself. It never produces answers and never approaches an end. It is life. We said a moment ago that the life I inquire into, my own, is not independent of my inquiry into it. The converse of this is also true: my inquiry into my life is part of my life. Or rather, it is not a part, it is ingredient in all of my life. Existential reflection is not a selfless mirroring of an independent fact, but a new level of existence. And by that I do not mean that it is poured on top, as if existence were a *pousse café*. The life of a reflective being is through and through reflective; the whole life rises to a new level. It becomes, if you will, thought thinking about thinking. As Hegel saw, subject and object are mutually dependent and relative, but their synthesis, reflective life itself, is absolute. Reflection is of course a form of knowing, but it is perhaps more important to keep reminding oneself that it is a level of being. Hegel was right: philosophy *is* the Absolute.

I conclude that phenomenology is, as Husserl claimed, an eidetic science, but that for that very reason it cannot be the method of existentialism, which is neither eidetic nor scientific.

Comments on Asher Moore's "Existential Phenomenology"[1]

I want to make two points at the outset. First, I am neither a phenomenologist nor an existentialist. I am strongly interested in the methodologies of various

[1] Read at the Western Division meeting of the American Philosophical Association, Chicago, Illinois, April 29, 1965.

philosophic points of view, if "methodology" is understood as inquiry into what kinds of evidence are cited,
what types of arguments are used, and what issues are
taken as central. Many of my comments will be directed
toward such themes. Second, I agree with Mr. Moore
that the differences between phenomenology and existentialism are great, and I share his suspicion of
linking them in so-called "existential phenomenology."
Perhaps my remarks would be more interesting to this
audience if I disagreed with Mr. Moore on that central
point.

Next, I wish to make a further preliminary remark
about my own philosophic orientation. Intellectually
and temperamentally I am opposed to what I will call
Mr. Moore's "romanticism." By that I mean the extreme
emphasis on himself, as revealed in the following quotations:

(a) "Strictly speaking . . . the existentialist is not in-
    terested in 'human beings.' As an existentialist, I
    am directly and immediately concerned with my-
    self—which, be it noted, is not the same as being
    concerned with myselfness . . ."
(b) "As an existentialist . . . my primary object is
    myself and my own life."
(c) "You are no more independent of my existential
    decisions than I am. If you were more than your
    impingement upon me, more than what I ex-
    perience you as being, you would to that extent
    not be *you*."

Perhaps because of my naturalistic anti-romanticism,
I have considerable difficulty grasping some of Mr.
Moore's points. The major part of my commentary will
be devoted to a discussion of those points:

(1) I am not at all confident I understand what he
means by "empirical science." At one point he says:
"Existentialism is the empirical science of you and me
and the others." The next sentence of his paper reads:
"In important ways, to be sure . . . it is seriously misleading to call existentialism a science." Shortly thereafter, he says "Existentialism is not a science at all,

but personal existence become reflective." Interpreted literally, that would seem to say that existentialism is an empirical science yet not a science. If this is not to be interpreted literally, I do not grasp what Mr. Moore intends.

(2) Early in the paper there is a passage that either I fail to understand, or if I do understand it, I think it is quite wrong:

A human being is not a universal structure or a set of universal structures. . . . A human being is unique, unrepeatable, and entirely particular. Or rather, since of course human beings *may* participate in or illustrate common structures, let us say that whether or not a particular person illustrates a certain structure is always a question of fact, to be determined by consulting him, never a question about men, to be settled by inductive inference from other men.

In view of later comments in his paper, I suspect that the emphasis on humans being unique, unrepeatable, and entirely particular is partly to indicate a basic difference between man and other objects in the world. But I have doubts. First, is man unique, unrepeatable, and particular? For example, I have been informed that some of the followers of Wittgenstein, even unto the third generation, have taken on not only his intellectual style, but also imitate his behavior, including his mannerisms. And biologically I should think men share many common structures. If the argument is that the total "configuration" of a human is what is unique, would not nonhuman objects also be unique? Two carbon molecules are remarkably similar, but at least they differ in their spatio-temporal locations. If we look at the total set of relations between an object and other objects, is not every object unique and unrepeatable? On the other hand, if we look at the world in a less inclusive way, neither humans nor nonhumans seem unique and unrepeatable.

I tend to agree with the statement that "whether or not a particular person illustrates a certain structure is always a question of fact," but I wonder what basis

Mr. Moore has for saying that such questions are "to be settled by consulting him [the man involved]"? I think we might use not only inductive inferences from other humans (ruled out by Mr. Moore), but also observation. Indeed, are there not cases where the least illuminating evidence would come from consulting the man involved, simply because he fails signally to understand his own behavior? A person whose difficulty is acute anxiety may think he is having a heart attack, and consulting him about his difficulty may be far less helpful for the therapist than what the therapist knows about the "common structure" of anxiety. Or we might get interesting responses from a person suffering religious delusions, but I daresay the "common structure" he "participates in" would be best grasped through observation, inductive inference, etc.

(3) Mr. Moore says: "There are no patterns or laws to which a human being's life must conform, no channels it must follow." A little later he says: "Since there is nothing which a human being must inevitably be or become to do . . ." Again, to take crude cases, I think it is rather close to inevitable that a given person was born, that he will change, and that he will die. And I assume that the consequences of certain kinds of surgery are also close to inevitable.

(4) Mr. Moore says: "What a human being is, in the sense of what universals he exemplifies, does not determine, but is determined by *who* he is." If I understand that statement correctly, it seems dogmatic. It is no mystery to me why nearly all French children speak French, and I think the basic factors in such cases are *what* factors, not *who* factors. In short, sociocultural factors often determine (to use Mr. Moore's language) what universals a person exemplifies, and not the other way around.

All along, then, I have been contrasting to Mr. Moore's romanticism a view which regards man as a biosocial organism. My attempts to explain human behavior may or may not provide more "leverage" for understanding both *what* man is and *who* he is than does existential romanticism. But the major question I have for Mr. Moore is how we settle such disagreements. What is the relevant evidence, and what criteria do we use to evaluate the evidence?

Lastly, a point where I think I understand Mr. Moore, but on which I believe he is wrong, and that the wrongness is important for his whole approach. He says: "Nor does the argument which has rightly driven us philosophers from one area after another of empirical inquiry—the argument that we lack special information and special training—apply to existential reflection." In my view, philosophers have often been driven from areas because they have used inappropriate methods. They may have tried to settle factual questions by logic, or have regarded as "conceptual" what was "empirical," or relied on common sense or intuition when (alas!) they should not have. If so, then existential reflection may also turn out to be incorrect on many occasions. I realize that the lure of introspection is great for many philosophers, but I think the history of the relation of philosophy and science ought to make us wary of attempts to establish through argument that certain areas of inquiry are forever closed to a scientific approach.

In summary, I have indicated some of the places in which I believe Mr. Moore is wrong. If my own philosophic orientation has blinded me to a correct understanding of his statements, I fall back on the general question of the basis Mr. Moore has for his statements. What kind of evidence can he cite to skeptics?

Reply To Rollo Handy

(1) When I said that "whether or not a particular person illustrates a certain structure is . . . to be determined by consulting him," I did not mean that one

should ask the subject's opinion. I was using the term *consulting* in the more generous sense in which one consults reference books, the facts, and one's conscience. What I meant was that one must attend to that man himself, not to other men or to Man.

(2) Mr. Handy takes exception to my statement that what a human being is, is determined by who he is, not *vice versa*. But Mr. Handy is using the term *to determine* in the sense of *to cause*, whereas I was using it in the sense *to render determinate*.

(3) I meant to say that existentialism differs from science in that science is an impersonal inquiry into objects which are independent of the personal circumstances of inquiry whereas existentialism is not. But I meant to say also that existentialism is, like scientific psychology but unlike phenomenology, empirical, and that, again like scientific psychology, it is addressed to existing things—you and me and the others.

(4) Because I emphasized the existentialist's concern with himself without always carrying along the complementary idea of his concern for the world insofar as it is *his* world, I deserve Mr. Handy's rebuke of romanticism. I did not really mean to endorse an exclusive preoccupation with oneself. Indeed, immediately after saying that, as an existentialist, I am directly and immediately concerned with myself, I went on to say that, "I am concerned with you, and with him and her, and with them, and possibly with thee. I am concerned with we and with us and with what *it* means to us." So my emphasis upon self was not always unguarded.

Also, while I of course think about many things other than myself, it is *I* who do the thinking. And while it is easy to draw unwarranted conclusions from this—as egoism has been mistakenly inferred from the comparable fact about motives and solipsism from its semantical counterpart—I believe the fact itself is philosophically crucial. Even here, however, I would concede that the "I" in question, while not a bare transcendental unity, is not always a sharply indi-

viduated ego either, but runs over into less focused
modes of subjectivity.

(5) Mr. Handy thinks that the history of philosophy
and science "ought to make us wary of attempts to
establish through argument that certain areas of inquiry are forever closed to a scientific approach," and
hence, by implication, reserved to philosophical reflection. I endorse this statement. I would observe,
however, that all it requires of us is wariness. No facts
of history can prove in advance that all areas of empirical fact *are* open to a scientific approach or that
they are closed to philosophical reflection.

On these matters, I doubt that Mr. Handy and I
have any differences which could not be resolved by
clearing up misstatements or misunderstandings on
the one side or the other. And clearing away these
matters allows to emerge into full view what I believe
to be Mr. Handy's really basic objections to my paper.

Mr. Handy thinks that human beings are subject to
causal laws—("It is no mystery to me why nearly all
French children speak French, and I think the basic
factors in such cases are *what* factors, not *who* factors. . . . In short, socio-cultural factors often determine. . . ."). As against this, I have argued elsewhere[2]
that human behavior is correlated not with causes but
with "motives," and that it is misleading to think of
a motive's determining an act, since both the motive
and the act express, and hence presuppose, the same
meaning. But the matter is a complex one which
cannot be adjudicated apart from a comprehensive
theory of motivation, choice, action, expression, and
personality. Secondly, Mr. Handy doubts that human
beings are unique and unrepeatable in any way in
which physical objects are not. This is of course the
problem of particularity and individuality, and its reso-
lution would require a detailed understanding of personal identity, of specific and numerical difference, and
of the relations among all of these, and between them
and spatio-temporal position. Thirdly, Mr. Handy,

[2] Inquiry, I (1961), 53–65.

pointing to death and to the consequences of certain
kinds of surgery, objects to my claim that "there is
nothing which a human being must inevitably be or
become or do. . . ." To pursue this objection to its
roots would involve the whole difficult distinction between my life and my situation—between my acts,
what I may "be or become or do," and the given
setting of my action, the "not mine" into which I am
thrown and within which I must live. For of course I
did not mean that nothing inevitable ever *happens*
to a human being.

Since these objections of Mr. Handy's are indeed
basic, I cannot possibly "reply" to them within the
present confines. Even if I had indefinite space and
time, I could do no more than continue our discussion
of them. Mr. Handy twice challenges me to produce
the evidence for my views, as if philosophical evidence
could be neatly and exhaustively codified in two
thousand words or less. But I think he himself indirectly
indicates to us the way that we in fact approach such
basic philosophical issues as the ones he raises. He does
this when, speaking of his own view of man as a biosocial organism, he says, "My attempts to explain human behavior may or may not provide more 'leverage'
for understanding both *what* man is and *who* he is
than does existential romanticism." Like Mr. Handy,
"leverage for understanding" is the only criterion of
evaluation which I can envisage. But to determine
which view in fact provides the greater leverage is not
the work of an afternoon or of one person. It is an
endless conversation which possibly leads only to the
suspicion that, while some theories give little or no
leverage, no one view balances on Archimedes' point.

PART III

Ethics and Responsibility

CHAPTER 9

TRUTH'S DEBT TO FREEDOM

WARNER WICK*

It is not our custom to regard the concept of freedom as being especially germane to the theory of knowledge or, to put it differently, to the philosophy of science. Freedom's normal associations are all with moral philosophy, sometimes as one chapter heading of ethical doctrine, sometimes as a principle of the whole enterprise. As the contrary of coercion, freedom demands the moralist's attention because it is both a condition and a goal of civilized life. And as the opposite of natural necessity, it is thought to be presupposed by moral philosophy as a whole. The usual story is that since the notion of freedom is of no use to us in understanding the course of nature, we should have had no cause to wonder about it had not the moral law and our idea of responsibility forced it upon our attention. As in the old tale, if it had not been for Eve and the awareness of good and evil, we might still be contemplating the world in innocence.

Plausible as this may be as an account of how we came to be concerned with freedom as a topic in the commonplace book of metaphysics, I want to argue that, whatever led to our interest in it, what Kant would have called transcendental freedom is as essential to speculative philosophy as it is to the practical variety.

No doubt the world, and all that we encounter in it, becomes intelligible to the degree that we can discover

* Warner Wick is a member of the Philosophy Department at the University of Chicago. This article first appeared in *Mind*, October 1964, and is printed here by permission of the editor and author.

regular connexions between one thing and another. Moreover, since we are also parts of nature, our own behaviour is likewise subject to this kind of explanation. As creatures of nature, we naturally ask how nature helped to make us what we are; and so if we want to understand ourselves we look to all the empirical sciences, from astronomy to zoology, and from genetics and physical anthropology to psychology.

But still, if I may ask an old-fashioned question, how are we to understand science itself? Is there also a scientific explanation of science, of our activities as scientists, and of all that these have added to our stature? In one perfectly straightforward sense, of course, there is. We can specify necessary conditions without which our understanding of the world and of ourselves would have been impossible. We must first have had certain genetic equipment: a certain complexity of the nervous system, the power of articulate utterance that could become speech, the prolonged incompetence of human offspring that makes some sort of family relation necessary for survival and, almost incidentally, has thereby made possible the development of society and culture—including the cultivation of knowledge.

In sum, provided we already know what sort of thing science is, all this helps explain how it could come to be. But to know what sort of thing a science is is rather different from knowing what sort of thing a parakeet or a paramecium is. Once in the proper situation and armed with the appropriate equipment, we can be pretty sure of encountering parakeets and paramecia. But sciences, instances of scientific inquiry, and even scientists as pursuers of scientific knowledge rather than as members of *homo sapiens* like the rest of us, are not among the things that we can encounter in the same sense.

In more technical language we may say that the concept of a bird or of a bacterium is an empirical concept in a sense in which the concept of an empirical science is not. We identify instances of the first by referring back to other instances that we have met, however complicated the references and the procedures of identification and classification may become. But to identify a scientist or an instance of scientific inquiry or explanation is rather like identifying a policeman, or a strategic play in a game. These are all identified in relation to what I should call a *canon*, rather than in relation to individuals previously observed. A policeman is not known by his flat feet or his blue suit, for he may be a motorized plain-clothesman, but by the role he plays; and anyway the uniform may clothe an impostor. The canon which determines a policeman's lot, whether or not it be a happy one, is in turn relative to his function, the conception of which we must have before we can recognize what accords with it. Similarly a scientist, though he be roughly identifiable on empirical grounds as a man, is not recognizable as a scientist except by the canon of the science which occupies him; and the concept of this is not empirical in the usual sense. It is, as we say, "only an idea," the archetype of a kind of norm-regulated activity. We have to understand the point of science and its standards—understand "the scientific game" just as we must understand the point of any ordinary game—before we can spot the observable activities that answer to it or the persons who engage in it.

This thesis can be generalized and illustrated by the way we identify the varied uses of language, for these too are recognized by reference to what I have been calling their respective canons. Indeed, this is why the idea of a language game has been so useful. How do we identify and describe describing, or persuading, or arguing, giving instructions, telling a story or questioning a hypothesis? Not, surely, by simply noting sequences of sounds, gestures, or other observable events. (For that matter, the concept of a *word*, as opposed to a sound, is not what I have called an empirical concept either, since it is defined by its role and function.) To be sure none of these things—cases of describing, persuading, drawing a conclusion, or answering a question—can occur apart from observable processes, but that is not my present point.

For consider a piece of narrative. Disregard for the moment the basic but easily overlooked fact that even a minimal "reading" requires far more than recognizing the design and order of words and letters. How do we tell by internal evidence whether what we have read is an eyewitness report of a slice of history, or a bit of fiction written as a "slice of life" in the manner of *The New Yorker*? Or how do we tell, on reading a student's examination, whether he has given us an argument (imperfect, but a rudimentary argument still) or whether he has inaccurately remembered a sequence of propositions which to him never hung together as an argument at all? These distinctions are not impossible to make, but making them is not just a matter of the observable facts. We also have to "get the idea."

So, in "reading" or interpreting any activity or the record of an activity, just as in identifying the big man in the blue suit as a policeman or an actor, we both note the appearances and refer them to the canon that defines what they are. To be sure, we do something *like* this in making any empirical judgment, because to see that visible blob as my next-door neighbour requires that I perceive the sensible appearance as falling under a concept. Hence the old metaphors about "reading the book of nature" and the hermeneutics of natural science. But what I wish to emphasize is the *difference* between the concept of a role, of a rule-governed activity or complex of them on the one hand, and on the other the empirical concept of my neighbour Robinson, whom I have met many times across the garden fence.

Now because every technique and every method, and similarly every practice and act of choice (to paraphrase the first line of a philosophical classic) must have an observable embodiment as well as a characteristic intelligible form, we *may* consider such activities as sequences of events. But because it is their intelligible form that determines what kind of practice, method, or technique each of them is, and because this form is in turn determined by the end for the sake of which of them "is" at all, it is more often this aspect that commands our attention and that is reflected in the way we talk about them.

For example, the events on a football field all have their physical, physiological, or psychological "explanations," although we would seldom refer to any of them if we set out to explain the goings-on to a novice. Indeed, they are so remote from what we think of as the game itself that it requires a rather specialized taste in any spectator who would succeed in paying close attention to them, especially if the game is a good one. The same is true of the events in the laboratory, the study, and the seminar room. Every hypothesis entertained, every conclusion drawn, every opinion ventured, has its psychological and psysiological conditions and "explanation"; but these would be scarcely relevant if one wanted to explain what these activities are and why they occur.

I have been arguing that science, whether as inquiry or as knowledge, whether as the capacity to establish a conclusion or as the ability to understand such a proof, all falls under the heading of activity directed to an end and subject to a canon. Keeping my eye on this, I now wish to ask about the relation between scientific activity in this sense and scientific activity as a natural process subject to the empirical conditions which fall within the scope of the natural and behavioural sciences. In particular, I want to ask whether these conditions have anything to do with the truth or falsehood of an opinion, the cogency of a conclusion, or the relevance of a hypothesis. And when I have satisfied myself on that point, I wish to explore some implications of the answer. I think the first question, about the relation between an activity as we ordinarily understand it and an activity as a natural process, can best be approached by some further remarks about explanation.

II

It should be clear from what I have been saying that we use the term "explanation" in two quite different senses when we apply it to the genus of activities, and that which sense we have in mind varies according to whether we are thinking of the activity as a process in the context of other natural processes—which we can always do—or whether we are focusing our attention on the specific characteristics it has as an intelligent activity with its own autonomous rules and aims.

Sometimes, for example, we "explain" the failure of an attempted field goal by the wind, which blew the ball too far to the left, or by the interfering arm of a player, which blocked the kick. But sometimes we "explain" it in a different sense by the quarterback's poor strategy or by his opponent's skill in breaking through the defence. Or, to take a more intellectual example, sometimes we explain a mistake in a scientific experiment by the investigator's faulty apparatus or by the emotional tantrum that made him misuse his equipment. But sometimes we attribute the error to a misconception of the problem or to a logical fallacy. Both kinds of explanation may be accepted at the same time: the investigator may have had a tantrum because of something his supervisor said and he may also have misconceived his problem. But at any rate, they are quite different as explanations. One is concerned with what happened as a sequence of events and goes in terms of the subject-matter of one of the empirical sciences that enables us to explain them as events. The other is concerned with what happened as an instance of intelligent activity and goes in terms of the canon of some art or discipline. It is a convenient simplification to say that in the latter case we explain by appealing to "reasons" rather than to "causes."

Furthermore, there is an interesting asymmetry in the way we apply these different types of explanation to the things we say we "do." We may give *reasons* for our successes and also for our failures; for we may employ our methods and skills well or badly according to our mastery of them. But we do not ordinarily cite *causes* or give psychological or other empirically "scientific" explanations of actions and activities except when things go wrong—when performance fails to measure up to intention. When we bring things off nicely, we take the credit for ourselves, accepting full responsibility for what "we did" despite the necessary co-operation of the circumstances. When our projects fail, we usually look first to the circumstances in order to excuse ourselves by the slings and arrows of outrageous fortune; and then, if the necessary empirical conditions for success were admittedly present, we have to admit an error in conception or execution. It is as if success could only have reasons, while causes can be invoked only for failures.

A pair of illustrations will indicate how stubbornly we resist admitting causes for success, either denying the success when the cause cannot be ignored or *vice versa*. A man sneezes on the rifle range, discharges his gun, and hits the bull's-eye. But unless he can keep his secret, this will win him no prize—it was an "accident" to the judges even though the ballistics expert would have found nothing irregular about it. On the other hand, did the "accidental" production of fluorescence (which again was no accident to those who understand what happened) "cause" the discovery of X-rays? I do not think it mere human vanity that makes us insist that it did not. We explain that discovery by the intellectual reasons why Wilhelm Röntgen perceived the significance of that phenomenon, and why he set out to discover what had made it that way, although we may concede that it was lucky that the accident occurred in the laboratory of so sagacious a man. I conclude from this that we ask and answer questions in terms of the causes of a process only to the degree that we do not regard what happened as an act, and that when we ask questions about intelligent achievements, answers framed in terms of phenomenal processes and their causes are at best only indirectly relevant.

Now consider these common questions: Why do you believe that? What makes you think so? Each one, in the asking, refuses to acknowledge truth, which would here be the relevant form of success. Each further suggests, if I do not read too much into these everyday expressions, that some cause or influence that is not quite appropriate to the problem at hand may have intervened to affect your thinking. The effect—your belief, the way you think—is taken as a phenomenon that can be explained by other psychological phenomena. It may have been something you ate, or an eruption of your impetuous and passionate nature. The connotations of both questions, then, are a bit insulting, suggesting that you are not in charge of your own thinking. They invoke a context in which the Freudian slip, the bias of your class, and similar bits of the psychopathology of everyday life are accepted as explaining and perhaps also as excusing your ineptitudes of thought and opinion.

But as the late John Austin observed (in his famous essay on "Other Minds"), we do not naturally substitute other verbs in these questions and ask, "Why do you know?" or "What makes you (causes you to) understand?" Instead, we ask *how* you know, how you understand the situation, and how you discovered the proof of that theorem. Each of these questions, in contrast to "What makes you think so?" and "Why do you believe that?" at least presumes the presence of knowledge or understanding and goes on to ask for the methods by which it was achieved or the grounds on which it may be certified. You know it by its colour; he proved the theorem by making this construction; I understand his condition as being a case of vitamin deficiency. Where "causes" are mentioned, such as the vitamin deficiency of the last example, they are not causes of the *knowledge* or understanding, but rather causes of the condition that needed explaining, of the thing known or understood. I understand it *by* its cause, which is not the cause *of* my understanding.

Finally, we do indeed ask "why" questions as well as "how" questions in cases where knowledge is conceded, but in doing so we ask about what is known, not about the knowledge. That is, we do not ask why someone knows, but why something is the case. These questions are about the subject matter of the problem we are concerned with, not about inquiry as an activity or about knowledge as an achievement. Why do projectiles follow a parabolic path? Because the distance of their fall toward the earth increases as the square of the time, whereas their travel along the axis of projection is a simple function of time. That is why it is so. How do I know it? By the experiments of Galileo, which I can repeat, and by the nature of the conic sections, which I can demonstrate for you. None of these why's or how's have anything to do with the psychology, history, or other circumstances of a knower. These have all dropped out of the picture, and what we have left is the canon by which we relate data to problem and premises to conclusion in a particular science.

Let me now collect these threads of argument and come to a preliminary conclusion. The intellectual activities of inquiry, the achievements of understanding, the powers of explanation and demonstration, that together make up the complex of practices that we call science, are all defined by and owe their existence to their characteristic aims and methods, their special standards and subject matters. The point of all of them is to be right in the appropriate respect, to get to the truth; and the criteria of being right are independent of anyone's state of mind or train of thought. They are in no way subverted if it happens that no one quite succeeds in living up to the demands of the science he professes.

At the same time every human activity, including those guided by a more or less clear conception of what science is, is a phenomenon of nature with all the empirical conditions science has so far identified as well as others without number that we have as yet no inkling of. And so every thought, whether true or false, *a propos* or "far out," is, as a psychological fact, explicable in the same way as any other. Their explanations as events give no clue to their truth or relevance. It is not *qua* truth, but only *qua* a state of mind, that truth has psychological causes. This is why, when we achieve truth and can certify the achievement, it does not occur to us to ask for its particular empirical conditions.

By way of illustration, consider my tape recorder, to which I have given a long, abstruse lecture. It profits so well from my "instruction" that it can answer any question about what I said with complete accuracy, if without much originality of expression. Then one day it says something false. Where I had told it that saying what is true is not the same as knowledge, it now says the contradictory, hesitating guiltily at the point where I had said "not," thus: "saying what is true is, uh, the same as knowledge." A little inspection discloses the trouble. A quarter-inch of tape had been erased, perhaps when I had caught my nephew fiddling with the switches. It was a simple thing to splice in a new "not," restoring its capacity to answer without mistakes.

I presume that whatever my recorder says, it is at every point behaving according to the conditions of its nature and the "information" on its tape. Whatever it says has a determinate explanation in terms of those conditions, but the difference between the true and the false has nothing to do with the conditions of sound production. Only when the true is independently discriminated from the false does it become possible to explain, in addition to the sounds, the so-called truths and errors of my machine. This simple model shows, then, how the determination of truth is independent of the correctnesses of utterance and is logically prior to them. Correct utterance is not knowledge, and meaningful reference is not a matter of fact concerning a relation between sounds or signs and other things. The recorder neither "knows" anything nor "says" anything, though I use it to reproduce what *I* say and know.

Consider next the illustrious calculating horse who, when asked to do simple sums, gave correct answers by pawing the floor the requisite number of times. He had been conditioned to respond to certain sensible cues, of which his trainer was in fact unaware. Whether he was taught to give answers that were true or false was all the same to the horse, and equally explicable in terms of the stimuli to which he responded. "Five" would have been the answer to "two plus two" if it had produced the rewarding lump of sugar. The horse, then, had no knowledge of arithmetic, and the truth or falsehood of his responses was a matter of the prior knowledge of the spectators and their capacity to interpret his pawings as signifying numbers.

Consider finally the student who is shrewd enough to know that success in school is measured by grades, which in turn depend—since his is a progressive school —on his ability to score on "objective" tests. By long practice he has at least qualified for the degree of S.T.T. (sophisticated test taker) and he has also studied his instructors very astutely. Result: a high incidence of correct answers, high grades rewarded by princely scholarships, and a good start in "life" as well. How does he differ from the horse?

For one thing, we might credit him with more intelligence. Highly motivated and self-determined within the limits of his narrow interests, he is really the master of an art. He knows how to play a prevalent academic game. His behaviour is not to be explained as the tape recorder's and, to a lesser degree, the horse's was, as the predetermined outcome of given conditions, since he adapts himself to shifting circumstances so as to achieve the objective of his special craft. Here we have, for the first time in these examples, the work of intelligence upon a problem, which is to achieve a goal of its own conceiving.

But there is a very important qualification: his intelligence is only that of a test-taker, and the grounds on which he selects the correct answers are entirely irrelevant to what those answers are about and therefore to the disciplines to which, as truths, they belong. *His* reasons have to do instead with the way multiple-choice questions are constructed, with the frequency of certain signs of acceptability in the true-false questions, and a perception of the sympathies of his instructors. These give no warrant for saying that he knows or understands even the rudiments of what he is certified as having "learned." His answers, then, have not succeeded in being right (although they may also be the right answers) unless he knows what makes them so—that is, unless he knows what they are about instead of knowing such useful things about them as their standing in his teachers' esteem. If he is to be right in a way that is significantly different from the horse, who had also learned to please his masters, he must be able to use the canons of the substantive disciplines as well as the precepts of his private art of answering.

The upshot of my argument, and of these examples of "correctness," is that all talk of truth (or even of art) would be utterly *pointless* if there were nothing to it but causal influences that induced me to say or think *this*, while causing you to opine *that*—nor indeed would it make any sense to talk of thinking or opining, which involve reference both to an object and to an objective, which is thinking what is in fact the case. I suspect that insufficient appreciation of this point is one reason why historical studies in the humanities are so often trivial. Too many scholars spend too much time at the dismal pastime of spotting "influences," such as the books an author may have read, instead of looking to the artistic principles by which his active intelligence had made something wonderful from the available materials. In this they are false to the genius of their craft as well as missing the genius of their subjects, for *Hamlet's* peculiar excellence owes nothing to the tale from which Shakespeare borrowed his story.

III

I am now all finished except for the summing up. Someone who wished to play at influence spotting with this essay might conclude correctly that I have been mainly occupied with ringing changes on the following proposition: while everything in nature happens according to rules, the activities characteristic of intelligence are aimed at being in accord with the conception of a rule. Sometimes the rule whose conception we follow is subordinated to an end apart from it; sometimes the end of action is simply to act as the rule prescribes. To think truly, for example, just *is* to think according to the canon of the appropriate science; while the rules of the test-taker's art are for the sake of high marks, by whatever standards the papers may be graded.

From this it follows that certain common characteristics and distinctions apply to all the works of intelligence acting according to rules it conceives for itself. For one thing, the fundamental rules cannot be empirical, although subordinate ones may. Thus the principles of logic are in no way empirical; for they constitute a canon prescribing how we ought to speak and think, whether we ever succeed in doing so or not. But logic may have empirical appendices, explaining why, as a matter of fact, we are often misled and why our failures tend to be of certain kinds. Given the canonical laws of logic, the empirical supplement yields useful rules for avoiding the chief sources of error; but it can never be the source of principles. Notice now that these distinctions apply similarly in moral philosophy. The principles of morals owe nothing to the facts of behaviour, for they too constitute a canon prescribing how we ought to act. But like logic in being corrupted by the introduction of empirical principles, ethics is also like logic in having its helpful empirical supplement, which notes the conditions under which what ought to happen frequently does not and indicates how we may take advantage of circumstances in order to avoid obstacles and exploit opportunities for the realization of what ought to be.

Further parallels extend to the different kinds of principles that, in ethics, have been recognized as imperatives. The principles of rhetoric are rules of skill as much as those of tailoring, though the materials of the former are entirely discursive in contrast to the materials of the needle trades; and the only reason for following the precepts of either would be an interest in their results. The principles of both, then, are hypothetical imperatives, as are those of the art of test-taking. This we saw to be especially interesting because it so easily counterfeits learning, its point being to give scientific responses on non-scientific grounds. As such, it has its everyday moral parallel in the calculated avoidance of jail or censure by doing what is right for nonmoral or even immoral reasons.

Furthermore, the theoretic use of intelligence has its categorical imperatives just as ethics does. Why should I care about the truth? There is no relevant reason, if by "reason" one means an ulterior motive different from the regard for truth itself; and the question, "Why should I be rational, or respect the canons of truth?" is an inane as "Why should I be moral, or respect the moral law?" Why indeed? If you have to ask, there is no answer that you would understand; yet since you do ask, I presume that you want a true answer, so your question must be disingenuous.

Finally, with regard to deliberate falsehood, theoretic and moral imperatives seem to be indistinguishable. To believe what one knows to be false is a contradiction. To fob off on others what one cannot accept himself is as inconsistent with the interests of knowledge as it is with those of justice, quite apart from any harm that may be done.

We have come to the point where we can see, in the words of a great philosopher, that "ultimately it can be only one and the same reason, which had to be distinguished merely in its applications." I have been arguing all along in support of his point that "we cannot possibly conceive a reason that consciously receives a bias in its judgments from any quarter, for then one would ascribe the determination of judgment not to one's own reason but to an impulse. Reason must then regard itself as the author of its principles . . . ." Correctness which is not self-determined is not truth; just as legality without autonomy is without virtue.

The autonomy of intelligence, or of "reason" as we used to call it, is thus the keystone of the whole edifice. What then does truth owe to freedom? Why, everything, of course!

CHAPTER 10

HOW TO DERIVE "OUGHT" FROM "IS"[1]

JOHN R. SEARLE[*]

••••➤◉◄••••

I

IT is often said that one cannot derive an "ought" from an "is." This thesis, which comes from a famous passage in Hume's *Treatise,* while not as clear as it might be, is at least clear in broad outline: there is a class of statements of fact which is logically distinct from a class of statements of value. No set of statements of fact by themselves entails any statement of value. Put in more contemporary terminology, no set of *descriptive* statements can entail an *evaluative* statement without the addition of at least one evaluative premise. To believe otherwise is to commit what has been called the naturalistic fallacy.

I shall attempt to demonstrate a counterexample to this thesis.[2] It is not of course to be supposed that a single counterexample can refute a philosophical thesis, but in the present instance if we can present a plausible

[*] John R. Searle is Professor of Philosophy at the University of California at Berkeley. This essay first appeared in *The Philosophical Review,* Vol. 73, No. 1 (January 1964), and is printed here by permission of the editors and the author.

[1] Earlier versions of this paper were read before the Stanford Philosophy Colloquium and the Pacific Division of the American Philosophical Association. I am indebted to many people for helpful comments and criticisms, especially Hans Herzberger, Arnold Kaufmann, Benson Mates, A. I. Melden, and Dagmar Searle.

[2] In its modern version. I shall not be concerned with Hume's treatment of the problem.

counterexample and can in addition give some account or explanation of how and why it is a counterexample, and if we can further offer a theory to back up our counterexample—a theory which will generate an indefinite number of counterexamples—we may at the very least cast considerable light on the original thesis; and possibly, if we can do all these things, we may even incline ourselves to the view that the scope of that thesis was more restricted than we had originally supposed. A counterexample must proceed by taking a statement or statements which any proponent of the thesis would grant were purely factual or "descriptive" (they need not actually contain the word "is") and show how they are logically related to a statement which a proponent of the thesis would regard as clearly "evaluative." (In the present instance it will contain an "ought.")[3]

Consider the following series of statements:

(1) Jones uttered the words "I hereby promise to pay you, Smith, five dollars."

(2) Jones promised to pay Smith five dollars.

(3) Jones placed himself under (undertook) an obligation to pay Smith five dollars.

(4) Jones is under an obligation to pay Smith five dollars.

(5) Jones ought to pay Smith five dollars.

I shall argue concerning this list that the relation between any statement and its successor, while not in every case one of "entailment," is nonetheless not just a contingent relation; and the additional statements necessary to make the relationship one of entailment do not need to involve any evaluative statements, moral principles, or anything of the sort.

[3] If this enterprise succeeds, we shall have bridged the gap between "evaluative" and "descriptive" and consequently have demonstrated a weakness in this very terminology. At present, however, my strategy is to play along with the terminology, pretending that the notions of evaluative and descriptive are fairly clear. At the end of the paper I shall state in what respects I think they embody a muddle.

Let us begin. How is (1) related to (2)? In certain circumstances, uttering the words in quotation marks in (1) is the act of making a promise. And it is a part of or a consequence of the meaning of the words in (1) that in those circumstances uttering them is promising. "I hereby promise" is a paradigm device in English for performing the act described in (2), promising.

Let us state this fact about English usage in the form of an extra premise:

(1a) Under certain conditions *C* anyone who utters the words (sentence) "I hereby promise to pay you, Smith, five dollars" promises to pay Smith five dollars.

What sorts of things are involved under the rubric "conditions *C*"? What is involved will be all those conditions, those states of affairs, which are necessary and sufficient conditions for the utterance of the words (sentence) to constitute the successful performance of the act of promising. The conditions will include such things as that the speaker is in the presence of the hearer Smith, they are both conscious, both speakers of English, speaking seriously. The speaker knows what he is doing, is not under the influence of drugs, not hypnotized or acting in a play, not telling a joke or reporting an event, and so forth. This list will no doubt be somewhat indefinite because the boundaries of the concept of a promise, like the boundaries of most concepts in a natural language, are a bit loose.[4] But one thing is clear; however loose the boundaries may be, and however difficult it may be to decide marginal cases, the conditions under which a man who utters "I hereby promise" can correctly be said to have made a promise are straightforwardly empirical conditions.

---

[4] In addition the concept of a promise is a member of a class of concepts which suffer from looseness of a peculiar kind, viz. defeasibility. Cf. H. L. A. Hart, "The Ascription of Responsibility and Rights," *Logic and Language*, First Series, ed. by A. Flew (Oxford, 1951).

So let us add as an extra premise the empirical assumption that these conditions obtain.

(1b) Conditions *C* obtain.

From (1), (1a), and (1b) we derive (2). The argument is of the form: If *C* then (if *U* then *P*): *C* for conditions, *U* for utterance, *P* for promise. Adding the premises *U* and *C* to this hypothetical we derive (2). And as far as I can see, no moral premises are lurking in the logical woodpile. More needs to be said about the relation of (1) to (2), but I reserve that for later.

What is the relation between (2) and (3)? I take it that promising is, by definition, an act of placing oneself under an obligation. No analysis of the concept of promising will be complete which does not include the feature of the promiser placing himself under or undertaking or accepting or recognizing an obligation to the promisee, to perform some future course of action, normally for the benefit of the promisee. One may be tempted to think that promising can be analyzed in terms of creating expectations in one's hearers, or some such, but a little reflection will show that the crucial distinction between statements of intention on the one hand and promises on the other lies in the nature and degree of commitment or obligation undertaken in promising.

I am therefore inclined to say that (2) entails (3) straight off, but I can have no objection if anyone wishes to add—for the purpose of formal neatness—the tautological premise:

(2a) All promises are acts of placing oneself under (undertaking) an obligation to do the thing promised.

How is (3) related to (4)? If one has placed oneself under an obligation, then, other things being equal, one is under an obligation. That I take it also is a tautology. Of course it is possible for all sorts of things to happen which will release one from obligations one has undertaken and hence the need for the *ceteris paribus* rider. To get an entailment between (3) and (4) we therefore need a qualifying statement to the effect that:

(3a) Other things are equal.

Formalists, as in the move from (2) to (3), may wish to add the tautological premise:

(3b) All those who place themselves under an obligation are, other things being equal, under an obligation.

The move from (3) to (4) is thus of the same form as the move from (1) to (2): If E then (if PUO then UO): E for other things are equal, PUO for place under obligation and UO for under obligation. Adding the two premises E and PUO we derive UO.

Is (3a), the *ceteris paribus* clause, a concealed evaluative premise? It certainly looks as if it might be, especially in the formulation I have given it, but I think we can show that, though questions about whether other things are equal frequently involve evaluative considerations, it is not logically necessary that they should in every case. I shall postpone discussion of this until after the next step.

What is the relation between (4) and (5)? Analogous to the tautology which explicates the relation of (3) and (4) there is here the tautology that, other things being equal, one ought to do what one is under an obligation to do. And here, just as in the previous case, we need some premise of the form:

(4a) Other things are equal.

We need the *ceteris paribus* clause to eliminate the possibility that something extraneous to the relation of "obligation" to "ought" might interfere.[5] Here, as in the previous two steps, we eliminate the appearance of enthymeme by pointing out that the apparently suppressed premise is tautological and hence, though

[5] The *ceteris paribus* clause in this step excludes somewhat different sorts of cases from those excluded in the previous step. In general we say, "He undertook an obligation, but nonetheless he is not (now) under an obligation" when the obligation has been *removed*, e.g., if the promisee says, "I release you from your obligation." But we say, "He is under an obligation, but nonetheless ought not to fulfill it" in cases where the obligation is *overridden* by some other considerations, e.g., a prior obligation.

formally neat, it is redundant. If, however, we wish to state it formally, this argument is of the same form as the move from (3) to (4): If E then (if UO then O); E for other things are equal, UO for under obligation, O for ought. Adding the premises E and UO we derive O.

Now a word about the phrase "other things being equal" and how it functions in my attempted derivation. This topic and the closely related topic of defeasibility are extremely difficult and I shall not try to do more than justify my claim that the satisfaction of the condition does not necessarily involve anything evaluative. The force of the expression "other things being equal" in the present instance is roughly this. Unless we have some reason (that is, unless we are actually prepared to give some reason) for supposing the obligation is void (step 4) or the agent ought not to keep the promise (step 5), then the obligation holds and he ought to keep the promise. It is not part of the force of the phrase "other things being equal" that in order to satisfy it we need to establish a universal negative proposition to the effect that no reason could ever be given by anyone for supposing the agent is not under an obligation or ought not to keep the promise. That would be impossible and would render the phrase useless. It is sufficient to satisfy the condition that no reason to the contrary can in fact be given.

If a reason is given for supposing the obligation is void or that the promiser ought not to keep a promise, then characteristically a situation calling for an evaluation arises. Suppose, for example, we consider a promised act wrong, but we grant that the promiser did undertake an obligation. Ought he to keep the promise? There is no established procedure for objectively deciding such cases in advance, and an evaluation (if that is really the right word) is in order. But unless we have some reason to the contrary, the *ceteris paribus* condition is satisfied, no evaluation is necessary, and the question whether he ought to do it is settled by saying "he promised." It is always an open possibility that we may have to make an evaluation in order to derive "he ought" from "he promised," for we may have to evaluate a counterargument. But an evaluation is not logically necessary in every case, for there may as a matter of fact be no counterarguments. I am therefore inclined to think that there is nothing necessarily evaluative about the *ceteris paribus* condition, even though deciding whether it is satisfied will frequently involve evaluations.

But suppose I am wrong about this: would that salvage the belief in an unbridgeable logical gulf between "is" and "ought"? I think not, for we can always rewrite my steps (4) and (5) so that they include the *ceteris paribus* clause as part of the conclusion. Thus from our premises we would then have derived "Other things being equal Jones ought to pay Smith five dollars," and that would still be sufficient to refute the tradition, for we would still have shown a relation of entailment between descriptive and evaluative statements. It was not the fact that extenuating circumstances can void obligations that drove philosophers to the naturalistic fallacy fallacy; it was rather a theory of language, as we shall see later on.

We have thus derived (in as strict a sense of "derive" as natural languages will admit of) an "ought" from an "is." And the extra premises which were needed to make the derivation work were in no cause moral or evaluative in nature. They consisted of empirical assumptions, tautologies, and descriptions of word usage. It must be pointed out also that the "ought" is a "categorical" not a "hypothetical" ought. (5) does not say that Jones ought to pay up if he wants such and such. It says he ought to pay up, period. Note also that the steps of the derivation are carried on in the third person. We are not concluding "I ought" from "I said 'I promise,'" but "he ought" from "he said 'I promise.'"

The proof unfolds the connection between the utterance of certain words and the speech act of promising and then in turn unfolds promising into obligation and moves from obligation to "ought." The step from (1) to (2) is radically different from the others and requires special comment. In (1) we construe "I hereby promise . . ." as an English phrase having a certain meaning. It is a consequence of that meaning that the utterance of that phrase under certain conditions is the act of promising. Thus by presenting the quoted expressions in (1) and by describing their use in (1a) we have as it were already invoked the institution of promising. We might have started with an even more groundfloor premise than (1) by saying:

(1b) Jones uttered the phonetic sequence: /ai⁺ hirbai+pramis+təpei+yu+smiθ+faiv+daIərz/

We would then have needed extra empirical premises stating that this phonetic sequence was associated in certain ways with certain meaningful units relative to certain dialects.

The moves from (2) to (5) are relatively easy. We rely on definitional connections between "promise," "obligate," and "ought," and the only problem which arises is that obligations can be overridden or removed in a variety of ways and we need to take account of that fact. We solve our difficulty by adding further premises to the effect that there are no contrary considerations, that other things are equal.

II

In this section I intend to discuss three possible objections to the derivation.

First Objection

Since the first premise is descriptive and the conclusion evaluative, there must be a concealed evaluative premise in the description of the conditions in (1b).

So far, this argument merely begs the question by assuming the logical gulf between descriptive and evaluative which the derivation is designed to challenge. To make the objection stick, the defender of the distinction would have to show how exactly (1b) must contain an evaluative premise and what sort of premise it might be. Uttering certain words in certain conditions just *is* promising and the description of these conditions needs no evaluative element. The essential thing is that in the transition from (1) to (2) we move from the specification of a certain utterance of words to the specification of a certain speech act. The move is achieved because the speech act is a conventional act; and the utterance of the words, according to the conventions, constitutes the performance of just that speech act.

A variant of this first objection is to say: all you have shown is that "promise" is an evaluative, not a descriptive, concept. But this objection again begs the question and in the end will prove disastrous to the original distinction between descriptive and evaluative. For that a man uttered certain words and that these words have the meaning they do are surely objective facts. And if the statement of these two objective facts plus a description of the conditions of the utterance is sufficient to entail the statement (2) which the objector alleges to be an evaluative statement (Jones promised to pay Smith five dollars), then an evaluative conclusion is derived from descriptive premises without even going through steps (3), (4), and (5).

Second Objection

Ultimately the derivation rests on the principle that one ought to keep one's promises and that is a moral principle, hence evaluative.

I don't know whether "one ought to keep one's promises" is a "moral" principle, but whether or not it is, it is also tautological; for it is nothing more than a derivation from the two tautologies:

All promises are (create, are undertakings of, are acceptances of) obligations,

and

One ought to keep (fulfill) one's obligations.

What needs to be explained is why so many philosophers have failed to see the tautological character of this principle. Three things I think have concealed its character from them.

The first is a failure to distinguish external questions about the institution of promising from internal questions asked within the framework of the institution. The questions "Why do we have such an institution as promising?" and "Ought we to have such institutionalized forms of obligation as promising?" are external questions asked about and not within the institution of promising. And the question "Ought one to keep one's promises?" can be confused with or can be taken as (and I think has often been taken as) an external question roughly expressible as "Ought one to accept the institution of promising?" But taken literally, as an internal question, as a question about promises and not about the institution of promising, the question "Ought one to keep one's promises?" is as empty as the question "Are triangles three-sided?" To recognize something as a promise is to grant that, other things being equal, it ought to be kept.

A second fact which has clouded the issue is this. There are many situations, both real and imaginable, where one ought not to keep a promise, where the obligation to keep a promise is overridden by some further considerations, and it was for this reason that we needed those clumsy *ceteris paribus* clauses in our derivation. But the fact that obligations can be overridden does not show that there were no obligations in the first place. On the contrary. And these original obligations are all that is needed to make the proof work.

Yet a third factor is the following. Many philosophers still fail to realize the full force of saying that "I hereby promise" is a performative expression. In uttering it one performs but does not describe the act of promising. Once promising is seen as a speech act of a kind different from describing, then it is easier to see that one of the features of the act is the undertaking of an obligation. But if one thinks the utterance of "I promise" or "I hereby promise" is a peculiar kind of description—for example, of one's mental state— then the relation between promising and obligation is going to seem very mysterious.

Third Objection

The derivation uses only a factual or inverted-commas sense of the evaluative terms employed. For example, an anthropologist observing the behavior and attitudes of the Anglo-Saxons might well go through these derivations, but nothing evaluative would be included. Thus step (2) is equivalent to "He did what they call promising" and step (5) to "According to them he ought to pay Smith five dollars." But since all of the steps (2) to (5) are in *oratio obliqua* and hence disguised statements of fact, the fact-value distinction remains unaffected.

This objection fails to damage the derivation, for what it says is only that the steps *can* be reconstrued as in *oratio obliqua,* that we can construe them as a series of external statements, that we can construct a parallel (or at any rate related) proof about reported speech. But what I am arguing is that, taken quite literally, without any *oratio obliqua* additions or interpretations, the derivation is valid. That one can construct a similar argument which would fail to refute the fact-value distinction does not show that this proof fails to refute it. Indeed it is irrelevant.

III

So far I have presented a counterexample to the thesis that one cannot derive an "ought" from an "is" and considered three possible objections to it. Even supposing what I have said so far is true, still one feels a certain uneasiness. One feels there must be some trick involved somewhere. We might state our uneasiness thus: How can my granting a mere fact about a man, such as the fact that he uttered certain words or that he made a promise, commit *me* to the view that *he* ought to do something? I now want briefly to discuss what broader philosophic significance my attempted derivation may have, in such a way as to give us the outlines of an answer to this question.

I shall begin by discussing the grounds for supposing that it cannot be answered at all.

The inclination to accept a rigid distinction between "is" and "ought," between descriptive and evaluative, rests on a certain picture of the way words relate to the world. It is a very attractive picture, so attractive (to me at least) that it is not entirely clear to what extent the mere presentation of counterexamples can challenge it. What is needed is an explanation of how and why this classical empiricist picture fails to deal with such counterexamples. Briefly, the picture is constructed something like this: first we present examples of so-called descriptive statements ("my car goes eighty miles an hour," "Jones is six feet tall," "Smith has brown hair"), and we contrast them with so-called evaluative statements ("my car is a good car," "Jones ought to pay Smith five dollars," "Smith is a nasty man"). Anyone can see that they are different. We articulate the difference by pointing out that for the descriptive statements the question of truth or falsity is objectively decidable, because to know the meaning of the descriptive expressions is to know under what objectively ascertainable conditions the statements which contain them are true or false. But in the case of evaluative statements the situation is quite different. To know the meaning of the evaluative expressions is not by itself sufficient for knowing under what conditions the statements containing them are true or false, because the meaning of the expressions is such that the statements are not capable of objective or factual truth or falsity at all. Any justification a speaker can give of one of his evaluative statements essentially involves some appeal to attitudes he holds, to criteria of assessment he has adopted, or to moral principles by which he has chosen to live and judge other people. Descriptive statements are thus objective, evaluative statements subjective, and the difference is a consequence of the different sorts of terms employed.

The underlying reason for these differences is that evaluative statements perform a completely different job from descriptive statements. Their job is not to describe any features of the world but to express the speaker's emotions, to express his attitudes, to praise or condemn, to laud or insult, to commend, to recommend, to advise, and so forth. Once we see the different jobs the two perform, we see that there must be a logical gulf between them. Evaluative statements must be different from descriptive statements in order to do their job, for if they were objective they could no longer function to evaluate. Put metaphysically, values cannot lie in the world, for if they did they would cease to be values and would just be another part of the world. Put in the formal mode, one cannot define an evaluative word in terms of descriptive words, for if one did, one would no longer be able to use the evaluative word to commend, but only to describe. Put yet another way, any effort to derive an "ought" from an "is" must be a waste of time, for all it could show even if it succeeded would be that the "is" was not a real "is" but only a disguised "ought" or, alternatively, that the "ought" was not a real "ought" but only a disguised "is."

This summary of the traditional empirical view has been very brief, but I hope it conveys something of the power of this picture. In the hands of certain modern authors, especially Hare and Nowell-Smith, the picture attains considerable subtlety and sophistication.

What is wrong with this picture? No doubt many things are wrong with it. In the end I am going to say that one of the things wrong with it is that it fails to give us any coherent account of such notions as commitment, responsibility, and obligation.

In order to work toward this conclusion I can begin by saying that the picture fails to account for the *different types* of "descriptive" statements. Its paradigms of descriptive statements are such utterances as "my car goes eighty miles an hour," "Jones is six feet tall," "Smith has brown hair," and the like. But it is forced by its own rigidity to construe "Jones got married," "Smith made a promise," "Jackson has five dollars," and "Brown hit a home run" as descriptive statements as well. It is so forced, because whether or not someone got married, made a promise, has five dollars, or hit a home run is as much a matter of objective fact as whether he has red hair or brown eyes. Yet the former kind of statement (statements containing "married," "promise," and so forth) seem to be quite different from the simple empirical paradigms of descriptive statements. How are they different? Though both kinds of statements state matters of objective fact, the statements containing words such as "married," "promise," "home run," and "five dollars" state facts whose existence presupposes certain institutions: a man has five dollars, given the institution of money. Take away the institution and all he has is a rectangular bit of paper with green ink on it. A man hits a home run only given the institution of baseball; without the institution he only hits a sphere with a stick. Similarly, a man gets married or makes a promise only within the institutions of marriage and promising. Without them, all he does is utter words or makes gestures. We might characterize such facts as institutional facts, and contrast them with noninstitutional, or brute, facts: that a man has a bit of paper with green ink on it is a brute fact, that he has five dollars is an institutional fact.[6] The classical picture fails to account for the differences between statements of brute fact and statements of institutional fact.

The word "institution" sounds artificial here, so let us ask: what sorts of institutions are these? In order to

[6] For a discussion of this distinction see G. E. M. Anscombe, "Brute Facts," *Analysis* (1958).

answer that question I need to distinguish between two different kinds of rules or conventions. Some rules regulate antecedently existing forms of behavior. For example, the rules of polite table behavior regulate eating, but eating exists independently of these rules. Some rules, on the other hand, do not merely regulate but create or define new forms of behavior: the rules of chess, for example, do not merely regulate an antecedently existing activity called playing chess; they, as it were, create the possibility of or define that activity. The activity of playing chess is constituted by action in accordance with these rules. Chess has no existence apart from these rules. The distinction I am trying to make was foreshadowed by Kant's distinction between regulative and constitutive principles, so let us adopt his terminology and describe our distinction as a distinction between regulative and constitutive rules. Regulative rules regulate activities whose existence is independent of the rules; constitutive rules constitute (and also regulate) forms of activity whose existence is logically dependent on the rules.[7]

Now the institutions that I have been talking about are systems of constitutive rules. The institutions of marriage, money, and promising are like the institutions of baseball or chess in that they are systems of such constitutive rules or conventions. What I have called institutional facts are facts which presuppose such institutions.

Once we recognize the existence of and begin to grasp the nature of such institutional facts, it is but a short step to see that many forms of obligations, commitments, rights, and responsibilities are similarly institutionalized. It is often a matter of fact that one has certain obligations, commitments, rights, and responsibilities, but it is a matter of institutional, not brute, fact. It is one such institutionalized form of obligation, promising, which I invoked above to derive

---

[7] For a discussion of a related distinction see J. Rawls, "Two Concepts of Rules," *Philosophical Review*, LXIV (1955).

an "ought" from an "is." I started with a brute fact, that a man uttered certain words, and then invoked the institution in such a way as to generate institutional facts by which we arrived at the institutional fact that the man ought to pay another man five dollars. The whole proof rests on an appeal to the constitutive rule that to make a promise is to undertake an obligation.

We are now in a position to see how we can generate an indefinite number of such proofs. Consider the following vastly different example. We are in our half of the seventh inning and I have a big lead off second base. The pitcher whirls, fires to the shortstop covering, and I am tagged out a good ten feet down the line. The umpire shouts, "Out!" I, however, being a positivist, hold my ground. The umpire tells me to return to the dugout. I point out to him that you can't derive an "ought" from an "is." No set of descriptive statements describing matters of fact, I say, will entail any evaluative statements to the effect that I should or ought to leave the field. "You just can't get orders or recommendations from facts alone." What is needed is an evaluative major premise. I therefore return to and stay on second base (until I am carried off the field). I think everyone feels my claims here to be preposterous, and preposterous in the sense of logically absurd. Of course you can derive an "ought" from an "is," and though to actually set out the derivation in this case would be vastly more complicated than in the case of promising, it is in principle no different. By undertaking to play baseball I have committed myself to the observation of certain constitutive rules.

We are now also in a position to see that the tautology that one ought to keep one's promises is only one of a class of similar tautologies concerning institutionalized forms of obligation. For example, "one ought not to steal" can be taken as saying that to recognize something as someone else's property necessarily involves recognizing his right to dispose of it. This is a constitutive rule of the institution of private property.[8] "One ought not to tell lies" can be taken as saying that to make an assertion necessarily involves undertaking an obligation to speak truthfully. Another constitutive rule. "One ought to pay one's debts" can be construed as saying that to recognize something as a debt is necessarily to recognize an obligation to pay it. It is easy to see how all these principles will generate counterexamples to the thesis that you cannot derive an "ought" from an "is."

My tentative conclusions, then, are as follows:

1. The classical picture fails to account for institutional facts.

2. Institutional facts exist within systems of constitutive rules.

3. Some systems of constitutive rules involve obligations, commitments, and responsibilities.

4. Within those systems we can derive "ought's" from "is's" on the model of the first derivation.

With these conclusions we now return to the question with which I began this section: How can my stating a fact about a man, such as the fact that he made a promise, commit me to a view about what he ought to do? One can begin to answer this question by saying that for me to state such an institutional fact is already to invoke the constitutive rules of the institution. It is those rules that give the word "pro-

[8] Proudhon said: "Property is theft." If one tries to take this as an internal remark it makes no sense. It was intended as an external remark attacking and rejecting the institution of private property. It gets its air of paradox and its force by using terms which are internal to the institution in order to attack the institution.

Standing on the deck of some institutions one can tinker with constitutive rules and even throw some other institutions overboard. But could one throw all institutions overboard (in order perhaps to avoid ever having to derive an "ought" from an "is")? One could not and still engage in those forms of behavior we consider characteristically human. Suppose Proudhon had added (and tried to live by): "Truth is a lie, marriage is infidelity, language is uncommunicative, law is a crime," and so on with every possible institution.

mise" its meaning. But those rules are such that to commit myself to the view that Jones made a promise involves committing myself to what he ought to do (other things being equal).

If you like, then, we have shown that "promise" is an evaluative word, but since it is also purely descriptive, we have really shown that the whole distinction needs to be re-examined. The alleged distinction between descriptive and evaluative statements is really a conflation of at least two distinctions. On the one hand there is a distinction between different kinds of speech acts, one family of speech acts including evaluations, another family including descriptions. This is a distinction between different kinds of illocutionary force.[9] On the other hand there is a distinction between utterances which involve claims objectively decidable as true or false and those which involve claims not objectively decidable, but which are "matters of personal decision" or "matters of opinion." It has been assumed that the former distinction is (must be) a special case of the latter, that if something has the illocutionary force of an evaluation, it cannot be entailed by factual premises. Part of the point of my argument is to show that this contention is false, that factual premises can entail evaluative conclusions. If I am right, then the alleged distinction between descriptive and evaluative utterances is useful only as a distinction between two kinds of illocutionary force, describing and evaluating, and it is not even very useful there, since if we are to use these terms strictly, they are only two among hundreds of kinds of illocutionary force; and utterances of sentences of the form (5)—"Jones ought to pay Smith five dollars"—would not characteristically fall in either class.

[9] See J. L. Austin, *How to Do Things with Words* (Cambridge, Mass., 1962), for an explanation of this notion.

CHAPTER 11

HE COULD HAVE DONE
OTHERWISE

RODERICK M. CHISHOLM*

SUPPOSE we say to a man, "This morning you could
have arranged things so that you would be in Boston
now but you didn't," meaning thereby that he had it
within his power this morning so to arrange things and
that he did not exercise this power. How is one to
understand this sense of "could" and of "in his power"?

First, I shall note certain things we need *not* be
implying when we thus say of a man that he could
have done otherwise. Secondly, I shall criticize certain
familiar answers to our question. And, thirdly, I shall
attempt to sketch what seems to me to be the proper
way to answer it.

I

When we say, "This morning you could have arranged things so that you would be in Boston now,"
we are not implying that the man was able to do
this at any other time. Conceivably he will have had

* Roderick M. Chisholm is a member of the Brown University Philosophy Department. His article was originally
published in the *Journal of Philosophy*, Vol. 64, No. 13
(July 6, 1967), and is printed here, with some minor
revisions by the author, by permission of the editor and
the author.

[1] Revised by the author.

only one opportunity in his life to arrange things so that he would be in Boston now, or even to arrange things so that he would ever be in Boston. And so we are not predicating of him a "general ability" to get to Boston, as one might, say, in the case of a lady who lives in Newton.

We are not implying that he *knew how* to exercise this power effectively. For we could consistently add: "What a pity you didn't know you should have traveled toward the east, for had you done so you would be in Boston now." (In this case, he may have known that he had the power without having known how to exercise it. For he may have known that he could travel in any direction and that one of them was such that if he were to travel in that direction then he would be in Boston now; but he may not have known which direction it was.)

Nor are we implying that he *knew that* he had the power. For "He could have" does not imply that he knew that he could have. When we say, "You could have arranged things so that you would be in Boston now," we may add, quite consistently: "And what a pity that you had no idea at the time that you could have." (In this case, although we can say "You could have," we cannot say "You could have if you had chosen." The latter statement, as Kurt Baier points out, would be true only if the agent's success would be due to his "skill, know-how, or practical knowledge, and not to luck."[2] But we can say to the man who didn't realize that getting to Boston had been in his power: "There were things such that, if you had chosen to bring *them* about, then you would be in Boston now.") It would not be entirely wrong to say that *most* of the things that are within our agent's power are things he knows nothing whatever about.

Nor does "He could have," in the present sense of the expression, imply that the act in question was in any sense morally or legally *permissible*. For having

---

[2] Compare Kurt Baier, "Could and Would," *Analysis*, XXIII (1961), supplement, pp. 20–29.

said, "You could have arranged things so that you
would be in Boston now," we may add, quite consistently: "And it is a very good thing that you didn't,
since, as you well knew, that was about the worst
thing you could have done this morning." (In this
case, one might *also* say, "This morning you *could not*
have done it," but taking "could" in its moral or legal
sense and not in the sense that now concerns us.)

II

Let us remind ourselves of certain familiar but (so
it seems to me) obviously unsuccessful attempts to
explicate the present sense of "could" and of "within
his power."

Our "could" is not the "could" of logical possibility.
If it were, we could say of the man we are now considering, "This morning he could have arranged things
so that he would now be on the moon," since what
such a statement expresses is something that is logically
possible. But the man *we* are considering could not
have so arranged things this morning.

Nor is our "could" the "could" of epistemic possibility. To say "You could have arranged things so that
you would be in Boston now" is not to say "Your
having arranged things so that you would be in Boston
now is consistent with everything that is known."[3] For
we may truly say that he could so have arranged things
even though we know in fact that he did not so arrange
them. Nor does "You could so have arranged things
this morning" mean the same as "You having arranged
them this morning is consistent with everything that

[3] Hobbes had said that we call propositions contingent
"because we do not yet know whether they be true or
false"; see *De Corpore,* chapter 10. Compare the criticism
of this view, and some of the others noted here, in Richard
Taylor, *Action and Purpose* (Englewood Cliffs, N.J.:
Prentice-Hall, Inc., 1966), ch. iv.

was known this morning." Suppose that, unknown to everyone this morning, the man had been locked in his room, sound asleep, and unable to move. In such a case it would be false to say that he could then have arranged things so that he would be in Boston now; but it might be true to say that his having so arranged them is consistent with everything that was known this morning.

Are we dealing, then, with a "could" that is "constitutionally iffy"? In saying "You could have arranged things this morning so that you would be in Boston now," are we saying: "If you had undertaken (chosen, willed, tried, set out) to bring it about that you are in Boston now, you would have succeeded"? Or, somewhat more plausibly: "There are certain things such that, if this morning you had undertaken (chosen, willed, tried, set out) to bring it about that those things would occur, then you would be in Boston now"? (The second formula is the more plausible because, unlike the first, it is applicable to the man who didn't know this morning that he could then arrange things so that he would be in Boston now.)[4]

Whichever of the two types of "if" statement we choose, there would seem to be things consistent with the "if" statement that are not consistent with our "could" statement. If this is true, the "could" statement cannot have the same meaning as the "if" statement. Consider, for example, those things which are such that, if this morning our agent had undertaken (chosen, willed, tried, set out) to bring them about, then he would be in Boston now. And let us suppose (i) that he *could not* have undertaken (chosen, willed, tried, set out) to bring any of those things about and (ii)

---

[4] There are objections to the first formula that do not apply to the second. Some of these were pointed out by J. L. Austin in "Ifs and Cans"; see his *Philosophical Papers* (Oxford: The Clarendon Press, 1961), esp. p. 166. In "J. L. Austin's Philosophical Papers," *Mind*, LXXIII, 289 (January 1964): 1–26, I noted that certain other objections are applicable to the first formula and are not applicable to the second; see esp. pp. 23–24.

that he would be in Boston now only if he *had* undertaken (chosen, willed, tried, set out) to bring them about. These suppositions are consistent with saying that he *would* be in Boston now *if* he had undertaken those things, but they are not consistent with saying that he *could* then have arranged things so that he would be in Boston now.[5]

Is our "could" the "could" of physical possibility? In saying "You could have done it" are we saying that your having done it is something that is, or was, physically possible? We must distinguish between two senses of the expression "physically possible."[6]

In saying of a certain state of affairs that it is "physically possible," one of the things we might mean is this: that the state of affairs is one such that the statement that it obtains is, by itself, consistent with

---

[5] Presumably it was for reasons such as these that George Washington was said to be unable to tell a lie. The point was, not that he lacked the wit or skill or opportunity to do it, but that he was so good that he couldn't bring himself to deceive. Bayle quotes a seventeenth-century Walloon theologian, one de Wolzogue, who pointed out that, although God would have no difficulty in deceiving if he chose to deceive, nonetheless he *cannot* deceive since he *cannot choose* to deceive. De Wolzogue wrote: "God can deceive if he will . . . but it is impossible for him to have such a will to deceive; it is also impossible for him to endeavor to employ his power for the execution of a deceit, whence I conclude that it is impossible for him to deceive." See Pierre Bayle, *A General Dictionary, Historial and Critical*, article "Rimini (Gregorio de)," note C. According to some Christians, an important point of difference between Mary and Jesus was that, while Mary could sin but never did, Jesus "has not merely actually sinned, but also could not sin," the point being, again, that he could not undertake (choose, will, try, set out) to sin. Compare Ludwig Ott, *Fundamentals of Catholic Dogma* (Cork: Mercier Press, 1952), p. 169. Compare St. Thomas's treatment of the question, "Can God Do What Others Do?" in *On the Power of God*, Question II, Article 4.

[6] The two senses of "physically possible" are clearly distinguished by Bruce Aune in the article, "Can," in *The Encyclopedia of Philosophy* (New York: Macmillan and the Free Press, 1967), ed. Paul Edwards, vol. II, pp. 18–20.

the laws of nature. In *this* sense of "physically possible," it is not only physically possible that our man this morning arranged things in such a way that he is in Boston now, but it is also physically possible that he then arranged them in such a way that he is now in a space capsule, orbiting the earth. But although such orbiting is "physically possible" in the sense in question, it is quite certain that, in our present sense of "could," the man we are talking about *could* not so have arranged things this morning that *he* is now thus orbiting the earth.

The other thing we might mean, when we say of a state of affairs that is "physically possible," is this: that no *other* states of affairs have obtained such that it is a law of nature that if such states of affairs obtain then the state of affairs in question does not obtain. Or, more exactly, if we say that it is physically possible, in this sense, for a state of affairs A to obtain at a certain time t, we mean that there have been no earlier states of affairs such that it is a law of nature that, if those earlier states of affairs obtain, then A does not obtain at t. In short, if A is physically possible, in this sense, then there is no sufficient causal condition for not-A. And so if it was physically possible for our agent to do otherwise, in the present sense of "physically possible," then there was no sufficient causal condition of his *not* doing otherwise.

Is our "could" thus one of simple indeterminism? In saying "You could have arranged things so that you would be in Boston now," are we saying merely: "Your *not* being in Boston now has no sufficient causal condition"? It would seem not. For it may well be that, although this morning the man could have arranged things so that he would be in Boston now, he has been in Chelmsford for the past 15 minutes. And this will mean that for the past 15 minutes, if not for considerably longer, there has been a set of conditions constituting a sufficient causal condition for his not being in Boston now.

Could we modify this indeterministic answer by

saying: "Even though for the past 15 minutes there has been a sufficient causal condition for your not being in Boston now, there *was* a time (say, 10 o'clock this morning) when there was *no* sufficient causal condition for your not being in Boston now"? This, too, seems wrong. Suppose that between 9 and 11 o'clock this morning a certain *other* man had it within *his* power, in this present indeterministic sense, to render our agent incapable of moving from the place where he then happened to be and that our agent was incapable of depriving him of this power; and suppose further that at 11 o'clock the other man exercised this power but without there being any sufficient causal condition for his so doing. These suppositions would be consistent with saying to our agent, "At 10 o'clock this morning there was no sufficient causal condition for your not being in Boston now." But they are not consistent with saying "At 10 o'clock this morning you could have arranged things so that you would be in Boston now."

We should remind ourselves, finally, that these indeterministic answers are frequently criticized in still another way. Thus there may be cases of indeterminism that are not cases of ability to do otherwise. Suppose then an atomic particle is so situated that there is a place such that there has been no sufficient causal condition for the particle *not* now being in that place. This fact alone would hardly imply that the particle *could* have made it happen that it is now in a place other than where it is in fact.

III

I shall now describe the type of answer that I shall propose to our question. Then I shall attempt to set it forth more precisely.

I shall assume that the agent himself is a causal factor. In other words, at least one of the events that is involved in any act is caused, not by any other event or set of events, but by the agent, by the man. Causation is thus a relation that holds, not only between states or events, but also between agents, as causes, and states or events, as effects. I shall also assume that the concept of an act is essentially teleological: action involves *endeavor* or *purpose*, one thing occurring *in order that* some other thing may occur. Purpose or endeavor is "intentional" in the philosophical sense of this term; from the fact that one thing occurs in order that some other thing may occur, it does not follow that the other thing does in fact occur.

In attempting to explicate the concept expressed by the words "He could have done otherwise," I shall make use of the intentional concept of *undertaking*, or *endeavoring*. The technical expression "He undertakes (or endeavors to make it happen that . . . will be used to mean, simply, that there is something that the agent makes happen with an end to making it happen that. . . . The blank may be filled by any propositional expression, e.g., "he goes to Boston."[7]

---

[7] I have discussed undertaking, or endeavoring, in greater detail in "Freedom and Action," in Keith Lehrer, ed., *Freedom and Determinism* (New York: Random House, 1966), esp. pp. 30–44. The following is a simplified statement of what I take to be the logic of this notion. We take as undefined, "He makes it happen that . . . in the endeavor to make it happen that . . ." where the blanks may be filled by propositional expressions. We assume with respect to any instance of this locution, i.e., any sentence formed by filling its blanks: (1) it implies "There is a p and a q such that he makes it happen that p in the endeavor to make it happen that q"; (2) it implies the corresponding instance of ". . ."; and (3) it implies the corresponding instance of "He makes it happen that, he makes it happen that . . . in the endeavor to make it happen that . . . in the endeavor to make it happen that. . . ." If we abbreviate "He makes p happen in the endeavor to make q happen" as "$M(p,q)$," we may summarize the third point by saying that "$M(p,q)$" implies "$M[M(p,q),q]$." We define the expression introduced above, viz., "He undertakes to make it happen that . . ." as "There is a p such that he makes p happen in the

The "could" I shall attempt to define will be indeterministic in this respect: our definitions will imply,
in effect, that if our agent had it within his power at
10 o'clock this morning to arrange things so that he
would be in Boston now, then there were certain
things such that at 10 o'clock this morning there was
no sufficient causal condition for his not then *undertaking* those things. (But presumably in the case of the
undetermined subatomic particle, the absence of the
equipment necessary for undertaking or endeavoring
constitutes a sufficient causal condition for *its* not undertaking anything, and our definitions, therefore, will
not apply to it.)

In addition to being thus indeterministic, our
"could" will also be constitutionally iffy. For the definitions will imply that *if* our agent had undertaken
some of the things just referred to, and *if* further conditions, which I shall try to specify, had obtained,
then he *would* be in Boston now.

But what we say must be consistent with the possibility that, for the past fifteen minutes, there has been
a sufficient causal condition for the fact that our agent
has not been in Boston now. To ensure this consistency
I shall attempt to make a technical distinction between
what we may describe as being "directly" in our agent's
power and what we may describe as being "indirectly"
in his power. Thus he may have had it *directly* within
his power at 10 o'clock this morning to take the first
step in a journey toward Boston, but he may have had
it only *indirectly* in his power then to arrange things

---

endeavor to make it happen that . . ." Instances of the
latter expression will not ordinarily imply the corresponding
instances of . . ."; for undertakings are intentional and
may not be successful. But, because of (3), "He undertakes" will imply "He makes it happen that he undertakes" (though not "he undertakes to undertake"). "He
makes it happen that . . ." would be defined as "There
is a *p* such that he makes it happen that . . . in the
endeavor to make it happen that *p*"; and "He intentionally
makes it happen that . . ." would be "He makes it happen
that . . . in the endeavor to make it happen that. . . ."

so that he would be in Boston now. And perhaps, although he then had it directly within his power to take the first step, he had it only indirectly in his power to take the second, and only indirectly in his power to take any of the others. But he may have been so situated that, if he *had* taken the first step, then he *would* have had it directly within his power to take the second, and if he had then taken the second, then he would have had it directly within his power to take the third, and so on, until he stepped into Boston. One could say that the first step "directly enabled" him to take the second (since taking the first put taking the second directly within his power) and that each step, had he continued the journey, would have directly enabled him to take the next.

I shall formulate three preliminary definitions: first a definition of what it is for our agent to be free to undertake a certain action; secondly, a definition of "directly within his power"; and thirdly, a definition of "indirectly within his power." Then we will be able to say that an act is in the agent's power, in the sense that we have been concerned with, just in case it is either directly or indirectly within his power.

IV

Our first definition, then, will be this: (D1) At *t* he is *free to undertake* to make it happen that . . . provided only: there is no sufficient causal condition at *t*, or prior to *t*, either for his undertaking at *t* to make it happen that . . . or for his not undertaking at *t* to make it happen that. . . . In other words, if the agent is free to undertake a certain act, then there is no sufficient causal condition for his undertaking it and there is no sufficient causal condition for his *not* undertaking it.[8]

---

[8] "There is no sufficient causal condition for his not undertaking to make it happen that . . ." would be spelled

The sense of "sufficient causal condition" that is here intended may be suggested by the following. If C is a *sufficient causal condition* for E, then C is a set of events no member of which begins after E begins and which is such that it is a law of nature, but not a law of logic, that if C were to occur then E would occur. (Ordinarily, when we say that one event "causes" another, we do not mean that the one event is a sufficient causal condition, in the present sense, for the other. We mean only that the one event is a "partial cause" of the other. An event that is a *partial cause* of an event E would be any proper subset of a "minimal" sufficient causal condition for E; and a "minimal" sufficient causal condition for E would be a sufficient causal condition for E.)

Our second definition concerns the technical concept, "directly within his power": (D2) It is *directly within his power* at t to make it happen that . . . provided only: there is a p such that (i) at t he is free to undertake to make it happen that p, and (ii) if he were to undertake at t to make it happen that p, he would make it happen that. . . .

It may be that our agent is free, in this sense, to undertake to get himself to the piano. It may also be that if he were now to undertake to get himself to the piano, then he would cause himself to be three feet closer to Boston. Our definition would allow us to say, therefore, that getting three feet closer to Boston is now directly within his power. But if he does not know that there is such a place as Boston, then he will not know that getting three feet closer to Boston is now directly within his power. Or if he knows that there is such a place but does not know where it is, then he may know that getting three feet closer to Boston is directly within his power (for he knows, say, that going three feet in any direction is directly within his

---

out in the technical locution we have introduced, as: "There is no sufficient causal condition for it not being the case that there is a p such that he makes it happen that p in the endeavor to make it happen that. . . ."

power) but he may not know what it is that he needs to undertake to get himself three feet closer to Boston. It is quite possible therefore, that although there are various things such that his undertaking any one of them would get him three feet closer to Boston, his undertaking to get three feet closer to Boston is not among them.

It may be noted, in passing, that the point just made is essential to marking off the sense of "could" and "can" that is implied by "ought." Consider a man in the position of Jimmy Valentine, for whom it is imperative to open the safe in the shortest time possible: he has it directly within his power to turn the dials to any one of the 10,000 possible combinations within 10 seconds (there being 100 positions for the left dial and 100 for the right) but he has no idea at all of what the proper combination is. Our definition would allow us to say that it is directly within his power to turn the dials to the proper combination within 10 seconds; for if he undertook to set the dials to L-84 and R-32, then he would have the proper combination. But it would be unjust to say to him: "You could have done it within 10 seconds; therefore you ought to have."

Unless our agent is very close indeed to Boston, it is not likely that getting to Boston is directly within his power in the sense just defined. But there is a clear sense in which it may be *indirectly* within his power. For, as we have noted, if he takes the first step, which is directly within his power, then he will put taking the second step directly within his power, and if he takes the second, then taking the third will become directly within his power, and so on until the trip is completed. We need, therefore, a definition of "indirectly within his power."

Our definition, in effect, should tell us this. If there is a certain state of affairs such that it is indirectly within our agent's power to make that state of affairs happen, then there is a possible series of successive acts, each of which is such that, either he *is* free to undertake it, or he *would* be free to undertake it if he undertakes all its predecessors in the series; and if he does undertake all of those acts then he will make happen the state of affairs in question. I suggest, therefore, the following definition: (D3) It is *indirectly within his power* at t to make it happen at t that . . . provided only: there is a p such that it is directly within his power at t to make it happen that p; there is a series of states of affairs, the first of which is his undertaking at t to make it happen that p, and each of the others of which is a state of affairs such that it would be directly within his power to make that state of affairs happen if he were to make its predecessors in the series happen; and if he were to make those states of affairs happen, then he would make it happen at t' that. . . .[9]

If these definitions are adequate, then we may say, of any given agent at any time, that his making a certain thing happen is *within his power* at that time if, and only if, his making that thing happen is either directly within his power or indirectly within his power at that time. (Strictly speaking, "directly" is here redundant, since our definition implies that what is directly within the agent's power is also indirectly within his power.)

We may also say that the agent's undertaking are among the things that he makes happen.[10] Thus

[9] An alternative procedure would be this: First, define "directly enabling" (e.g., "his making p happen would directly enable him to make q happen provided only: if he makes p happen, then his making q happen will be directly within his power) and then use this concept to formulate a definition of "indirectly within his power" patterned after Frege's definition of the ancestral. Thus we might say: "It is indirectly within his power at t to make it happen at t' that . . . provided only: (a) there is a state of affairs p such that his making p happen is directly within his power at t; and (b) its happening at t' that . . . is a member of every class of states of affairs C such that (i) p is a member of C and (ii) whatever any member of C directly enables him to make happen is also a member of C."

[10] This follows from the third assumption referred to in footnote 7 above.

Suarez had said: "If we understand the term 'effect' so that it includes not only the thing produced but also everything that flows from the power of the agent, then we may say that the action itself is in a certain sense the effect of the agent."[11] And we may also say that these undertakings are among the things that are within his power to make happen. But we need not say that, if an agent undertakes to make a certain thing happen, he thereby *undertakes to undertake* to make that thing happen (". . . to say, I can will if I will, I take to be an absurd speech."[12])

And so what do we mean when we say, "This morning you could have arranged things in such a way that you would be in Boston now, but you didn't"? We mean that, although the agent did not make it happen this morning that he so arranged things, nevertheless it was then within his power to make it happen. The "could," as definition (3) makes clear, is constitutionally iffy, and the proposed explication is consistent with saying that for some time now there has been a sufficient causal condition for the agent's not being in Boston now. But the "could" is also indeterministic. For we are saying that this morning the agent was free to undertake such arrangements. And this means, according to definition (1), that there was no sufficient causal condition for his undertaking them and no sufficient causal condition for his not undertaking them.

The things that our agent *can* make happen, therefore, will be those things which are within his power to make happen. And so to say of him, "He could have done otherwise," is to say that there was a time at which his doing otherwise was within his power.

---

[11] F. Suarez, *Disputationes Metaphysicae*, Disp. XVIII, Sec. 10, para 6.

[12] Thomas Hobbes, in *The Questions concerning Liberty, Necessity, and Chance*; the quotation may be found on page 42 of the excerpt reprinted in Bidney Morgenbesser and James Walsh, *Free Will* (Englewood Cliffs, N.J.: Prentice-Hall, Inc., 1962).

CHAPTER 12

ON SAYING THE ETHICAL THING[1]

WILLIAM K. FRANKENA*

Morality could not become a science without a radical reconstruction of the very uses of such terms as "good" and "right"; but such a reconstitution would no longer enable us to say (or do) "the ethical thing."

H. D. AIKEN, *Reason and Conduct*

I

AT this moment I cannot help wishing that we were all sitting around a banquet table as we did in times past. In defence of banqueting, Kant once wrote,

Although a banquet is a formal invitation to intemperance in both food and drink, there is still something

* William K. Frankena is in the Philosophy Department at the University of Michigan. This essay was given as the Presidential Address of the Western Division of the American Philosophical Association, Spring 1966, and is printed here by permission of the *Proceedings and Addresses of the American Philosophical Association*, Vol. 39 (1966), published by the Antioch Press. The author has also granted permission for the use of this slightly revised version.

[1] Presidential address delivered, with some omissions, before the Sixty-Fourth Annual Meeting of the Western Division of the American Philosophical Association in Minneapolis, Minnesota, May 5–7, 1966. Slightly revised by the author.

in it that aims at a moral end, beyond mere physical well-being: it keeps a lot of people together for a long time so that they may exchange their ideas.[2]

We, however, have rejected this transcendental deduction, just as we have rejected the others, and so have brought to an end the old association of philosophy with feasting. The Platonic archetype was a dinner plus a panel of several speakers. This was changed to a dinner with one speaker, or, alternatively, to a symposium of three speakers without dinner. Now we have no dinner and only one speaker. As the speaker, I must hope that this is the end of the line, for only one more step remains: no dinner and no speaker. I shudder to think that this speech may result in that step's being taken.

For this address will be an essay in metaethics, and I know that some have complained that moral philosophers today do too much metaethics and too little normative ethics. But, whatever may be said about my analytical friends and relations, I think I have done enough normative ethics lately to deserve at least one more metaethical fling. There are also some who have attacked the distinction itself that I and my sisters and my cousins and my aunts have made between normative ethics and metaethics. Perhaps both groups of critics will be placated if I tell them that what I am going to do is *normative metaethics*, that is, "betta" metaethics. I take this occasion as an invitation to say something more about what I think than I have so far. What I shall have to say is not new in any of its parts, but I believe that it has some novelty of form and that the resulting whole is of some interest. In any case, it needs saying, now more than ever, even if I shall not do so with the rigor that would be called for at another time.

[2] I. Kant, *The Doctrine of Virtue* (New York and London, 1964), pp. 91–92.

II

Let me explain the phrase "normative metaethics." By a *normative* inquiry, I mean one that aims at and results in conclusions to the effect that something is desirable, good, bad, right, wrong, or ought to be done. By a *metaethical* inquiry, I mean one that asks about the meaning and justification of such conclusions. Now, a metaethical inquiry may and usually does take a descriptive, elucidatory, or reportive form, that is, it may seek simply to lay bare what we actually mean when we judge that something is good or right or what our actual logic is for justifying such judgments. But it may also be normative, telling us what our meanings and our logic should be; and then it may be either *conservative*, bidding us to go on using our normative terms and justifying our normative judgments as we have, or *revisionary*, proposing that we reconstruct our meanings or our logic, more or less radically. This last possibility was suggested by P. F. Strawson some years ago in a very interesting passage:

There is another kind of thinking which might be called the creative or constructive work of the philosophical imagination. To engage in this kind of thinking is to consider how . . . we . . . might conduct our discourse . . . in forms different from, though related to, those which we actually use.[3]

I am not against purely elucidatory metaethics, and I believe that such neutral inquiry is in principle possible. Some form of intuitionism, emotivism, or even naturalism *might* be true as an account of our actual judgments and reasoning when we use terms like "right" and "good." However, I think that, in fact, metaethics has always been normative, for even those

[3] See D. F. Pears, *et al.*, *The Revolution in Philosophy* (London and New York, 1956), p. 107.

who are or claim to be elucidating the rules of our
normative discourse have implied that we should go on
following those rules—in short, they have been conservatively normative. Some of them have actually
been more revisionary than they pretended to be.
This is not said in criticism, as others have said it, for
I see nothing wrong in being normative in metaethics,
even if there are those who tell us to leave our language alone, and I propose to be normative, though
not in any drastically revisionary way. If one is going
to be normative, let him be so openly!

It does not follow at once that the distinction between normative ethics and metaethics breaks down.
Non-normative metaethics still may be possible, and,
moreover, an inquiry into the meaning and logic of
moral discourse may be normative without being moral.
Normative judgments and proposals are not necessarily
moral; they may be aesthetic, prudential, technical,
methodological, and what not. Hence, the findings of
metaethics need not be construed as moral judgments
even if they are normative. There might be a normative
meta-science or a normative meta-history, telling us
how to do science or history, and its conclusions would
not necessarily be moral, or even scientific or historical.
Meta-disciplines are not *ipso facto* parts of the disciplines they are meta to; and they are not parts of
morality simply because they are normative. G. H. von
Wright may be right in maintaining that conceptual
analysis in the area of practical philosophy must be
normative,[4] though I myself doubt that it must be; but,
even if he is, it does not follow that such conceptual
analysis must make *moral* commitments. It may still
be that it will turn out to be committed to some moral
judgment or other, but this must be shown and not
assumed. *Prima facie*, it is at least possible that there
are two levels of normative judgments—the first level
ones occurring in normative ethics or aesthetics, and
the second level ones occurring in metaethics or meta-
aesthetics.

[4] See *The Varieties of Goodness* (London, 1963), pp. 3–6.

In truth, there is at least an air of paradox in the notion of a normative metaethics. For it will purport to tell us that we ought to use our normative discourse in certain ways (for example, in the same ways in which we have been using it), but then it is itself using the normative term "ought," and it may seem that this is somehow illegitimate. But *is* there really some kind of legerdemain going on here, because one is making normative statements about normative discourse? After all, one can, without any logical inconsistency, advocate the use of Esperanto in English or order silence in a loud voice. One would come closer to paradox if one were to say, as some views to be mentioned later do, that we *ought* to stop using normative discourse altogether, but even then one could appeal to a theory of types of normative judgment. One could also cite a famous text about throwing away one's ladder after having climbed up it.

What, then, is it that normative metaethics would be doing? Two questions have traditionally been central in metaethics:

1. What are the meanings, uses, or functions of words like "good" and "right" or of sentences in which they occur?

2. What are the principles of ethical reasoning? What is the logic of moral reasoning? How can statements using "good" and "right" be justified, if at all?

These questions, however, are ambiguous. The first may mean either:

1a. What are the *actual* meanings, uses, or functions of sentences using words like "good" and "ought"? Or:

1b. What meanings, uses, or functions *should* we assign to such sentences?

The second, likewise, may mean either:

2a. What is the *actual* logic by which we conduct our reasoning about normative matters? Or:

2b. What conception *should* we have of the justification of normative statements?

1a and 2a are for present purposes the main questions of descriptive or elucidatory metaethics, and I see no reason why the answers to them must be any more normative than the answers to similar questions involving history or science. 1b and 2b, on the other hand, will be the main questions of normative metaethics and will require normative answers.

Since the questions and conclusions of normative metaethics are not descriptive, it follows that its methods and arguments must be different from those of descriptive metaethics. For example, the open question argument is stated by R. M. Hare as follows:

. . . if "right" meant the same as "in accordance with the will of God," then, "whatever is in accordance with the will of God is right" would mean the same as "whatever is in accordance with the will of God is in accordance with the will of God"; but according to our actual use of the words, it seems to mean more than this mere tautology.[5]

Taken in this form, if the argument is good at all, it is good only against a definist metaethics that purports to be elucidating our "actual use" of words; it will have little or no cogency against one that proposes to redefine our words in a certain way—as R. B. Perry, for example, proposes to do. In order to operate in the field of normative metaethics, the open question argument must run as follows (using Hare's example):

If we take "right" as meaning the same as "in accordance with the will of God," then we must take "whatever is in accordance with the will of God is right" as meaning the same as "whatever is in accordance with the will of God is in accordance with the will of God," but surely this is not a desirable use of words.

But then the argument is not obviously and immediately decisive, as it is usually taken to be; it simply begs the question. In general, answers to questions of normative metaethics cannot be established wholly by

[5] *The Concise Encyclopedia of Western Philosophy and Philosophers*, ed. by J. O. Urmson (London, 1960), p. 139.

the methods of descriptive elucidation. No metaethical Ought can be logically inferred from any metaethical Is alone.

Even though this is true, it must be allowed that the descriptive finding that we do use our normative words in certain ways may be used as *an* argument (and a good one) for the (conservative) normative conclusion that we should go on using them in that way. Even then, however, this normative conclusion will not follow from the descriptive premise alone, but only from that taken together with a desire to communicate or with a belief that nothing important is to be gained by revising our language. No doubt we should in normative meta-ethics presume that revisions are not to be advocated unless necessary (Notice, this is a normative judgment, but is it a moral one?), but some revisions may be necessary if we are to avoid the ambiguity, looseness, and vagueness of our actual discourse.

III

Consider now question 1b, namely, "What meanings, uses, or functions *should* we assign to such terms as 'good' and 'right' or to sentences in which they occur?" Several types of answers are possible, paralleling the usual types of answers to question 1a. (1) A normative ethical intuitionist would answer that we ought to use "good" or "right" or both as standing for simple non-natural properties and sentences involving them as ascribing such properties to certain objects. (2) A normative ethical definist, naturalistic or metaphysical, would argue that we should use the terms in question, if we use them at all, to mean "being in accordance with the will to God," "being an object of interest," *et cetera*, and sentences involving them as ascribing such empirical or metaphysical properties to things. (3) A normative ethical non-cognitivist or non-descriptivist would hold that we should assign some other use to ethical expressions than that of standing for or ascribing properties.

It may be worth mentioning that one might give one type of answer to question 1a and a different type of answer to question 1b. For example, one might contend that we *actually* use our ethical terms as if they stood for simple non-natural properties, but *ought* to use them simply to express our attitudes or emotions or to evoke similar ones in others. This position was virtually put forward at one time by Richard Robinson.[6] It would combine intuitionism in descriptive metaethics and emotivism in normative metaethics.

However this may be, just what is at issue between the various types of normative metaethics? Is it merely the question whether the noises "right," "good," and the like, should be used in certain ways rather than others? Even if it were in this sense verbal or terminological, it would not necessarily be trivial, since the noises in question are already in use. But the issue is not so simple as all that. For it involves a question, not only about the use of "right" and "good," but also about many other forms of expression in English, as well as about good corresponding expressions in other languages—not to mention gestures, inflections, and other linguistic or non-linguistic devices for doing what "good" and "right" do or might be used to do. No, I suggest that the issue is not just one about the use of certain sounds or printed shapes; it is, rather, one about the status, function, or desirability of a whole "symbolic form," "type of discourse," or "realm of meaning."

This is vague, and we must now try to see more fully just what the issue is. In doing so, we may adapt an image borrowed from Michael Oakeshott.[7] He has a very interesting conception of "human activity and intercourse" as "a conversation which goes on both

[6] "The Emotive Theory of Ethics," *Proc. Arist. Soc., Supp. Vol. XXII* (1948), pp. 79–106.

[7] See *Rationalism in Politics* (London, 1962), pp. 197ff, 327f.

in public and within each of ourselves" and is made up of a number of "voices," namely, those of poetry, history, science, practical activity, and philosophy. Let us likewise conceive of human discourse as a conversation involving at least the following three voices:

Voice A: This is the language of so-called descriptive or factual assertions or statements, or of what J. L. Austin prefers to call "constatives," for example, such sentences as:

> The book is red.
> Lord Raglan won the battle of Alma.
> All snow geese migrate to Labrador.
> The hose burst because of the pressure.
> Many people enjoy skiing.
> The Greeks approved of courage.
> Love of parents is commanded by God.

I can no more define this voice accurately than Austin could, and must hope that the illustrations given will indicate which one I mean.

Voice B is more varied, for it consists of such utterances as:

> Ouch!
> Shut the door!
> Be careful!
> Hello!
> Hurrah for Michigan!
> Let's go to a movie!
> Would that we were all sitting around a banquet table!
> I promise to return the book.
> You make me sick! I hate you!
> How white the wall is!
> Oh, how love I Thy law! It is my meditation all the day.

And many more—all imperatives, all expressions of emotion, attitude, or commitment, many of Austin's various kinds of performatives,[8] *et cetera.*

---

[8] See J. L. Austin, *How to Do Things With Words* (Oxford, 1962), p. 150. His "verdictives" probably combine Voices B and C.

Voice C I must describe even more vaguely, partly to avoid begging questions. It includes linguistic acts that are at least *prima facie* different from those of the two Voices, namely, acts of grading, commending, recommending, appraising, approving, evaluating, or criticizing. Many would list acts of prescribing here also, and some of these certainly belong to Voice C, but others seem to belong to Voice B. Estimating and assessing may also be of two kinds, as Austin pointed out, but at least some such acts would belong to Voice C. Perhaps the same thing is true of acts of advising, praising, blaming, enjoining, and the like.

Four remarks are apposite at this point. (a) Roughly speaking, but only roughly, each Voice involves a vocabulary and a syntax, if we use these terms in a broad sense. (b) It seems possible that two of these Voices may be blended in a single utterance. "I hate you!", for example, may be a blending of Voices A and B. (c) It may be that there are still more Voices to be recognized. Where, for instance, are we to put modal utterances, epistemic statements, the statements of logic and mathematics, or analytic sentences? On the other hand, it has at least been suggested that such statements are basically normative and so belong to the kind of discourse we are discussing the status of. (d) It might be argued, of course, that this normative discourse, ethical or non-ethical, should itself be regarded as a fourth Voice distinct from the three described. However, since it is precisely the status of normative discourse that we are discussing, we cannot begin by assuming that it represents a separate Voice. In fact, since Voices are surely not to be multiplied beyond necessity, there may even be a presumption that it does not (Actually, in what follows, I shall place it with Voice C).

It will, no doubt, have been observed that Voice A will include all of the sentences regarded by ethical definists as equivalent to sentences of normative discourse, for example, "Skiing is an object of positive interest" or "Love of parents is in accordance with the

will of God"; that Voice B will contain all of the
sentences or utterances held by emotivists, impera-
tivists, *et cetera,* to be equivalent to sentences of normative discourse, for example, "Do not kill!" and
"Stealing! Bah!"; and, finally, that Voice C will cover
the various other kinds of speech acts to which less re-
ductionistically-minded philosophers have sought to
assimilate moral and other kinds of normative judgments. This is, of course, not an accident but a bit of
beneficence aforethought. For we are now in a position
to say more adequately what the issue under debate in
normative metaethics is (or would be if people were
actually to debate it).

Let us see, in the terms that are before us, just what
each of the parties to that debate would say. Consider
first the ethical naturalist.[9] It is sometimes alleged by
his opponents that he simply assumes that the conversation of mankind is and is to be carried on in Voice A
alone—that he is deaf to the multi-functionality or
multi-vocality of language. However, while this may
have been true of some naturalists, it need not be
true of them all. A naturalist may perfectly well admit
the existence and desirability of Voice B and possibly
even of Voice C. What he cannot allow is that normative discourse (that is, discourse using words like
"good," "right," "ought," "should," their opposites, or
their equivalents) should belong anywhere but with
Voice A. Actually, the normative ethical naturalist
could take *either* of two positions. (a) He might maintain that we should simply drop our normative discourse entirely and use instead only such sentences as
are already contained in Voice A, for example, "Skiing
is an object of interest" or "Love of parents is commanded by God." (b) He might take the more moder-
ate view naturalists in fact always take, namely, that
we should keep our normative vocabulary but use it
simply as an alternative way of asserting and describing
facts for which we already have another vocabulary.

---

[9] The same will, of course, be true of the metaphysical
or theological definist.

For example, we should use "Skiing is good" as merely another way of saying "Skiing is an object of positive interest" or "The people who do it enjoy it." In this case, he will not object to our using normative expressions like "right" and "good" to guide choice and action, but must insist that the guidance-potential of sentences in which they appear should be thought of as exactly equivalent to that of sentences like "*x* is an object of interest" or "*y* is commanded by God."

The normative intuitionist agrees with the second kind of naturalist in retaining our normative vocabulary and assigning it to Voice A. But he believes that there are brave non-natural properties and facts of a very special kind, that we are aware of them, and that we do and should use our normative discourse as a way of ascribing such properties and asserting and communicating such facts. Like the naturalist, he may allow Voices B and C a role in the conversation of mankind. He may also allow that sentences like "*x* is good" and "*y* is right" may be used to guide action, but must insist that they are action-guiding in their capacity of reporting a fact, albeit a fact of a very special kind. And, to explain this, he may hold either that an apprehension of such a fact is directly "practical" or that it is so only in conjunction with a desire awakened by it.

In opposition to both definists and intuitionists, some non-cognitivists or non-descriptivists would maintain that, if we are to keep our normative discourse at all, we should assimilate it, not to Voice A, but to Voice B. In fact, like the naturalist, such a non-cognitivist may hold *either* (a) that we should simply drop our normative discourse entirely and use instead only such sentences as are already contained in Voice B, for example, "Do not kill!", "Hurrah for promise-keeping!", "How wonderful!", "Would that more people were benevolent!", *or* (b) that we should retain our normative vocabulary but use it simply as an alternative way of expressing our sentiments and uttering commands, that is, use (say) "Killing is wrong" as merely another way of saying "Do not kill!", "Killing, no!", or "Would that people would stop killing one another!"

Other non-descriptivists will cry a plague on all of these houses, contending that we cannot be satisfied with Voices A and B, but must have Voice C as well, and that our normative utterances should be construed as belonging to Voice C. In Euripides' play, *Alcestis*, King Admetus, stricken with grief, cries, "What can I say? All language is too poor!" For this second group of non-cognitivists, without Voice C, all language is too poor—too poor, that is, to say the ethical or normative thing. For this, they claim, we must have a vocabulary and a syntax in which we can do something besides reporting, describing, or explaining, something besides uttering commands, ejaculating, or expressing emotions and attitudes, namely, such things as grading, commending, evaluating, and advising.[10]

These being the positions of the parties to the debate in normative metaethics, it becomes clear that the issue in that debate is composed of the following questions: (a) Should we retain our normative vocabulary? (b) What voices should we admit to the conversation of mankind? (c) To which of these voices should normative discourse (saying the ethical thing) be assigned?

Now, in connection with the first of these questions, it will be recalled that, on some of the views just described, our so-called normative discourse is merely an alternative way of saying or doing something we already have an adequate way of saying or doing. It might, then, be argued that if our normative discourse is simply a second language of this sort, then we should dispense with it, even if it is stylistically desirable to have more than one way of saying the same thing. This contention certainly is plausible, but it may be replied that in fact we are hardly likely at this time of day to stop using such words as "good," "right," and

[10] Cf., e.g., P. W. Taylor, *Normative Discourse* (Englewood Cliffs, N.J., 1961), pp. 257–258.

the like, and that, if we are going to have them always
with us (like the poor), then we had better assign
them some profitable or at least innocuous employment.
As one naturalist expresses it,

. . . the terms "value," "good," "bad," and their equivalents . . . could now be dispensed with and nothing of
empirical consequence would be lost, though many
rich literary connotations would vanish, . . . there is no
need to use the terms "good" and "value," and . . . con-
fusions vanish as soon as these terms are eliminated.
For without them, we are referred directly to the facts.
. . . Then why not do without these terms? Because
they are convenient. And because it is safer to keep
them equated with the various selective systems than
floating loose where ingenious men [like Moore] may
note their freedom from attachment and proceed to
hypostatize facts for them to refer to.[11]

Some such thought as this, no doubt, is the reason why
the actual elimination of our normative vocabulary has
never (well, hardly ever!) been proposed. Omitting,
then, the views that propose its elimination, we may
take the following positions as the live options by way
of answer to question 1b (taken normatively, of
course):

1. Definist theories holding normative discourse to
   be an alternative mode of saying something
   already in Voice A,
2. Intuitionism,
3. Emotive and imperativist theories holding normative discourse to be an alternative way of expressing emotion, uttering commands, *et cetera*,
   in short, part of Voice B,
4. Other non-descriptivist views, that is, those
   denying that normative discourse should be assimilated to Voices A or B.

[11] S. C. Pepper, *The Sources of Value* (Berkeley and Los
Angeles, 1958), pp. 689–690. Cf., p. 269. Pepper's metaethics is really normative in my sense, even though he calls
his definitions of ethical terms "descriptive."

IV

We must now consider these views and what we should say about the issues between them, namely, which voices should be admitted to the conversation of mankind, and to which of those voices should our normative discourse (that is, the use of "good," "right," their equivalents and opposites) be assigned?

About intuitionism, to which I long subscribed even though I was always suspicious of the naturalistic fallacy charge and the open question argument, I shall say little. I still do not think that the usual arguments against it, for example, those of Hare and Nowell-Smith,[12] are as fatal as they are thought to be. However, the existence of the special properties and facts that intuitionists believe in raises such epistemological and ontological problems that it seems to me we must look for a view that saves the insights of intuitionism but does away with these difficulties.

What about emotivism and other similar views? They strike me as being clearly inadequate as accounts of our actual ethical and value judgments. I do not deny that, when we apply ethical and value terms to things, we are normally taking and putting into words some attitude or other for or against them, nor do I wish to propose that we should stop doing so if we can. But it seems obvious to me that in our actual ethical and value judgments, when we are not frightened out of our normative wits by the relativists, subjectivists, and sceptics, we are not merely exclaiming, commanding, expressing emotion, evoking a response, or committing ourselves; rather, we are claiming some kind of status,

[12] Cf., Hare, *The Language of Morals* (Oxford, 1952), pp. 29-30; P. H. Nowell-Smith, *Ethics* (London, 1954), pp. 36-43; Carl Wellman, *The Language of Ethics* (Cambridge, Mass., 1961), pp. 81-87.

justification, or validity for our attitudes or judgments. Others have said this very well before me. To quote:

Amidst all the reputed vagueness and ambiguity of ethical terms [emotive theorists] have found one constant element, the expression of the speaker's approval, and have seized upon this as the meaning of ethical statements. But at least one other factor is equally constant; ethical statements are always understood to be supported by reason. They imply the claim made is one that a reasonable man would willingly allow. Ethical statements make claims upon us, but claims advanced as impersonal and rationally justifiable.[13]

Or again:

. . . the new approach takes seriously, as the emotive theory does not, the fundamental distinction between moral judgments, which profess a certain objectivity and impersonality, and mere expressions of taste or interest which neither have nor claim to have any interpersonal "authority" over the judgments or conduct of others. . . . The terms of moral discourse, are, in use, not such wildly "open-textured" expressions of emotion as the emotivists contend. Governing the use of ethical terms . . . are rules of application. . . . Such rules . . . set limits to the sort of judgment we are prepared to countenance as "ethical." Each time we apply moral rules, we are not simply "venting" our own passing sentiments or wishes; rather, we are in such a case invoking an impersonal linguistic ritual which serves to keep practical deliberation and disagreement within certain socially acceptable bounds.[14]

If someone rejoins here that normative judgments are not peculiar in this respect, that in all we desire, do, or say, we always claim some kind of justification or validity, then I am not really concerned to confute him. For one who answers thus is not so much assimilating normative judgments to utterances in Voice B as the reverse. In any case, however, what these

[13] A. Sesonske, *Value and Obligation* (Berkeley and Los Angeles, 1957), p. 16.
[14] H. D. Aiken, *Reason and Conduct* (New York, 1962), pp. 21–23.

passages say about ethical judgments is, in my opinion, true in some manner of all utterances in Voice C. This is precisely why it is so plausible to hold that normative discourse is an idiom belonging to that Voice.

If what such passages say is true, then it is clear why we cannot seriously propose to reduce normative judgments to interjections, imperatives, emotional expressions, or even ultimate commitments. For, if we were to do so, we would be debarred from doing something we very much want to do, something it would be less than human not to want to do, namely, to claim for ourselves at least a modicum of impersonal rationality and validity. All language would be too poor—too poor for distinctively human words!

Again, if what such passages say is true, then normative judgments *are* proper judgments, as A. C. Ewing and other cognitivists have insisted; and terms like "true" and "false," "valid" and "invalid," and perhaps also logical connectives, may be applied to them, as many antidescriptivists have themselves allowed since the salad days of logical positivism and emotivism. Shall we conclude, then, that such judgments belong to Voice A after all, that some form of definism is true, that perhaps we may now roll away the stone from before the tomb in which naturalism has lain ever since that dread day when the earth trembled under the naturalistic fallacy and the rocks were rent by the open question? Actually, I should not be much disturbed if it were to appear that the reports of the death of naturalism have been grossly exaggerated; the view I shall be advocating is, as we shall see, akin to a certain form of naturalism. However, the usual kinds of naturalism criticized by Moore and others do strike me as unsatisfactory, whether they are cast in a descriptive-elucidatory or in a normative form. As R. M. Chisholm puts it,

... these attempted reductions are entirely implausible; the sentences expressing our ostensible ethical knowledge *seem* at least to express considerably more than is expressed by any of their ostensible empirical translations.[15]

For one thing, the proposed translations (constatives in Voice A) express only belief, not such pro or con attitudes as ethical judgments normally give voice to. There is a taking of sides, different from mere belief, in a first hand normative judgment that is not necessarily present in any judgment in Voice A, though one may combine such a taking of sides with a statement in Voice A, as the Thin Woman of the Inis McGrath does when she says to her philosopher-husband, returning empty-handed and hungry from a day's contemplation, "Your stir-about is on the hob. I hope there's lumps in it."

One might, of course, contend that, while this is indeed true, we should not build this taking of an attitude for or against into the meaning of "*x* is good" or "*y* is wrong" any more than we should build an act of believing into the meaning of "*z* is square." But, even if this contention is correct, we must remember that attitude-taking is just as closely bound up with "*x* is good" or "*y* is wrong" as believing is with "*z* is square." How close this is is indicated by the paradox involved in my saying, "*z* is square, but I don't believe it." Still, however this may be, there remains a difference between normative judgments and pure constatives in Voice A that should be preserved in our language if we mean to go on saying the ethical thing. The difference may be spelled out as follows. A pure constative like "The table is square" does not merely express the speaker's belief that the table is square; it makes a claim that this belief is true, warranted by the evidence, or rationally justifiable. This claim is explicit in "(The table is square) is true," for saying that something is true is not just endorsing it, as P. F. Strawson once suggested, but the claim is also present in "The table is square." There is, in fact, a kind of equivalence

---

[15] *Theory of Knowledge* (Englewood Cliffs, N.J., 1966), p. 60.

between "S is P" and "(S is P) is true." Constatives in
Voice A and normative utterances are thus alike in
being status-seekers—in making what Carl Wellman
has called the "critical" claim that something is true,
valid, or justifiable (or the opposite) in some interpersonal sense.[16] To this extent, the naturalists (and
intuitionists) are right. A pure constative, however,
makes this claim only for the *belief* that S is P, not
for *feelings, attitudes, choices,* or *actions* with respect
to S, P, or S's being P. But the question whether
feelings, attitudes, choices, and actions are justifiable
or rationally defensible may also be asked—human
beings apparently cannot help but ask it—and it is in
asking and answering *this* question that normative discourse (and in general, Voice C) finds and should
continue to find its main function.

What I propose, then, in opposition to naturalism
(and intuitionism) is that we construe and employ
Voice A to express *beliefs* and claim a certain status
for them and Voice C (including normative discourse)
to express *other* states of mind and claim a similar
status for them—and I mean this both as an account
of our actual use of language and as a recommendation for the future. Naturalism and other forms of
definism (and intuitionism), if we read them as proposing that normative judgments shall be construed and
used merely as alternative ways of formulating certain
constatives, would limit us to claiming justifiability or
rationality for such beliefs as "*x* is an object of interest," or "*y* is forbidden by God," *et cetera.* They would
not allow us, through the use of "good," "right," and
the like, to claim justifiability or rationality for actions,
decisions, or preferences, *et cetera.* Indeed, pushed to
the hilt, they would seem to allow us no way of commending, recommending, advising, no way of "guiding," as distinct from "goading," except by the use of
Voice A—no way of doing any of the things Voice C
may be used to do, since all of these things involve

[16] Cf. *op. cit.,* Ch. X.

an appeal to reason in favor of something that is not just a belief. Speaking of advice, W. D. Falk writes:

"Do this" may be used in the sense of "my advice to you is, do this"; it may express a *recommendation*. . . . As advice, it is not direct pleading [or "goading"], in spite of its grammatical form. . . . It is . . . logically assured here that none but rational methods will be used in support. Advice . . . is understood to set out . . . purely to "guide," to make people act as they would have valid and sufficient reasons for acting. . . . One follows advice when one thinks it sound, believing its claim that there are valid reasons for doing the thing suggested. One can give advice without stating this claim. . . . But, also, one might as well have explicitly made it, as certainly the hearer must take it to have been made. . . .[17]

That is, advice (of this kind) belongs to the form of discourse in which, not beliefs, but actions, attitudes, dispositions (other than beliefs), decisions, or emotions are claimed, at least implicitly, to "have valid and sufficient reasons." And the pure definist, like the pure emotivist, is in effect proposing that we do without this form of discourse, conversing in future only in Voices A and B. Perhaps this is what "the naturalistic fallacy" really comes to: advocating that we drop Voice C and use our normative vocabulary simply as an alternative way of formulating constatives in Voice A. Even then, however, as I once said about that fallacy in an earlier rendering of it, it cannot be assumed to be a fallacy, but must be shown to be one by some independent argument. I shall, however, not use this occasion—or the little that is left of it—to mount such an independent argument (In fact, I am not clear what form such an argument would take;[18] if I were, I should certainly present it, regardless of time). Instead,

[17] "Goading and Guiding," *Mind*, LXII (1953). Reprinted in R. Ekman, *Readings in the Problems of Ethics* (New York, 1965). See pp. 226–227.

[18] Part of it, perhaps, would be the contention that, if we cast out Voice C, then Voice B will enter and dwell in its place, so that our last state will be worse than our first.

I shall take it as obvious that the conversation of mankind would be a sorry symphony if only Voices A and B could be heard in it—that, without Voice C, or a voice in which we articulate, not beliefs, but other states of mind, and in which we claim rationality, not for beliefs, but for these other states of mind or for actions and decisions in line with them, all language would, indeed, be too poor to say what we want to say.[19]

V

With this I align myself, except for a point to be mentioned later, with the anti-descriptivists or noncognitivists of what Aiken calls "the new approach," though I put matters more in a normative and less in a descriptive-elucidatory form than they are wont to do—and, hence, also in a more speculative one. If there were time, I would take up two related features of normative discourse (and perhaps of Voice C in general) which were noticed already by Moore and emphasized more recently by Hare, namely, that marked by the notion of universalizability on the one hand and that marked by the notion of consequentiality or supervenience on the other. Instead, I shall conclude the discussion of question 1b by making one more point. I have, in effect, assimilated normative discourse to Voice C and my main point has been that discourse in this voice is and should be used to perform a special function—that of expressing the speaker's partialities and commitments and especially that of claiming justification or rationality (or the opposite) for attitudes, actions, and decisions, not necessarily the speaker's.

[19] I do not mean to deny that sentences like "He is a good man" may have *both* descriptive and evaluative meaning, as Hare thinks (*op. cit.*, pp. 24ff.). But, if they do, then they claim rationality *both* for a belief and for something else.

That we have a *conatus* toward rationality is shown by our penchant for rationalization, though claiming rationality is not necessarily rationalization. It is also shown, I think, by the very fact that words like "good," "right," and "true" have the emotive meaning some recent philosophers have made so much of, for these words would hardly have the particular expressive and evocative force they have if they made no claim to justification and rational validity.

The point I wish to make is largely borrowed from P. W. Taylor.[20] It is that the reasons (and hence the rationality) claimed by normative judgments may be of various sorts: aesthetic, legal, moral, prudential, perhaps even religious. Each of the terms involved— "good," "ought," *et cetera*—has the same meaning in these various contexts but the grounds or reasons claimed are of different kinds. Whether a judgment is moral or aesthetic, for instance, depends on the kind of reason given for it or suggested by it in its context. In fact, the same sentence, "You ought to go to see your grandmother" will be moral if the reason supporting it is "because you promised to," prudential if it is "because she may remember you in her will if you do."[21] Each type of reason may be conceived of as related to a "point of view," and each type of normative judgment claims that something is justified or rational (or the opposite) from some such point of view. The point of view may be that of a simple desire; or it may be something more complex, like "the farmer's point of view," "the prudential point of view (self-love)," "the aesthetic point of view," or "the moral point of view"; possibly it may even be a point of view that overarches all other interests and positions.[22] In short, in making a normative judgment, besides voicing our partiality, we at least suggest that there are

[20] *Op. cit.*, preface, pp. 107–114, 299ff.
[21] Cf., J. Xenakis, "A Mistaken Distinction in Ethical Theory," *Philosophical Studies*, VIII (1957), pp. 69–71.
[22] In short, it may be any one of Pepper's "selective systems," *op. cit.*, pp. 663, 673.

good reasons for a certain action or attitude, and we usually have in mind more or less clearly a certain type of reason, that is, we are taking a certain point of view and claiming that one who is rational from that point of view would or would not have that attitude or perform that action.

Now, however, a possible criticism may be raised. This is that my view is a kind of cognitivism after all, and probably a form of naturalism. For it asserts that a normative judgment entails a claim that one who takes a certain point of view and is rational within that point of view (that is, knows the facts, is clear-headed, *et cetera*) will take a certain attitude, perform a certain action, or at least subscribe to the same judgment. And this claim, if meaningful, is either true or false. In fact, it will be said, my view comes close to saying that "x is good" means "x would be favored (from some point of view) by anyone who is rational." But then one can ask the open question: one can sensibly say, "This is favored (from some point of view) by anyone who is rational, but is it good?"

I answer (1) that, as already indicated, I would not be much troubled if my view turned out to be a form of cognitivism or even of naturalism, as long as it also turned out to be tenable. (2) It would, at least, not be a form of pure cognitivism, since it insists that making a normative judgment involves taking a stand that is not simply a belief (even *if* to believe p is to be prepared to act on p). (3) This means that a normative judgment is not so much a constative assertion on my view as an *act* of approval (*et cetera*) *from* a certain point of view. It implies or presupposes that there are reasons for approving (*et cetera*) which would convince anyone who is rational and takes that point of view, but the fact that it "implies" or "presupposes" this does not mean that it "asserts" this. (4) It does follow that there is a great similarity between constative judgments in Voice A and normative ones, and I do wish to stress this, but it is not clear that this commits me to any definist position of the form that ". . ." means ". . . . .". (5) If my view is nevertheless a form of naturalism, then it is a naturalism of a rather special kind, since, if it is defining "good" and "right" at all, it is defining them by reference to the concept of "rationality," which is also involved in the definition of "true," not by reference to notions like "being an object of interest," "being demanded by society," or even "being in accordance with the will of God."[23] (6) As for the use of the open question against such a form of definism—it would mean arguing that one can sensibly say "This is rational to favor (do) from said point of view, but is it good (right)?" And, of course, one can, for one may be asking if it is rational from some *other* point of view. The question is: Can one sensibly say "This is rational to favor (do) from said point of view, but is it good (right) from that point of view?" But this, I submit, it is not obviously sensible to say. One can, of course, say it; as C. H. Langford used to observe, one can close one's eyes and grit one's teeth and say anything. It does not follow that what one says is sensible.

VI

We come finally to question 2b: what should be our conception of the justification of normative statements? The answer to it depends largely on the answer to question 1b, and may be brief, as indeed it must. On the position taken above, the justification of a normative judgment, in its most general terms, involves taking a certain point of view, actually or at least hypothetically, and trying one's utmost to be rational (informed, clear-headed, and so forth) within it—just as the justification of "The table is square"

[23] For such a special kind of naturalism, see R. G. Turnbull, "Imperatives, Logic, and Moral Obligation," *Philosophy of Science*, 27 (1960), pp. 374–390.

does. It does not involve a "statistical" enquiry into the reaction of rational observers, as some naturalists and their opponents have supposed—any more than the verification of "The table is square" does. Of course, there may be different views about the nature of the point of view in question—different views about the nature of the moral or of the aesthetic point of view. The details of the process of justification will depend, not only on the point of view in question, but also on the position taken about its nature. These are questions we cannot go into now.

There are, however, two matters about which something must still be said. The first is the business of going from Is to Ought (Good, *et cetera*). On the view sketched above, contrary to the usual dictum, there will be a sense in which one can go from an Is to an Ought. According to it, one cannot make a first-hand normative judgment of any kind unless one is taking, at least hypothetically, some aesthetic or practical point of view (not simply one of belief or disbelief), and is claiming to be rational within it. But, if one does take some such point of view and does claim to be rational within it, then there is a sense in which one may appropriately conclude that something is good, right, or should be done, and claim that this conclusion is justified by the facts (Is) alone. For example, if I am building a bookcase and am concerned that it should be secure, then, if I learn that screws hold more securely than scotch tape or even nails, I may correctly conclude that I should use screws. For, on the view suggested, Ought-talk, Good-talk, and Voice C generally, simply *are* the appropriate mode for expressing oneself when one is taking a conative point of view and meaning to be rational within it. One cannot logically or even reasonably go from Is to Ought (Good, *et cetera*) *simpliciter*, but, in the presence of an aesthetic or practical point of view one may reasonably do so—indeed, it would be unreasonable, perhaps also a misuse of language, not to do so—though even then the "inference" would not be a logically valid one (unless "logical inference" is redefined to include it, as some have suggested). To say, without this qualification, that we must not go from Is to Ought is in effect to say that we must do without Voice C, and, in reply, I am minded to ask simply, "By what compulsion must we?" Or perhaps even more simply, "*Can* we?"

The second matter is the business of relativism. It is a prevailing view that the normative sphere of discourse is infected by a difficulty, namely, that, if two people hold conflicting normative judgments, it may be impossible to determine who is right. In fact, it is sometimes thought that both may be right—that no amount of being rational can decide between them and both judgments may be justified or rational. Some such relativistic position could, I think, be accommodated within the framework of what has been said here. But now I wish to propose that it be regarded as of the essence of a normative judgment to claim that it is justified, rational, or valid (as well as the act or attitude it is about) and that conflicting judgments are not—that normative discourse claims that there is a right answer to a normative question and only one, however hard it may be to determine what it is.

"Well," it may be said, "we have in the past so conceived of our normative discourse, at least implicitly. That is why the relativistic position has always come as a shock. Now, however, we know that attitudes are not all rooted in beliefs, that ultimate disagreements are possible in normative matters, and so on. Hence, if we go on using normative discourse (and Voice C) at all, we should use it without laying claim to any kind of final interpersonal validity. Except for the truth-claims involved in using Voice A, we should either drop all claims to justification or rationality (in effect, limit ourselves to Voices A and B) or at least confine ourselves to making only modest and non-absolutistic ones. This is not a failure of normative nerve but only the better or more rational part of valor."

Now, there is a sense in which rational men may

justifiably or rationally differ in normative matters. It may be rational for Peter to hold that x is right when it is also rational for Paul to hold that x is wrong, if they have different beliefs or evidence about x. Here the rationality is analogous to what is sometimes called subjective or probable rightness. But "objective rationality" may be and should continue to be conceived as absolute, not only in the case of constative assertions in Voice A, but also in that of utterances in Voice C and of the acts and attitudes they somehow refer to— so I wish to maintain. This involves the claim that rational men who take the same point of view will agree on normative matters if they are fully informed, clear-headed, *et cetera* (The *"et cetera"* here is intentional; I am not sure how it should be filled out, though I am also not ready to grant that it cannot be adequately filled out without making the claim analytically true). It has *not* been established that this claim is false; we do *not* know that disagreements in attitude are not rooted in disagreements in belief or that ultimate normative disagreements, if they exist, will continue to exist as knowledge grows from more to more among rational men who share the same point of view. There is even some rough evidence to the contrary; historically, religious people who have theological beliefs of certain sorts tend to adopt the ethics of love, and, today, it begins to appear that, as the people of the world come to share more and more the same points of view and the same factual beliefs, they also come to regard the same things as desirable. At any rate, so long as the case against the absolutist claim is not better established than it is, we may still make that claim; it may take some temerity, but it is not unreasonable. As for me and my house, therefore, we will continue to serve the Lord—or, as others may prefer to say, the Ideal Observer. For Tennyson seems to me to be right in a sense (not his own) when he says,

The good, the true, the pure, the just—
Take the charm "Forever" from them
and they crumble into dust.

Take from them the claim to an eventual agreement of
all rational beings and they collapse into mere expressions and tools of feeling, desire, and will (Voice
B).

VII

I have now said my piece on saying the ethical
(normative) thing. Having said it, I know I have no
prospect of ending up in the black. But I have no
wish to finish in the red either, and so I choose to
close in purple. In saying my piece, I have a sense of
preaching a counterreformation two hundred years
too late. For there seems to be a drift, by no means
wholly unconscious, away from the use of Voice C or
of any form of discourse claiming interpersonal authority or validity, and, especially, away from the notion that any such authority or validity is somehow
final. That is what makes Hannah Arendt's title, "What
Was Authority?", so *a propos*.[24] I have in mind cultural
relativism, irrationalism, psycho-analysis, existentialism,
"the new morality," "the new immorality," "adversary
culture," post-modernism, the God-is-dead line, whatever that is, "the end of ideology," and many other
things—including even the prevailing position among
the moral philosophers of "the new approach" with
whom I have associated myself. I cannot help but feel
that they all somehow conspire against saying the
ethical thing as I have construed it, that is, against
the appearance of Voice C in the conversation of man-

24 Cf., C. J. Friedrich (ed.), *Authority* (Cambridge,
Mass., 1958), pp. 81–112.

kind, and that the final outcome of the drift they illustrate must be a conversation beyond culture, beyond modernity, beyond morality, beyond everything. Therefore, like the hero of a play set in a century to which I and those who are with me no doubt belong, I cry,

> What's that you say? Hopeless?—Why very well!
> . . . What's that? No! Surrender? No!
> Never—Never! . . .
> No! I fight on! I fight on! I fight on!